Global Communication and Collaboration

Klaus-Dieter Gronwald

Global Communication and Collaboration

Global Project Management, Global Sourcing, Cross-Cultural Competencies

Springer

Klaus-Dieter Gronwald
School of Engineering
University of Applied Sciences and Arts Northwestern Switzerland
Windisch, Luzern, Switzerland

ISBN 978-3-662-53149-5 ISBN 978-3-662-53150-1 (eBook)
DOI 10.1007/978-3-662-53150-1

Library of Congress Control Number: 2016963587

Springer

Printed on acid-free paper

This Springer imprint is published by Springer Nature
The registered company is Springer-Verlag GmbH Berlin Heidelberg
The registered company address is: Heidelberger Platz 3, 14197 Berlin, Germany

For

Inge
Alexandra
Victoria

Preface

With a decade of experience working for two India-based global services providers, as Head Enterprise Application Services Europe at Wipro Technologies and as Country Manager Germany at Mahindra Satyam (today Tech Mahindra), complemented by a couple of years with the Germany-based IT business software company SAP responsible for their global university liaison program with more than 450 academic institutions around the globe, I experienced the issues of working with emerging economies from Bangalore to Cochin, from Hyderabad to Chennai dominated by cross-cultural challenges from Abu Dhabi to Helsinki, from Stanford to Beijing, from Zurich to Sydney concluding that perception and prejudice are dominating when we start forming global teams.

At the India Week Hamburg (Germany) 2011 was an event organized by the Hamburg German Indian Society and the German Indian Round Table (GIRT) with the title "Dance with the Tiger – The Indian Tiger has awakened. Whoever wants to compete with him needs to sharpen his claws". When I showed it to my Indian colleagues, the immediate reaction was: "Tigers don't dance! – Why don't they take the peacock? It is the symbol of grace, joy, beauty and love and it is the national bird of India". There is obviously a significant difference how we perceive people from other cultures and how they perceive themselves and how they believe the rest of the world perceives them. India's Ministry of Tourism has been running a campaign "Incredible India" over the years. One of their advertisements shows the close-up of a tiger's face with the headline "Not all Indians are polite, hospitable and vegetarian", assuming, that the rest of the world shares their sense of humor. At least the Germans might take this serious.

At the same event, there was a session with the title "Renewable Energies in Hamburg and India" organized by the Hamburg Chamber of Commerce. They invited CEOs from regional solar energy companies, mostly SMEs and start-ups and representatives from the Federation of India Chamber of Commerce & Industry (FICCI). The Indian delegation offered "huge opportunities for German SMEs doing business in Rural India", implicitly assuming, that the Germans knew about Rural India. The Germans were very interested, implicitly assuming that the Indians knew about Rural Germany, so it could not be that different. The result of the event was that both sides did not understand each other because they still perceived what they wanted to perceive.

Cross-cultural sensitivity has turned out to be the most demanding area when leading global teams, especially in times of polarization when tolerance is decreasing. It starts with respect, learning about each other's cultural sensitivity and it is bidirectional. During my time as Country Manager Germany for Mahindra Satyam one of my team members was arrested by the police one day, because he had decorated his apartment with swastikas. The swastika was used by the Nazis and its use is prohibited in Germany and there is still a significant emotional potential in Western Europe for an EU-wide ban of the symbol. European Hindus are opposing these attempts. The swastika is an ancient Hindu symbol representing luck and prosperity and is one of the most popular ways of decorating rooms during Diwali, India's festival of light. What happened? My Indian colleague had been living in Germany with his family for three years already and was socially well integrated into the German neighborhood. With the door to his apartment left open, a neighbor saw the swastikas and called the police. A cross-culturally mature reaction would have been that the German neighbor explained the sensitivity of the swastika in German society while respecting religious practices without calling the police and my Indian friend being more discreet respecting local sentiments. I worked in teams with Christians, Muslims, Hindus, Buddhists, Sikhs and Jews. We were celebrating Christmas and Diwali and respected Ramadan. There is additional conflict potential when people from culturally more tolerant societies are working in teams with people from less tolerant societies. While people from less tolerant societies are expecting "integration", people from more tolerant societies are expecting "tolerance".

Culturally induced different work styles have direct impact on the team performance. European customers had problems to accept Indians as project or program managers. Prejudices like "Indians are too soft, they cannot say NO ", were common. I even had the same complaints from a German customer about one of my top French program managers. One of the generic cultural differentiators is time management, a critical factor for successful project execution. I experienced German project teams as time oriented with fixed milestones while the Indians appear more target oriented with variable milestones. Both methods can result in successful project executions (on time, on target, on budget) when managed properly. Germany, Switzerland, U.S. are monochronic time (M-time) cultures. That is one-thing-at-a-time, following a linear form. Monochronic cultures stress a high degree of scheduling and an elaborate code of behavior built around promptness in meeting obligations and appointments. India, the Arab part of Middle East, Latin America belong to polychronic time (P-time) cultures. Many things may occur at once since many people are involved in everything, and interruptions are frequent. Human relationships and interactions are valued over "arbitrary" schedules and appointments. Imagine what happens when Germans (M-time) and Indians (P-time) are working in a joint project team with an Indian program manager without cross-culture training. Well, it happened to me and it was the trigger for this book.

After returning to academia I started sharing my experiences teaching "The Issues and Challenges of Operating within the Context of an Emerging Economy" at the University of Strathclyde in Glasgow, United Kingdom, followed by a more formal, scientific didactical approach developing the course "Global Communication and Collaboration" at the University of Applied Sciences and Arts Northwestern Switzerland in Windisch for computer science students.

Six phases to develop the necessary competencies for successfully managing global virtual teams have been derived from interacting with more than 180 students in an evolutionary process: selecting the best global sourcing strategy and partner, risk assessment of working with emerging economies, developing best practices for intercultural competencies, applying professional international project management methods, optimize virtual teams, and develop international conflict management strategies.

Parallel to this course I developed a new combined learning concept in business informatics with a holistic view of the linked business process chain ERP-SCM-CRM-BI-Big Data as combined roleplay, online business simulation/serious gaming, and a text book "Integrated Business Information Systems" in German (http://www.springer.com/de/book/9783662437193) and English (http://www.springer.com/us/book/9783662532904) funded by Lucerne University of Applied Sciences and Arts, Lucerne, Switzerland. Enterprise Resource Planning (ERP), Supply Chain Management (SCM), Customer Relationship Management (CRM), Business Intelligence (BI) and Big Data Analytics (BDA) are business related tasks and processes, which are supported by standardized software solutions. This requires business oriented thinking and acting from IT specialists and data scientists. It is a good idea to let students experience this directly from the business perspective, for example as executives of a virtual company in a serious gaming environment. The course simulates the stepwise integration of the linked business process chain ERP-SCM-CRM-BI-Big Data of four competing groups of companies. The course participants become board members with full P&L responsibility for business units of one of four beer brewery groups each from production to retailer.

The story is a combination of facts and fiction. Global and local beer markets are occupied by beer giants. Four investor groups have acquired the independent breweries including their entire supply chains (Alpha Beer, Green Beer, Royal Beer, Wild Horse Beer). Each group has four retail chains distributed all over the country. There is a typical post merger situation right after the foundation of the four groups with business units having different business processes, product portfolios, rules, tools and IT infrastructures.

With the strategic goals of an ERP implementation (standardizing business processes, standardization of master data, optimization of the IT infrastructure) the post merger situation will be cleared. The next step is to optimize the supply chains introducing Supply Chain Management (SCM) techniques. With a focus on sales and marketing Customer Relationship Management (CRM) is implemented initiating the direct competition of the four groups. Real time Big Data Analytics is the final step for the successful implementation of Integrated Business Information Systems. Roleplay and gaming phases alternate gradually, starting with the formation of the business units and the analysis of the initial business situation. That finishes the course.

The virtual gaming environment www.kdibis.com is the web based business simulation system created specifically for these courses. It is complementary to the book with templates for decisions and presentations including simulation result.

Global Communication and Collaboration represents phase five of the implementation of the process chain ERP-SCM-CRM-BI-BIG DATA: outsourcing of IT and Business Services. The story continues: the four beer groups Alpha Beer, Green Beer, Royal Beer, Wild Horse Beer have grown into global beer giants with a global presence on almost all continents. They are the avatars for Anheuser-Busch InBev, Carlsberg, Heineken, SABMiller. All of them have outsourced their IT and Business Services to captive centers. Alpha Global IT & Business Services, Green Global IT & Business Services, Royal Global IT & Business Services, and Wild Horse Global IT & Business Services have become profit centers in our simulation. Additional they have decided to offshore parts of their services to one or two India-based global service providers (gdigservices and idktech).

Students will become the leadership teams with roles as service cluster heads for ERP, SCM, CRM, Big Data Analytics (BDA) headed by a Program Manager. IT & Business Service Centers are profit centers contributing directly to the profitability of the business. After developing the necessary competencies, teams will make strategic decisions for each of the six phases in the kdibis business simulation to gain competitive advantage and increase the market share for their respective company. The instructor is included into the roleplay as chairperson discussing the performance of each team in formal board review meetings.

Team sizes can vary from ten persons with at least two competitors up to forty persons with four companies and two students per role. The ideal size is twenty, four teams with one person per role. The ideal class room would be a room with four separate round or squared tables for eight to ten people. Those “learning islands”, one for each company, have turned out to be extremely important for an immediate identification of the groups with their company, developing their own group dynamics from day one, while sensing the other groups in the room. It is a noisy experience with a lot of emotions, laughter and fun.

I have the same experience with my MBA classes at City University of Seattle in Lucerne, teaching Essentials of Business Management and Business Strategy using the Capsim Business Simulation (www.capsim.com) with up to 30 students from around the globe, a real multi cultural experience. And it works right from the beginning. It is the first course they are taking just a couple of days after they arrived in Switzerland without knowing each other. That changes immediately after the first day of working together. And it is proof that with the right leadership and coaching you can build successful teams without sending them into boring team building programs, just focusing on the tasks at hand.

In the end, we all have more in common than some people want to make us believe. And what differentiates us makes the world just more colorful and interesting.

Thank you to all my students at University of Applied Sciences and Arts Northwestern Switzerland, who helped me finding the right way, and I apologize to all of you, who suffered from some of my experiments gone wrong.

Contents

1 Introduction 1
1.1 Introduction 1

Part I Role Based Business Simulation 5

2 Preparation and Initiation 7
2.1 Preparation 7
2.2 Game Structure and Organization 7
2.3 Step 1: Supervisor Registration 8
2.4 Step 2: Creating Classes 8
2.5 Step 3: Creating Games 9
2.6 Step 4: Register Students 10
2.7 Student Login 10
2.8 The Story 10
2.8.1 History 10
2.8.2 The Presence 11
2.9 The Game 11
2.9.1 Phase 1: Global Sourcing Initiative 13
2.9.2 Phase 2: Emerging Economies 13
2.9.3 Phase 3: Intercultural Competence 13
2.9.4 Phases 4, 5: International Project Management, Virtual Teams 13
2.9.5 Phase 6: Conflict Management in International Projects 14
2.10 Roleplay 14
References 14

Part II Course Content and Theory 15

3 Global Sourcing Initiative 17
3.1 Global Sourcing Principles 17
3.2 Global Sourcing Strategies 18
3.2.1 Delivery Model 18
3.2.2 Client-Vendor Partnership 19
3.3 Supplier Consolidation: Status 19
3.4 Gdigservices 20
3.4.1 Gdigservices Profile and Delivery Model 20
3.4.2 Gdigservices Capabilities Evaluation 20
3.5 Idktech 20
3.5.1 Idktech Profile and Delivery Model 20
3.5.2 Idktech Capabilities Evaluation 25
3.6 Sourcing Objectives 25
3.6.1 Performance Objectives 25
3.6.2 Financial Objectives 26
3.6.3 Relationship Objectives 26
3.7 Final Vendor Selection Process 26
3.7.1 Phase 1: Paired Comparison Method 26
3.7.2 Phase 2: Scoring Model 26
3.8 Engagement Roadmap: Maturity in Engagement Governance 27
3.9 Organizational Readiness 27
3.10 BS7799 and ISO20000 30
3.11 ITIL: Information Technology Infrastructure Library 31
3.12 Capability Maturity Model Integration 34
3.12.1 CMMI: Capability Level 34
3.12.2 CMMI: Maturity Level 35
3.12.3 CMMI: Services 36
3.13 Six Sigma 37
3.14 Lean IT 38
3.15 Decisions: Paired Comparison Method and Scoring Model 39
3.16 Decisions: Global Sourcing Priorities 39
3.17 Assigned Reading 39
References 41

4 The Challenges of Working with Emerging Economies 43
4.1 How to Identify Emerging Economies 43
4.2 The Gini Index 44
4.3 The Educational Challenge 45
4.4 Global Sourcing Risk Assessment 47
4.4.1 The Infosys Case (GadgetsNow 2010) 47
4.4.2 The Satyam Case 47

4.5 Emerging Economies and Innovation ... 48
4.6 Decisions – Emerging Economy Risks ... 48
4.7 Assigned Reading ... 48
References ... 49

5 Intercultural Competencies ... 51
5.1 Environment of International Cooperation ... 51
5.1.1 The Traditional Approach: International Trade, Foreign Direct Investment and Firm Internationalization (Morgan and Katsikeas 1997) ... 51
5.1.2 Global, Transnational, International and Multinational Companies (Hines 2007) ... 53
5.2 Theory in International Business (Grosse and Behrman 1992) ... 54
5.3 Generation "D" as Synonym for the Future International Manager (Gooderham et al. 2013) ... 55
5.4 The Cage Distance Framework (Ghemawat 2001) ... 56
5.5 About Globalization: People's Voice (Jim 1999) ... 57
5.5.1 Globalization: Positive Aspects ... 57
5.5.2 Globalization: Negative Aspects ... 58
5.6 Globalization: China's Big Mac Attack (Watson 2000) ... 59
5.7 Manage Generic Cultural Differences ... 61
5.7.1 The Process of Management (Littrell 2008) ... 61
5.7.2 The Problem of Planning (Littrell 2008) ... 61
5.7.3 Monochronic and Polychronic Time (Hall E and Hall M 1990) ... 62
5.7.4 Time Orientation (Hall E and Hall M 1990) ... 62
5.7.5 High and Low-Context Cultures (Hall E and Hall M 1990) ... 63
5.8 Decisions: Intercultural Competencies ... 63
5.9 Assigned Reading ... 64
References ... 64

6 International Project Management ... 67
6.1 Stakeholder Management ... 67
6.1.1 Why Projects Fail ... 67
6.1.2 Project Success ... 68
6.2 Stakeholder Engagement Approaches (stakeholdermap.com 2016) ... 68
6.3 Virtual Teams ... 69
6.3.1 Five Challenges to Virtual Team Success (Kirkman et al. 2002) ... 70
6.3.2 Managing Virtual Teams (Reiche 2013) ... 72
6.3.3 Making Virtual Teams Work (Watkins 2013) ... 74

6.4 Innovation in Global Delivery and Virtual Teams (Neumann 2012) 77
6.5 Decisions: Virtual Team Best Practices 77
6.6 Assigned Reading 78
References 78

7 Conflict Management in International Projects 79
7.1 Hofstede's Dimensions of National Culture (Hofstede 2001) 79
7.2 Differences Between Cultures on the Value Dimensions (Hofstede 2016) 81
7.3 Thomas & Kilman's Conflict Management Styles (Thomas and Kilmann 2015) 82
7.4 Culture and Conflict Management (Mohammed et al. 2008) 84
7.4.1 Competitor 84
7.4.2 Accommodator 84
7.4.3 Avoider 84
7.4.4 Collaborator 85
7.4.5 Compromiser 85
7.4.6 Conflict Management Style Ranking Total Average 86
7.5 Decisions: Conflict management style ranking 86
7.6 Assigned Reading 87
References 88

Part III Course Material 89

8 Papers and Cases 91
8.1 Lionel Messi's shoes: 'The greatest insult in Egyptian history?' (CNN 2016) 91
8.2 Airbus Industries (Airbus 2015) 92
8.3 CRM Contributes to a Scary Halloween for Hershey (techtarget 2004) 95
8.4 Global Sourcing: Shifting the Focus from Cost Saving to a Strategic Set-up (Gronwald 2012) 96
8.5 Successful People Strategies for Innovation in Global Delivery and Virtual Teams (Neumann 2012) 102
8.6 Advancing Intercultural Competencies for Global Collaboration (Messner and Schaefer 2012) 110
References 121

9 Company Profiles 125
9.1 Global Results 125
9.2 Global and Regional Revenue Market Share 125
9.2.1 Global Revenue Market Share 125
9.2.2 Market Share Americas by Revenue 125

9.2.3 Market Share Europe by Revenue ... 125
9.2.4 Market Share Africa by Revenue ... 125
9.2.5 Market Share Asia Pacific by Revenue ... 129
9.3 Global Volume Market Share ... 129
9.3.1 Global Market Share by Volume ... 129
9.3.2 Market Share Americas by Volume ... 129
9.3.3 Market Share Europe by Volume ... 131
9.3.4 Market Share Africa by Volume ... 131
9.3.5 Market Share Asia Pacific by Volume ... 131
9.4 Global EBITDA Market Share ... 133
9.4.1 Global Market Share by EBITDA ... 133
9.4.2 Market Share Americas by EBITDA ... 133
9.4.3 Market Share Europe by EBITDA ... 133
9.4.4 Market Share Africa by EBITDA ... 135
9.4.5 Market Share Asia Pacific by EBITDA ... 135
9.5 Alpha Beer ... 135
9.5.1 Alpha Beer Results ... 136
9.5.2 Global Presence Alpha Beer ... 136
9.5.3 Alpha Beer Market Share ... 136
9.5.4 Alpha Beer Portfolio ... 137
9.5.5 Alpha Group Organization Chart ... 139
9.5.6 Alpha Global IT & Business Servicers ... 140
9.6 Green Beer ... 140
9.6.1 Green Beer Results ... 140
9.6.2 Global Presence Green Beer ... 141
9.6.3 Green Beer Market Share ... 142
9.6.4 Green Beer Portfolio ... 142
9.6.5 Green Group Organization Chart ... 143
9.6.6 Green Global IT Organization Chart ... 144
9.7 Royal Beer ... 145
9.7.1 Royal Beer Results ... 146
9.7.2 Global Presence Royal Beer ... 146
9.7.3 Royal Beer Market Share ... 146
9.7.4 Royal Beer Portfolio ... 146
9.7.5 Royal Group Organization Chart ... 149
9.7.6 Royal Global IT Organization Chart ... 149
9.8 Wild Horse Beer ... 150
9.8.1 Wild Horse Beer Results ... 150
9.8.2 Global Presence Wild Horse Beer ... 151
9.8.3 Wild Horse Beer Market Share ... 151
9.8.4 Wild Horse Beer Portfolio ... 154
9.8.5 Wild Horse Group Organization Chart ... 154
9.8.6 Wild Horse Global IT Organization Chart ... 154

10 Global Service Provider Profiles 157
10.1 Gdigservices: Profile and Delivery Model 157
10.1.1 History 157
10.1.2 Global Footprint 157
10.1.3 Building Right Capability and Leadership 158
10.1.4 Globally diversified service portfolio 158
10.1.5 Engagement Roadmap 159
10.1.6 Investing in Optimized Global Delivery Model 160
10.1.7 Gdigdelivery: Applied Innovation to Application Support 161
10.1.8 Outsourcing Challenges and Traditional Delivery Models 161
10.1.9 gdigDelivery Versus Traditional Outsourcing Challenges 162
10.1.10 Organizations suited for gdigDelivery 162
10.1.11 gdigDelivery Service Offerings 163
10.1.12 Gdigservices Execution model 164
10.1.13 Gdigservices Tools 165
10.1.14 Pricing Models 165
10.1.15 Operational Model: Security and Ticket Allocation 165
10.1.16 Value Proposition 166
10.1.17 Governance Structure 167
10.1.18 Governance Organization 167
10.2 Idktech: Profile and Delivery Model 168
10.2.1 History 168
10.2.2 Global Presence 169
10.2.3 Associates 169
10.2.4 Process Models 170
10.2.5 Full Life Cycle Offering 170
10.2.6 Lines of Business 171
10.2.7 Advanced Shared Competency Delivery Model: ASCDM 171
10.2.8 ASCDM: Utilization with Maximized Profitability and Zero Bench 172
10.2.9 Advanced Shared Competency Delivery Versus Dedicated Support 172
10.2.10 Advanced Shared Competency Delivery Model Comparison 172
10.2.11 Competency Tower based Service Delivery 173
10.2.12 Advanced Shared Competency Delivery Benchmark 174
10.2.13 ASCDM Tool Support 175
10.2.14 Sourcing Model 177
10.2.15 Governance Model 178
10.2.16 Governance Participants 178

Index 179

List of Figures

Fig. 2.1 Supervisor eligibility check ... 9
Fig. 2.2 Company logos ... 11
Fig. 2.3 Kdibis student cockpit ... 12

Fig. 3.1 Sourcing models, Gronwald (2012) ... 18
Fig. 3.2 Gdigservices logo ... 20
Fig. 3.3 Gdigservices global footprint ... 21
Fig. 3.4 Gdigservices talents and competencies ... 21
Fig. 3.5 Gdiservices portfolio ... 22
Fig. 3.6 Idktech logo ... 22
Fig. 3.7 Idktech – global presence ... 23
Fig. 3.8 Idktech associates ... 24
Fig. 3.9 Idktech portfolio ... 24
Fig. 3.10 Paired Comparison Model ... 27
Fig. 3.11 Scoring model ... 28
Fig. 3.12 Engagement roadmap ... 29
Fig. 3.13 Sourcing roadmap ... 29
Fig. 3.14 Engagement maturity evolution ... 30
Fig. 3.15 Process models ... 30
Fig. 3.16 The Service lifecycle, Source: www.itil.org ... 31
Fig. 3.17 ITIL service lifecycle stages, source: www.itil.org ... 32
Fig. 3.18 ITIL service operation, www.itil.org ... 33
Fig. 3.19 Service level definition ... 34
Fig. 3.20 Six Sigma ... 37
Fig. 3.21 Lean IT, source: McDonald M 2010, A Model for the Lean IT Organization, Gartner ... 39
Fig. 3.22 Decisions – paired comparison method and scoring method ... 40
Fig. 3.23 Decisions – global sourcing priorities ... 41

Fig. 4.1 The Gini Index, Source: FindTheData (2016) 44
Fig. 4.2 Income distribution India, Source: Hindustan Unilever Limited, CLSA Investors' Forum, Hong Kong, September 2012 45
Fig. 4.3 Emerging economy risks 49

Fig. 5.1 Demographic GDP, source: The CIA Factbook, http://www.cia.gov/library/publications/the-world-factbook 52
Fig. 5.2 Plot of International Business Strategies adapted from Charles Hill 53
Fig. 5.3 CAGE Distance framework, source: http://www.slideshare.net/dxbugs/the-cage-framework 57
Fig. 5.4 Intercultural competencies 64

Fig. 6.1 Challenges of working in virtual teams, Source: experteer Magazine (2014) 70
Fig. 6.2 Virtual team success pyramid, source: Shaw (2012) 71
Fig. 6.3 Team Bonding, source: Wipro Technologies (2004) 73
Fig. 6.4 Virtual team best practices 77

Fig. 7.1 Conflict management styles, Source: (Thomas and Kilmann 2015) 82
Fig. 7.2 Conflict management style ranking – Competitor 85
Fig. 7.3 Conflict management style ranking – Accommodator 85
Fig. 7.4 Conflict management style ranking – Avoider 86
Fig. 7.5 Conflict management style ranking – Collaborator 86
Fig. 7.6 Conflict management style ranking – Compromiser 87
Fig. 7.7 Conflict management style ranking total average 87
Fig. 7.8 Conflict management style ranking 88

Fig. 8.1 Positioning of the developing world in the science and technology landscape 104
Fig. 8.2 Invisible innovation 105
Fig. 8.3 Global innovation systems 106
Fig. 8.4 Perceived cultural differences 111
Fig. 8.5 Key intercultural competencies 114
Fig. 8.6 Demographic information 116
Fig. 8.7 Relative importance of intercultural competencies 117
Fig. 8.8 Intercultural dimensions 118
Fig. 8.9 Q methodology 120

Fig. 9.1 Global results 126
Fig. 9.2 Global revenue market share 127
Fig. 9.3 Revenue market share Americas 127
Fig. 9.4 Revenue market share Europe 128
Fig. 9.5 Revenue market share Africa 128
Fig. 9.6 Revenue market share APAC 129
Fig. 9.7 Global volume market share 130

Fig. 9.8 Volume market share Americas 130
Fig. 9.9 Volume market share Europe 131
Fig. 9.10 Volume market share Africa 132
Fig. 9.11 Volume market share APAC 132
Fig. 9.12 Global EBITDA market share 133
Fig. 9.13 EBITDA market share Americas 134
Fig. 9.14 EBITDA market share Europe 134
Fig. 9.15 135
Fig. 9.16 EBITDA market share APAC 136
Fig. 9.17 Alpha Beer results 137
Fig. 9.18 Alpha Beer Global presence 137
Fig. 9.19 Revenue market share Alpha Beer 138
Fig. 9.20 Volume market share Alpha Beer 138
Fig. 9.21 EBITDA market share Alpha Beer 139
Fig. 9.22 Portfolio Alpha Beer 139
Fig. 9.23 Group organization chart Alpha Beer 140
Fig. 9.24 Global IT services organization chart Alpha Beer 141
Fig. 9.25 Green Beer results 141
Fig. 9.26 Global presence Green Beer 142
Fig. 9.27 Revenue market share Green Beer 143
Fig. 9.28 Volume market share Green Beer 143
Fig. 9.29 EBITDA market share Green Beer 144
Fig. 9.30 Portfolio Green Beer 144
Fig. 9.31 Group organization chart Green Beer 145
Fig. 9.32 Global IT services organization chart Green Beer 145
Fig. 9.33 Royal Beer results 146
Fig. 9.34 Global presence Royal Beer 147
Fig. 9.35 Revenue market share Royal Beer 147
Fig. 9.36 Volume market share Royal Beer 148
Fig. 9.37 EBITDA market share Royal Beer 148
Fig. 9.38 Portfolio Royal Beer 149
Fig. 9.39 Group organization chart Royal Beer 150
Fig. 9.40 Global IT services organization chart Royal Beer 150
Fig. 9.41 Wild Horse Beer results 151
Fig. 9.42 Global presence Wild Horse Beer 151
Fig. 9.43 Revenue market share Wild Horse Beer 152
Fig. 9.44 Volume market share Wild Horse Beer 152
Fig. 9.45 EBITDA market share Wild Horse Beer 153
Fig. 9.46 Portfolio Wild Horse Beer 153
Fig. 9.47 Group organization chart Wild Horse Beer 154
Fig. 9.48 Global IT services organization chart Wild Horse Beer 155

Fig. 10.1 Gdigservices logo 158
Fig. 10.2 Gdigservices global footprint 158
Fig. 10.3 Gdigservices building right capability and leadership 159

Fig. 10.4 Gdigservices globally diversified service portfolio 159
Fig. 10.5 Gdigservices engagement roadmap 160
Fig. 10.6 Gdigservices investing in optimized global delivery model 160
Fig. 10.7 Gdigservices outsourcing challenges 161
Fig. 10.8 gdigDelivery versus traditional outsourcing challenges 162
Fig. 10.9 Gdigservices execution model 164
Fig. 10.10 Gdigservices tools 165
Fig. 10.11 Gdigservices pricing models 166
Fig. 10.12 Gdigservices governance structure 167
Fig. 10.13 Gdigservice governance organization 168
Fig. 10.14 Idktech logo 169
Fig. 10.15 Idktech global presence 169
Fig. 10.16 Idktech associates 170
Fig. 10.17 Idktech full life cycle offering 171
Fig. 10.18 Idktech utilization 173
Fig. 10.19 Idktech ASCDM versus dedicated support 173
Fig. 10.20 Idktech shared competency delivery model comparison 174
Fig. 10.21 Idktech competency tower based service delivery 174
Fig. 10.22 Idktech sourcing model 177
Fig. 10.23 Idktech governance model 178
Fig. 10.24 idktech governance participants 178

List of Tables

Table 3.1 Gdigservices capabilities evaluation scores 22
Table 3.2 Idktech capabilities evaluation scores 25
Table 3.3 CMMI – Comparison of Capability and Maturity Levels, CMMI (2010) 35

Table 5.1 Patterns between cultures with different time use systems (Hall E and Hall M 1990) 63
Table 5.2 64

Table 10.1 Idktech ASCDM benchmark 175

Chapter 1
Introduction

Abstract Global sourcing is about working in virtual teams in a global, multicultural environment. It requires a significant amount of organizational and behavioral change of people and organizations. Understanding cultural differences in working styles is key for successful global project management. Theories of international management, company internationalization, cultural dimensions and distances are helping to develop cross-cultural competencies and conflict management styles for international project managers. This course simulates the stepwise outsourcing of global IT and business services to shared services centers as profit centers of four global beer groups.

1.1 Introduction

Global sourcing is about working in virtual teams in a global, multicultural environment. It requires a significant amount of organizational and behavioral change of people and organizations. Organizational change management is the method to eliminate resistance against change and improve organizational readiness. Organizational readiness is the measure for the changeability of an organization.

There are four key factors which have significant impact on global collaboration:

- Speed
- Social change
- Historical inheritance
- Cultural gaps

Understanding cultural differences in working styles is key for successful global project management. Theories of international management, company internationalization, cultural dimensions and distances are helping to develop cross-cultural competencies and conflict management styles for international project managers. They will understand modern theories and methods of international management and will be able to apply these to practical project management problems. They understand the benefits and challenges of international cooperation and know how to identify modes of cooperation that are relevant to the needs of international

K. Gronwald, *Global Communication and Collaboration*,
DOI 10.1007/978-3-662-53150-1_1

teams. High attrition in the IT services industry in emerging economies requires a focus on knowledge retention rather than people retention. Attrition and rotation of highly skilled and experienced talents add to the challenges to build and work in virtual teams.

This course simulates the stepwise outsourcing of global IT and business services to shared services centers as profit centers of four global beer groups Alpha Beer, Green Beer, Royal Beer, Wild Horse Beer. They are the avatars for Anheuser-Busch InBev, Carlsberg, Heineken, SABMiller. All of them have outsourced their IT and Business Services to captive centers. Alpha Global IT & Business Services, Green Global IT & Business Services, Royal Global IT & Business Services, and Wild Horse Global IT & Business Services have become profit centers in our simulation. Additional they have started the process to offshore parts of their services to India. The course begins in a phase when two India-based global service providers (gdigservices and idktech) have already been selected and the integration of the offshore providers has started.

Students will become the leadership teams with roles as service cluster heads for ERP, SCM, CRM, Big Data Analytics (BDA) headed by a Program Manager.

IT & Business Service Centers are profit centers contributing directly to the profitability of the business. After developing the necessary competencies, teams will make strategic decisions for six phases in the kdibis business simulation (www.kdibis.com) to gain competitive advantage and increase the market share for their respective company.

Phase 1: Select the best global sourcing strategy and partner.
Phase 2: Risk assessment of working with emerging economies.
Phase 3: Develop best practices for intercultural competencies.
Phase 4: Implement professional international project management standards.
Phase 5: Optimize virtual teams.
Phase 6: Develop international conflict management strategies.

Each phase finishes with a set of decisions to be made by each team in the online business simulation system kdibis. Those decisions are based on real studies and surveys, but are not included in the book. They will be disclosed only after the teams made their respective decisions online to compare their results with the reality. The closer students' match the real surveys, the bigger becomes their market and profitability gain. Since the beer market is saturated and actually shrinking year by year, growth can only be achieved by stealing market shares from the competition.

This makes the book and the online simulation mandatory components for the course.

The instructor is included into the roleplay as chairperson discussing the performance of each team in formal board review meetings.

The book is separated into three parts.

Part I: Role based business simulation. Introduction of the role based simulation environment *kdibis*, the story, methods and background information for the online simulation including the registration process and game initiation.

Part II: Course content for the six phases for building competency. The online decisions complete each phase.

Part III: Complementary course material including case studies and company profiles of the virtual kdibis world.

All other course material like templates for presentations and review meetings are available as downloads from kdibis.

Part I
Role Based Business Simulation

Abstract

Introduction of the role based virtual simulation environment *kdibis*, the story, methods and background information for the online simulation including the registration process and game initiation.

Chapter 2
Preparation and Initiation

Abstract Introduction of the role based virtual simulation environment *kdibis*, the story, methods and background information for the online simulation including the registration process and game initiation.

2.1 Preparation

In order to log in to the *Global Sourcing Game* as integrated part of this text book you must be registered either as a supervisor or a student. The supervisor registration is not required for participation in a course. The student authorization will be carried out by the supervisor.

In order to register as a supervisor this book is mandatory. Vice versa the full utilization of this book requires the game, since the decisions as exercises at the end of each chapter will be mapped against industries' best practices which will only be disclosed after students performed these exercises online.

The complete registration process is described in a separate online manual as download:

1. Go to http://www.kdibis.com and click *Login*.
2. Select *Global Sourcing Game English*.
3. Login as *guest* and enter the *IT and Business Service Center in the brewery building*.
4. In the lobby click the kdibis logo right of the elevator door to get into the visitor center.
5. Go to the check-in and then select *downloads* and download the supervisor manual. There you will find detailed instructions for the registration, for building your own course environment and how to run the Games.

2.2 Game Structure and Organization

Games are organized in classes. Each supervisor account can create a virtually unlimited number of classes.

K. Gronwald, *Global Communication and Collaboration*,
DOI 10.1007/978-3-662-53150-1_2

Each class can create a virtually unlimited number of games, but only one game can be active at any time. Games can be archived and reloaded if needed.

Each class has a number of registered students. Students are organized in teams (Alpha, Green, Royal, Wild Horse). Each team member has a specific role (Head IT Services, Cluster Head ERP, Cluster Head SCM, Cluster Head CRM, Cluster Head BDA). The ideal team size is five. There can be more than one member per role, ideally not more than two. All roles have the same privileges except the Head IT Services.

Supervisor are identified by their email address. There can be one supervisor registration per email address only. The same email address can be used as user name to be registered in a virtually unlimited number of classes as student, but only in one role per class.

There are four steps to initiate a course and game.

2.3 Step 1: Supervisor Registration

The detailed registration process is described in the supervisor manual (see Sect. 2.1):

1. Go to http://www.kdibis.com and click *Login.*
2. Select *Global Sourcing Game English.*
3. Click *register*, complete the registration form and *Submit.*
4. A confirmation mail will be sent to the registration email address which will serve as user name and an automatically generated passcode. This passcode cannot be changed.
5. With clicking the *activation link* the supervisor registration is completed.
6. Since the free unlimited use of the kdibis gaming site is linked to this text book, an eligibility check is required the first time a supervisor is logging in (Fig. 2.1). A random set of four images from the book will have to be identified with their correct figure number in the right sequence. If one of the answers is not correct, a new set of four images will be generated.

2.4 Step 2: Creating Classes

The detailed registration process is described in the supervisor manual (see Sect. 2.1):

1. Go to http://www.kdibis.com and click *Login.*
2. Select *Global Sourcing Game English.*
3. Login as supervisor and enter the *IT and Business Service Center in the brewery building*.
4. In the lobby click the Alpha Beer logo on the left side of the elevator. Click *Access Control.* When your login was successful you should be identified as

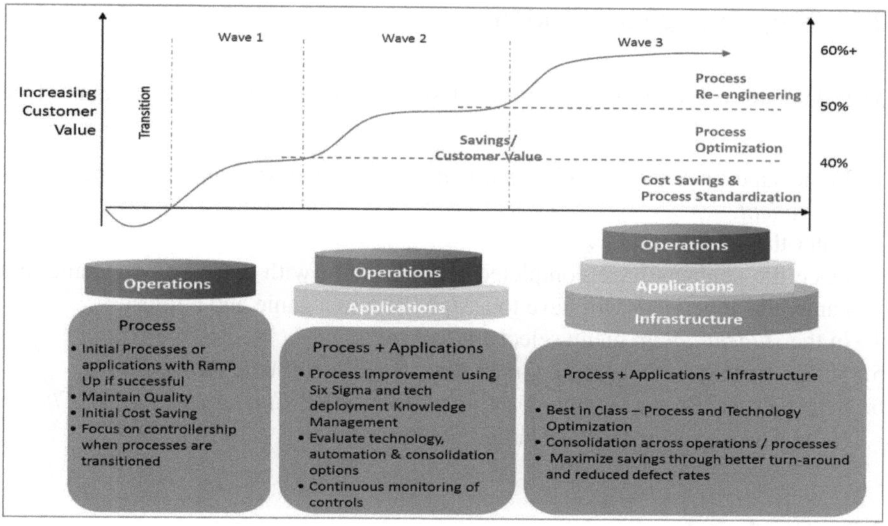

Fig. 2.1 Supervisor eligibility check

Chairperson and the palm scanner left should be green. Click the green button, go to the offices, and click the kdibis icon on the screen.

5. In the supervisor menu click *administrator* and select *class admin*, then *create class*.
6. Enter a *Class Title* and *Submit*. When successful, a registration mail was sent to the supervisor with an activation link.
7. Once done, go back to the supervisor menu and select the just generated class as *active class*. If there are more than one classes., the actual active class will be active during the entire session.
8. See the supervisor manual for more class admin options.

2.5 Step 3: Creating Games

The detailed game creation process is described in the supervisor manual (see Sect. 2.1):

1. In the supervisor menu click *administrator* and select *game admin*, then *new game*.
2. For each of the four teams *Alpha*, *Green*, *Royal*, *Wild* select the active class.
3. The game type is *CULT – Cross Culture*, enter institution and a game title and *Create Game* for all four teams.
4. See the supervisor manual for more game admin options.

2.6 Step 4: Register Students

The detailed registration process is described in the supervisor manual (see Sect. 2.1):

1. In the supervisor menu click *administrator* and select *student admin*, then *register student*.
2. Enter the student email.
3. Once the students have completed the activation with entering first name and name, the supervisor will have to assign them to a game and a role.
4. In the *student admin* menu select *student role*.
5. Select the team (*Alpha Beer, Green Beer, Royal Beer, Wild Horse Beer*).
6. Select a role (*Program Manager, Cluster Head ERP, Cluster Head SCM, Cluster Head CRM, Cluster Head BDA* and *Submit*).

2.7 Student Login

Once students have registered for an active game and assigned to a team and role, they can login with their credentials:

1. http://www.kdibis.com => login => Global Sourcing Game English.
2. Login with email address and password.
3. Enter the IT and Business Service Center in the brewery building.
4. In the lobby click the logo of your company (*Alpha, Green, Royal, Wild Horse*) on the left side of the elevator. Click *Access Control*.
5. When your login was successful you should be identified with your role and the palm scanner left should be green.
6. Click the green button, go to the office, and click the kdibis icon on the screen.

The student cockpit (Fig. 2.3) will be used for the decisions in Chaps. 3 to 7 (*Global Sourcing Initiative, Emerging Economies, Intercultural Competence, International Project Management, Conflict Management in International Projects*).

2.8 The Story

2.8.1 History

A couple of years ago 4 investors had acquired four breweries including their entire supply chains with 4 retail groups, distributor, wholesaler, and factory each (*Alpha Beer, Green Beer, Royal Beer, Wild Horse Beer*) (Fig. 2.2). In a four phases process they implemented the linked business process chain ERP-SCM-CRM- BI-BIG DATA. ERP for the standardization and consolidation of business processes, master data, and IT infrastructures. SCM for the optimization of the supply chains with the goal of minimizing inventory while guaranteeing delivery. CRM as marketing

Fig. 2.2 Company logos

instrument for demand generation, and finally BI-BIG DATA for the realtime analysis of markets and competitors. This is part of the text book *Integrated Business Information Systems* in German (Gronwald 2015) and English (Gronwald 2017), and the *kdibis business game* (www.kdibis.com).

2.8.2 The Presence

Global Communication and Collaboration represents phase five of the implementation of the process chain ERP-SCM-CRM-BI-BIG DATA: outsourcing of IT and Business Services. The story continues: the four beer groups Alpha Beer, Green Beer, Royal Beer, Wild Horse Beer have grown into global beer giants with a global presence on almost all continents. They are the avatars for Anheuser-Busch InBev, Carlsberg, Heineken, SABMiller. All of them have outsourced their IT and Business Services to captive centers. Alpha Global IT & Business Services, Green Global IT & Business Services, Royal Global IT & Business Services, and Wild Horse Global IT & Business Services have become profit centers in our simulation. Additional they have decided to offshore parts of their services to one or two India-based global service providers (gdigservices and idktech).

Students will become the leadership teams with roles as service cluster heads for ERP, SCM, CRM, Big Data Analytics (BDA) headed by a Program Manager.

The instructor is included into the roleplay as chairperson discussing the performance of each team in formal board review meetings.

2.9 The Game

IT & Business Service Centers are profit centers contributing directly to the profitability of the business. After developing the necessary competencies, teams will make strategic decisions for six phases in the kdibis business simulation to gain competitive advantage and increase the market share for their respective company. At the end of each phase the supervisor will grant access to the corresponding exercise in the student cockpit (Fig. 2.3).

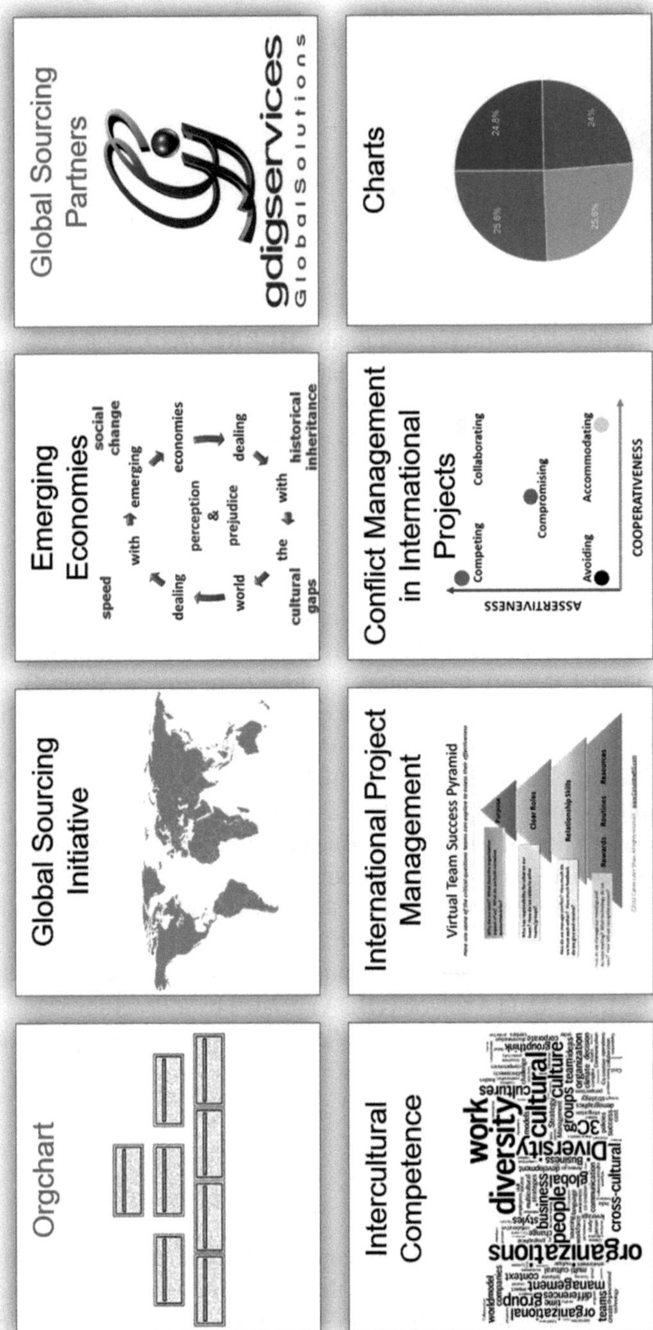

Fig. 2.3 Kdibis student cockpit

Each phase finishes with a set of decisions to be made by each team in the online business simulation system kdibis. Those decisions are based on real studies and surveys, but are not included in the book. They will be disclosed only after the teams made their respective decisions online to compare their results with the reality. The closer students' match the real surveys, the bigger becomes their market and profitability gain.

2.9.1 Phase 1: Global Sourcing Initiative

Select the best global sourcing strategy and partner. This phase has two decisions:

1. Paired comparison method and scoring model (Sects. 3.17 and 3.7). The result will be the decision for a single or a multi vendor model and in case of a single vendor which one.
2. Global sourcing priorities (Sect. 3.18). Students will rank twelve criteria and mark the impact of each decision as high or low. The results will be mapped against industry best practices and will have impact on the market shares of the four competitors.

2.9.2 Phase 2: Emerging Economies

Decisions are to be made about the priorities of emerging economy risks (Sect. 4.4). The results will be mapped against industry best practices and will have impact on the market shares of the four competitors. Students will rank fourteen criteria and mark the impact of each decision as high or low.

2.9.3 Phase 3: Intercultural Competence

Students will rank six job preferences and mark the impact of each decision as high or low (Sect. 5.6). The results will be mapped against the results of international studies and will have impact on the market shares of the four competitors.

2.9.4 Phases 4, 5: International Project Management, Virtual Teams

Decisions are to be made about the priorities of virtual team priorities (Sect. 6.4). Students will rank eighteen criteria and mark the impact of each decision as high or low. The results will be mapped against industry best practices and will have impact on the market shares of the four competitors.

2.9.5 *Phase 6: Conflict Management in International Projects*

Students will rank five conflict management styles for fifteen countries (Sect. 7.5). The decisions will be compared with the results of a survey and will have impact on the market shares of the four competitors.

2.10 Roleplay

For each Chaps. 2–7 templates team review meetings and presentations are available online.

1. http://www.kdibis.com => login => Global Sourcing Game English.
2. Login with email address and password.
3. Enter the IT and Business Service Center in the brewery building.
4. In the lobby click the kdibis logo right from the elevator door and enter the visitor center.
5. Go to the check-in and then select the appropriate templates from *downloads*.

References

Gronwald K (2015), Integrierte Business Informationssysteme, Springer, http://www.springer.com/de/book/9783662437193. Accessed 20 September 2016

Gronwald K (2017), Integrated Business Information Systems, Springer, http://www.springer.com/us/book/9783662532904. Accessed 20 September 2016

Part II
Course Content and Theory

Abstract

Global sourcing initiative, the challenges of working with emerging economies, intercultural competencies, international project management, working in virtual teams, conflict management in international projects are the six phases for developing competencies for the success of global virtual teams as combination of theory, role play and serious gaming.

Chapter 3
Global Sourcing Initiative

Abstract The global sourcing initiative introduces global sourcing principles, global sourcing strategies, delivery models and client vendor partnerships. The final vendor selection process includes discussions of engagement roadmaps, organizational readiness and process models, completed by decisions for a vendor and for global sourcing priorities.

3.1 Global Sourcing Principles

Although there has been quite a common understanding among various authors about the distinction between offshoring and outsourcing, in daily business they are often used "almost as synonyms" (Agerfalk and Fitzgerald 2008) (Fig. 3.1).

In order to be more precise, offshoring is linked to location, while outsourcing is about governance (see Davis et al. 2004) or ownership (see Miroudot et al. 2009). In other words, offshoring does not require an external service provider, while outsourcing can be done anywhere.

In-house offshoring, without the involvement of an external service provider, captive centers, is dominating shared services still. According to these definitions, there is no difference between offshore and nearshore, both are the same: delivering services from a foreign country.

The selection criteria for the location of an offshore center are linked to costs, logistics, availability of resources, taxes, legal restrictions, political stability, etc., but they do not have impact on the governance or delivery model needed for running an offshore center; the same rules apply to any location.

Outsourcing, on the other hand, does have significant impact on the governance, delivery system and the firm's organization (onsite or captive). Thus, the basic question when it comes to sourcing models is not so much where, but what, why and how.

There are some observations which are misleading the discussion about the right sourcing model inside a firm and between a firm as a customer and an outsourcing vendor.

Many sourcing discussions still are about nearshore versus offshore, although there is no difference between them. Both represent one and the same sourcing model: a location outside the firm's premises in a foreign country (but not necessarily outside the firm's boundaries) (see Miroudot et al. 2009).

K. Gronwald, *Global Communication and Collaboration*,
DOI 10.1007/978-3-662-53150-1_3

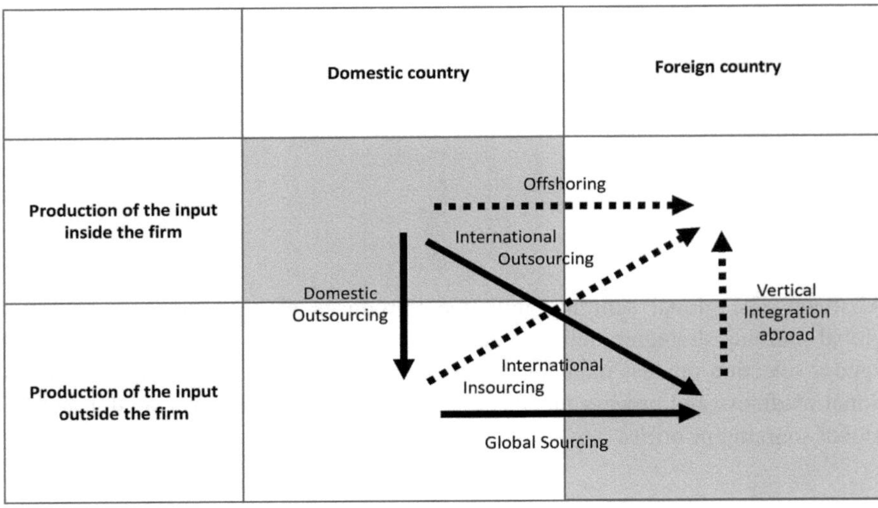

Fig. 3.1 Sourcing models, Gronwald (2012)

Many research and statistics do not make any difference between what to offshore or outsource, "service functions" like IT and administration (cost factors) or "product functions" like R&D, engineering services, innovation or product development. But, this distinction has a significant impact on the right decision when it comes to outsourcing.

According to Peeters et al. (2010), cost savings have been the main arguments for offshoring and outsourcing decisions on vendor and on customer's side with offshoring into low-cost countries and out-sourcing discussions about labor arbitrage and rate cards. This implicitly suggests that service functions would be the major offshoring/outsourcing components traditionally and product functions have come into the discussion only recently. It is just the opposite.

Although less than 10 % of the companies were going offshore until 1998–1999, two functions have been dominating since the beginning: IT as cost factor, and innovation services (R&D, engineering, product design) as production factors (see Manning et al. 2008; Peeters et al. 2010). Innovation services were the leading offshored services between around 1993 and 1996. Between 1998 and 2000, when the offshoring wave started on a larger scale, IT became the dominating offshored service, but still followed by innovation services.

3.2 Global Sourcing Strategies

3.2.1 Delivery Model

Global sourcing of talent as procurement centric task, a company not a service provider driven activity, has evolved into *global sourcing* as integrated part of vendor's delivery model, based upon the traditional *global delivery model*, expanded into an *advanced shared competency delivery model* which integrates support, maintenance and project execution, providing services using virtualized delivery centers across the globe with a standard platform of tools and processes (Gronwald 2012).

The model serves the major market demands of global sourcing:

- Cost savings,
- Flexible capacity,
- Gaining access to new technology

with a

- Dedicated customer facing team,
- Virtually zero bench

and is based on the principles of *knowledge retention* versus *people retention* accepting attrition as part of the process.

Teams can share knowledge, locate the best resources, and manage projects in real-time from anywhere in the service provider's global network. Those company's DNA is *task* based, not *geographically* based. The best resources for a specific project may be anywhere on the global delivery network; for example, Microsoft.Net and Java experts in Shanghai; ERP resources in Buenos Aires; finance and accounting expertise in Bangalore; and shared services for testing in Budapest and Chennai (Cognizant 2012).

3.2.2 Client-Vendor Partnership

Many relationships between customers and vendors are built on mutual *mistrust*:

- Bringing in a second vendor as competitor, because the current one has become *lazy*,
- Playing vendors against each other in order to gain *the best price*,
- *Reward-penalty* driven performance system,
- The most negotiated clauses in outsourcing contracts: *warranty and liability*.

3.3 Supplier Consolidation: Status

The vendor selection process has been finished with two of three phases.

Phase 1 reduced the number of suppliers, defined key suppliers and the delivery concept.

- 12 key suppliers group by Infrastructure, Application Management Services, and IT Governance Consulting.

Phase 2 identified the key suppliers having best fit.

- Request for Information (RFI) round early last year
- From 12 key suppliers down to 2 strategic supplier candidates
- Defined cross-organizational service packages for Application Management Services (ERP, SCM, CRM, BI, Big Data)

- Each service package assigned to selected candidate strategic supplier for competition
- Two finalist have been identified: *Gdigservices* and *Idktech*

3.4 Gdigservices

3.4.1 Gdigservices Profile and Delivery Model

First finalist – India-based global service provider Gdigservices (Fig. 3.2). For the complete profile see Sect. 10.1.

- Delivery centers in 54 countries with 50 global delivery centers and 25 near-shore centers (Fig. 3.3).
- More than 90,000 associates in 54 countries (Fig. 3.4).
- The service portfolio includes application development, business process outsourcing, testing services, package implementation, consulting, and technology infrastructure services (Fig. 3.5).

3.4.2 Gdigservices Capabilities Evaluation

Gdigservices capabilities evaluation scores (Table 3.1).

3.5 Idktech

3.5.1 Idktech Profile and Delivery Model

Second finalist – India-based global service provider Idktech (Fig. 3.6). For the complete profile see Sect. 10.2.

Fig. 3.2 Gdigservices logo

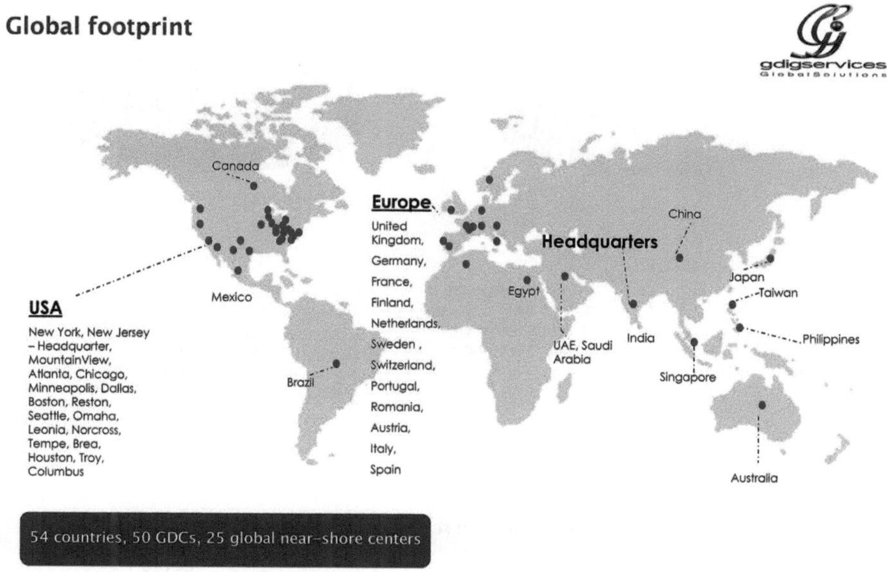

Fig. 3.3 Gdigservices global footprint

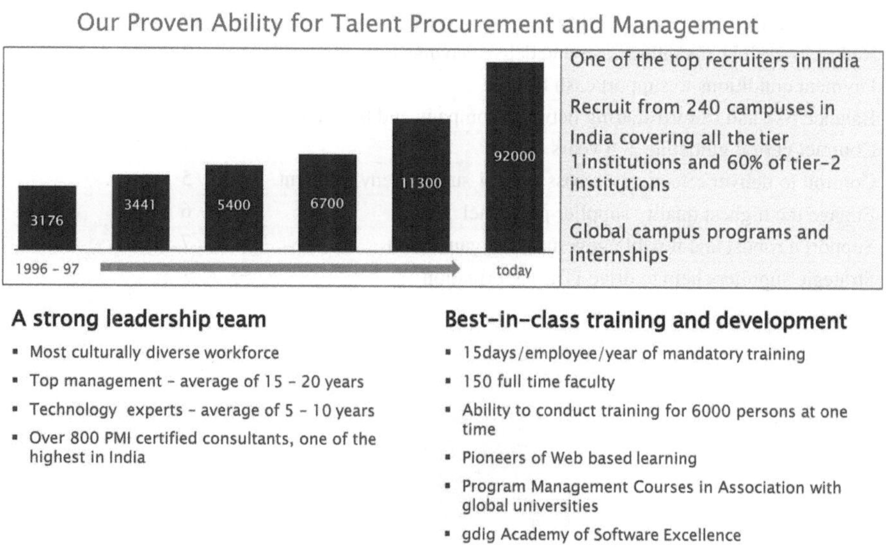

Fig. 3.4 Gdigservices talents and competencies

- Idktech presence in 34 countries with global development and solution centers in 75 locations (Fig. 3.7).
- Globally 29,000 employees, more than 60 nationalities, 80 % with more than three years experience (Fig. 3.8).
- Idktech portfolio includes outsourcing, consulting, and IT services (Fig. 3.9).

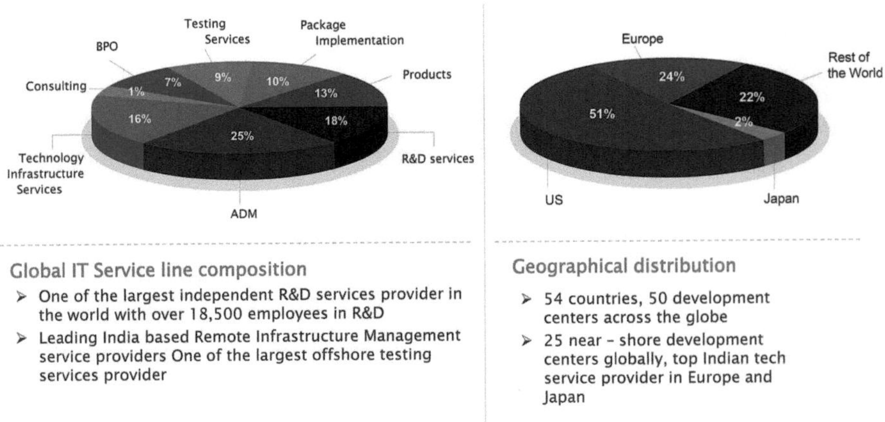

Fig. 3.5 Gdigservices portfolio

Table 3.1 Gdigservices capabilities evaluation scores

Gdigservices Criteria	Score
Improve efficiency to invest in innovation	5
Increase productivity for application maintenance services	7
Leverage the expertise and economy of scale of the supplier	7
Increase service and cost flexibility	9
Reduce overall IT operating costs and deliver savings from day 1 onwards	6
Payment conditions to support cash flow	8
Balance risk and reward sharing between company and the supplier	9
Contract period guideline 3–5 years	10
Commit to deliver effectively across a multi-supplier environment	5
Engage the highest quality supplier personnel	6
Support a robust and flexible governance organization	7
Strategic suppliers help to drive IT transformation	8

idktech
Global IT Services
Flexible application outsourcing for maximum business value

Fig. 3.6 Idktech logo

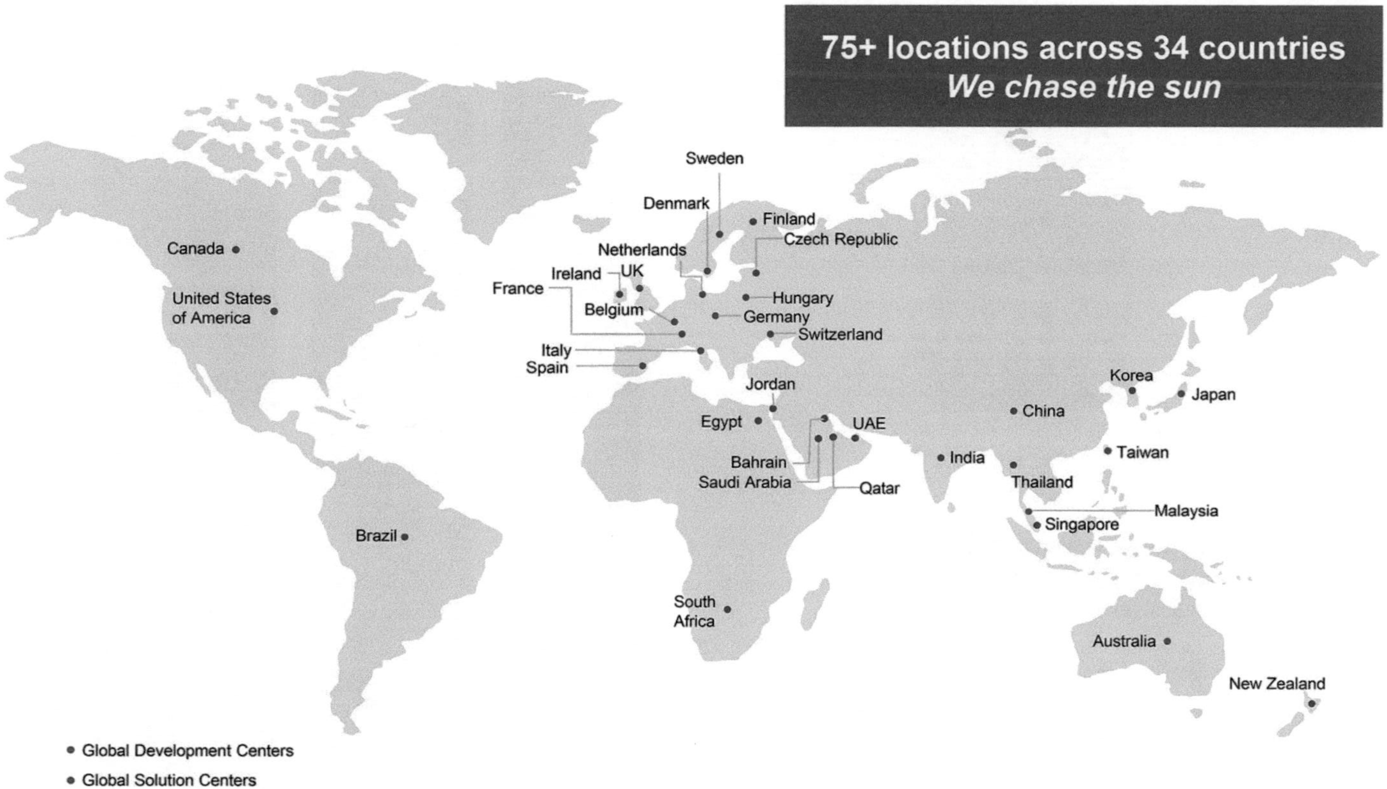

Fig. 3.7 Idktech – global presence

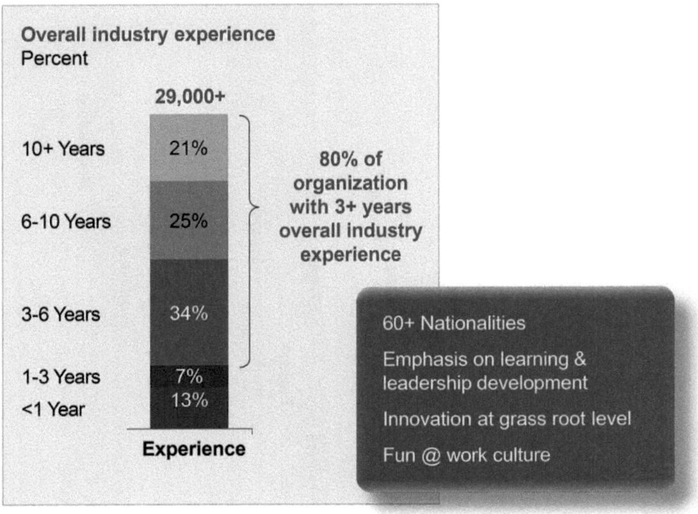

Fig. 3.8 Idktech associates

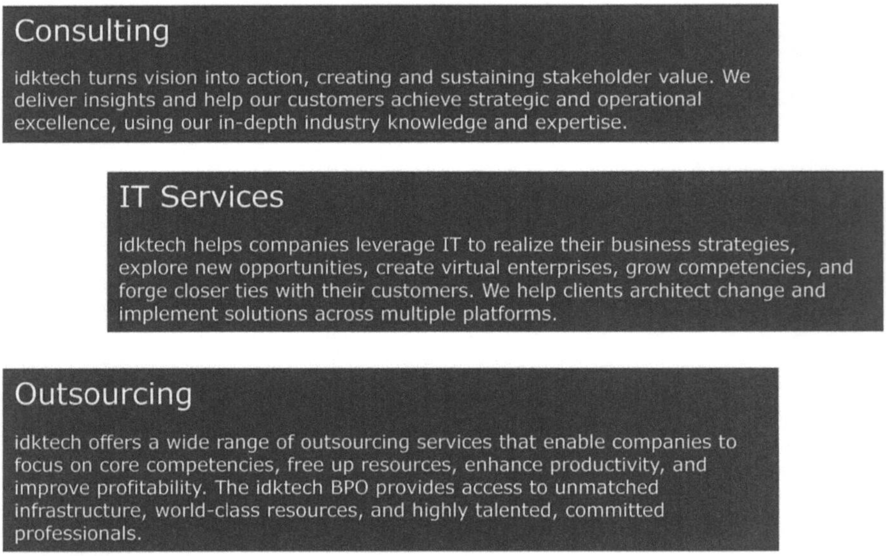

Fig. 3.9 Idktech portfolio

3.5.2 *Idktech Capabilities Evaluation*

Idktech capabilities evaluation scores (Table 3.2).

3.6 Sourcing Objectives

A set of objectives for outsourcing of IT services has been identified in three categories (sourcing, performance, and finance) but were not yet prioritized (Sects. 3.4.1, 3.4.2, 3.4.3). In the vendor selection process these objectives were used to identify those with the best fit. On a scale of one to ten two vendors were selected which scored at least five in all criteria.

The final vendor selection process includes the decision for a single or multi vendor model and in case of a single vendor the selection of the outsourcing partner.

A combination of two methods will be used: *paired comparison method* and *scoring model.*

3.6.1 *Performance Objectives*

- Improve efficiency to invest in innovation
- Increase productivity for applications maintenance services
- Leverage the expertise and economies of scale of the supplier

Table 3.2 Idktech capabilities evaluation scores

Idktech Criteria	Score
Improve efficiency to invest in innovation	8
Increase productivity for application maintenance services	7
Leverage the expertise and economy of scale of the supplier	6
Increase service and cost flexibility	5
Reduce overall IT operating costs and deliver savings from day 1 onwards	10
Payment conditions to support cash flow	9
Balance risk and reward sharing between company and the supplier	8
Contract period guideline 3–5 years	6
Commit to deliver effectively across a multi-supplier environment	9
Engage the highest quality supplier personnel	7
Support a robust and flexible governance organization	7
Strategic suppliers help to drive IT transformation	5

3.6.2 Financial Objectives

- Increased service and cost flexibility
- Reduce overall IT operating costs and deliver savings from Day 1 onwards
- Payment conditions to support cash flow
- Balance risk and reward sharing between company and the supplier
- Contract period guideline 3–5 years

3.6.3 Relationship Objectives

- Commit to deliver effectively across a multi-supplier environment
- Engage the highest quality supplier personnel
- Support a robust and flexible governance organization
- Strategic suppliers help to drive IT transformation

3.7 Final Vendor Selection Process

3.7.1 Phase 1: Paired Comparison Method

Paired comparison involves pairwise comparison of entities in pairs to judge which is preferable or has a certain level of some property (Fig. 3.10).

Step 1: Compare row criteria (A) with column criteria (B) and judge their importance. If AC1 is less important than BC2, rate the corresponding field 0. That makes AC2 more important than BC1. The field is marked with 2. If a row and a column are seen as equally important, both corresponding fields will be marked 1.

Step 2: Column C *Value* is the sum of fields C1-C12 of each row. It totals at the bottom line (E). Column D *Weight* is calculated as percentage of the total (E).

3.7.2 Phase 2: Scoring Model

The evaluation scores (Figs. 3.6 and 3.11) of the two finalists, Gdigservices and Idktech, will be multiplied with the weights (Fig. 3.11D) of the paired comparison method. The results are the weighted scores (Fig. 3.11G, I). They will be summarized (Fig. 3.11K, L) and the results are the final scores. The vendor with the highest final score is the preferred partner.

Paired Comparison

	Criteria	C1	C2	C3	C4	C5	C6	C7	C8	C9	C10	C11	C12	Value	Weight %
C1	Improve efficiency to invest in innovation		0	1										1	16.7%
C2	Increase productivity for applications maintenance services	2		2										4	66.7%
C3	Increased service and cost flexibility	1	0											1	16.7%
C4	Reduce overall IT operating costs and deliver savings from Day 1 onwards														
C5	Payment conditions to support NSN cash flow														
C6	Balance risk and reward sharing between NSN and the supplier														
C7	Contract period guideline 3-5 years														
C8	Commit to deliver effectively across a multi-supplier environment														
C9	Engage the highest quality supplier personnel														
C10	Support a robust and flexible governance organization														
C11	Strategic suppliers help NSN to drive its IT transformation														
C12	Leverage the expertise and economies of scale of the supplier														
	Total	3	0	3										6	

Fig. 3.10 Paired Comparison Model

3.8 Engagement Roadmap: Maturity in Engagement Governance

The engagement roadmap starts with the transition phase, an investment from both client and vendor (Fig. 3.12). Wave 1 focuses on cost savings and process standardization. As the maturity of the engagement grows, wave 2 adds to the customer value with process optimization followed by wave 3 with active process re-engineering. This is closely linked to the sourcing roadmap (Fig. 3.13) and the engagement maturity evolution (Fig. 3.14).

The sourcing roadmap is an evolutionary process, starting with a simple staff augmentation and evolving into a risk share partnership (Fig. 3.13).

3.9 Organizational Readiness

Working in virtual global teams requires a significant amount of organizational and behavioral change of people and organizations. That requires that organizations and people are changeable. Organizational readiness is the measure for the changeability

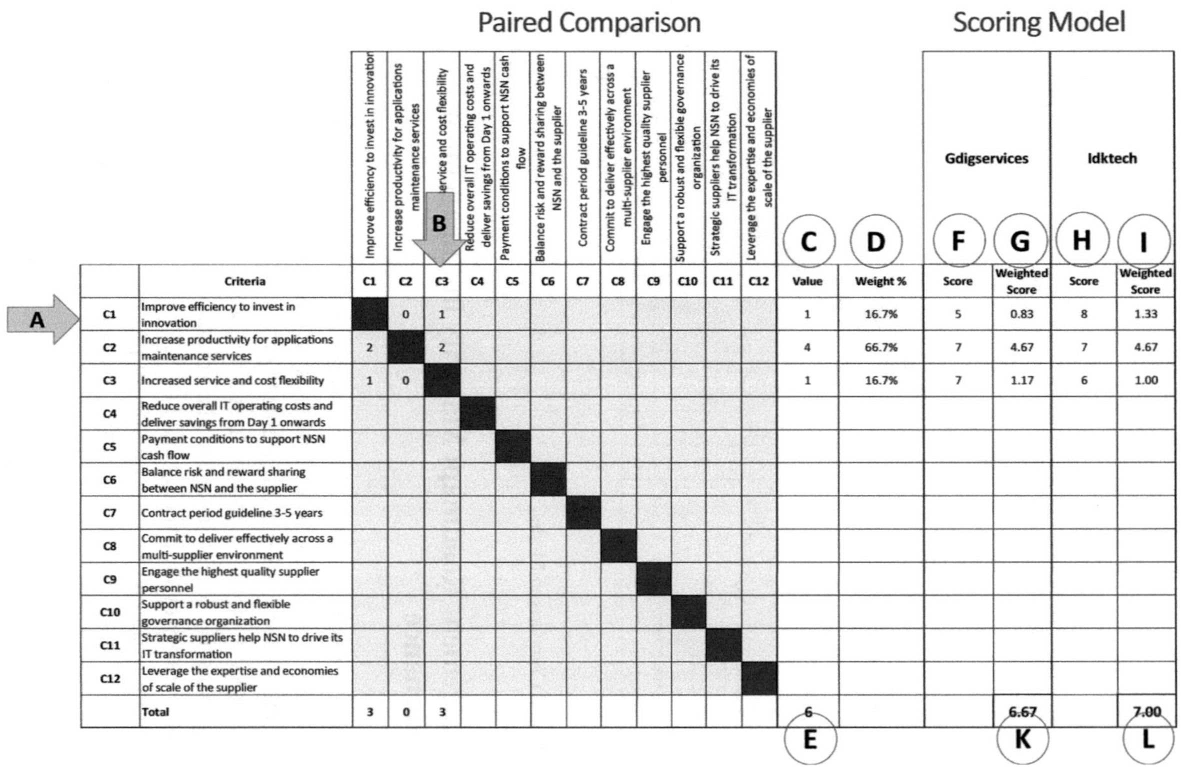

Fig. 3.11 Scoring model

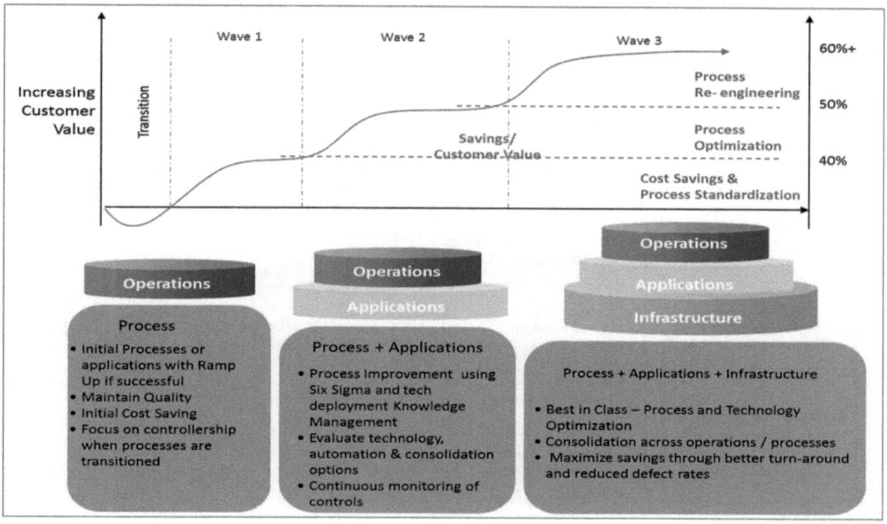

Fig. 3.12 Engagement roadmap

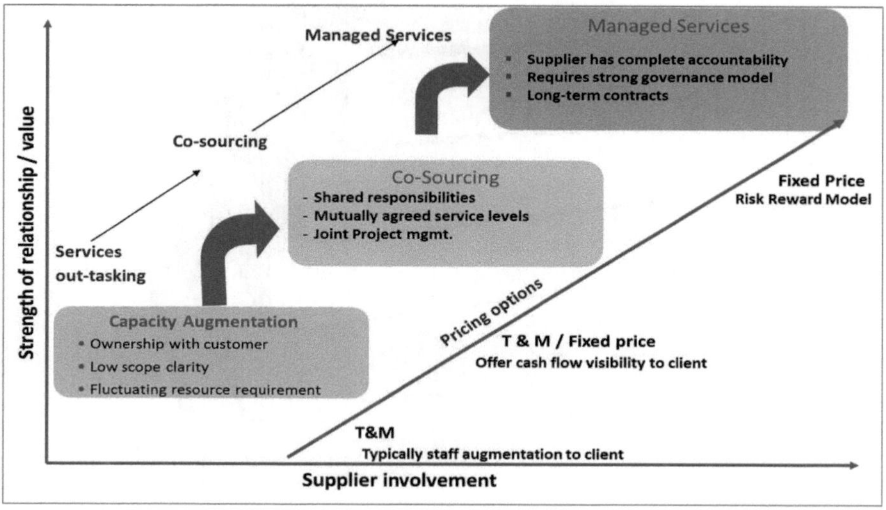

Fig. 3.13 Sourcing roadmap

of an organization. Organizational change management is the method to eliminate resistance against change and improve organizational readiness. The degree of organizational readiness can be measured and controlled by a set of established quality and process models (Fig. 3.15).

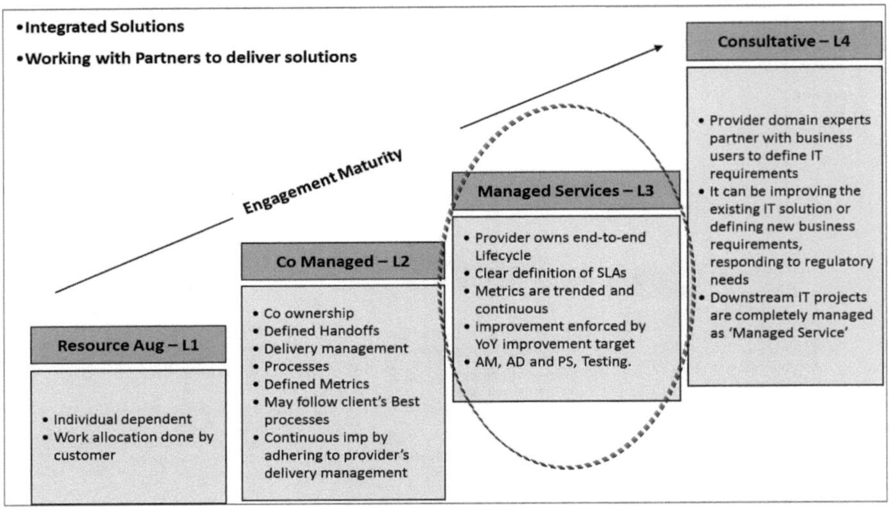

Fig. 3.14 Engagement maturity evolution

Fig. 3.15 Process models

3.10 BS7799 and ISO20000

The basis is the standard for information security management BS7799 (ISO 17799, ISO27001) (http://iso-17799.safemode.org/index.php?page=BS7799-2). The ISO9000 quality standard was for years the standard for quality management.

It has been superseded by ISO20000, used today by many global IT service providers. It has become the standard for IT service management and is close to ITIL (ISO/IEC20000 2012).

3.11 ITIL: Information Technology Infrastructure Library

ITIL provides a framework of Best Practice guidance for IT Service Management and since its creation, ITIL has grown to become the most widely accepted approach to IT Service Management in the world.

Core publications within ITIL (Figs. 3.16 and 3.17):

- Service Strategy
- Service Design
- Service Transition
- Service Operation
- Continual Service Improvement.

With the increasing integration of business and IT ITIL has become the basis for the transformation of an IT organization from providing technology and infrastructure to a customer-oriented service provider.

The term *service provider* can refer to internal or external organizations. There are three different types of services providers (Bucksteeg 2012):

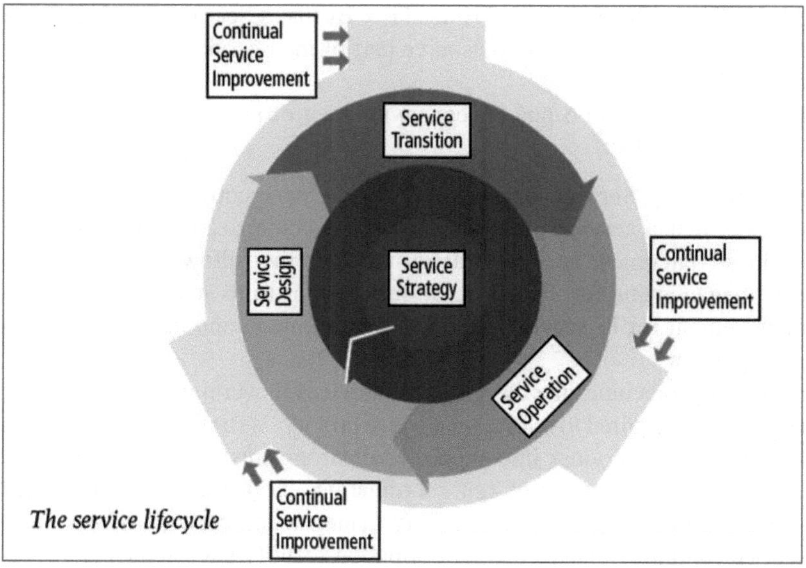

Fig. 3.16 The Service lifecycle, Source: www.itil.org

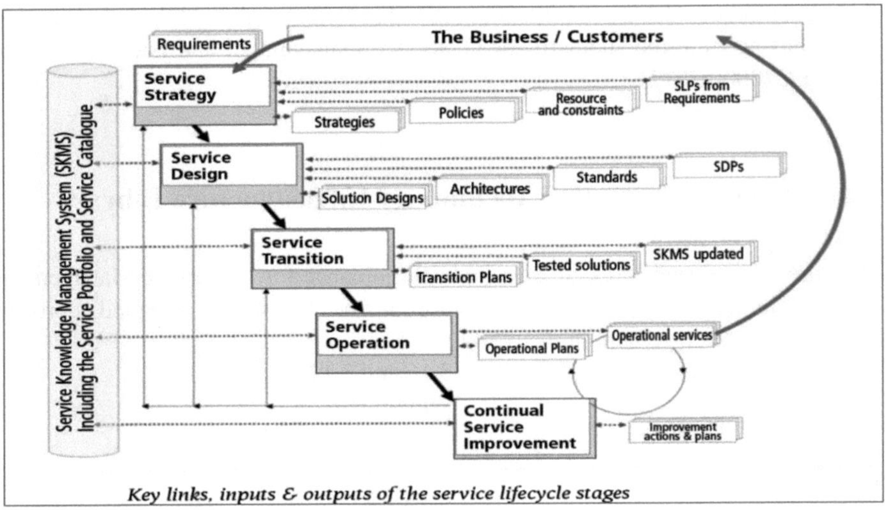

Fig. 3.17 ITIL service lifecycle stages, source: www.itil.org

Internal Service Provider is an IT service provider, who belongs to the same business unit as the client.

Shared Services Provider is an internal service provider, who provides services to more than one business unit of the same company.

External Service Provider is an IT service provider, who belongs to another company than the client.

Alpha, Green, Royal and Wild Horse IT & Business Services are shared services provider. They are planning to outsource part of their services to two external service providers.

ITIL is structured in 5 phases, each with a set of processes and sub-processes (ITIL Glossary 2011):

Service Strategy Service strategy defines the perspective, position, plans and patterns that a service provider needs to execute to meet an organization's business outcomes. Service strategy includes the following processes: strategy management for IT services, service portfolio management, financial management for IT services, demand management, and business relationship management.

Service Design includes the design of the services, governing practices, processes and policies required to realize the service provider's strategy and to facilitate the introduction of services into supported environments. Service design includes the following processes: design coordination, service catalogue management, service level management, availability management, capacity management, IT service continuity management, information security management, and supplier management.

Service Transition ensures that new, modified or retired services meet the expectations of the business as documented in the service strategy and service design stages of the lifecycle. Service transition includes the following processes: transition planning and support, change management, service asset and configuration management, release and deployment management, service validation and testing, change evaluation, and knowledge management.

Service Operation coordinates and carries out the activities and processes required to deliver and manage services at agreed levels to business users and customers. Service operation also manages the technology that is used to deliver and support services. Service operation includes the following processes: event management, incident management, request fulfilment, problem management, and access management. Service operation also includes the following functions: service desk, technical management, IT operations management, and application management (Figs. 3.18 and 3.19).

Continual Service Improvement ensures that services are aligned with changing business needs by identifying and implementing improvements to IT services that support business processes. The performance of the IT service provider is continually measured and improvements are made to processes, IT services and IT infrastructure in order to increase efficiency, effectiveness and cost effectiveness. Continual service improvement includes the seven-step improvement process.

Two ITIL processes overlap with CMMI:

- Service Level Management (phase Service Design)
- Improvement Process (phase Continual Service Improvement)

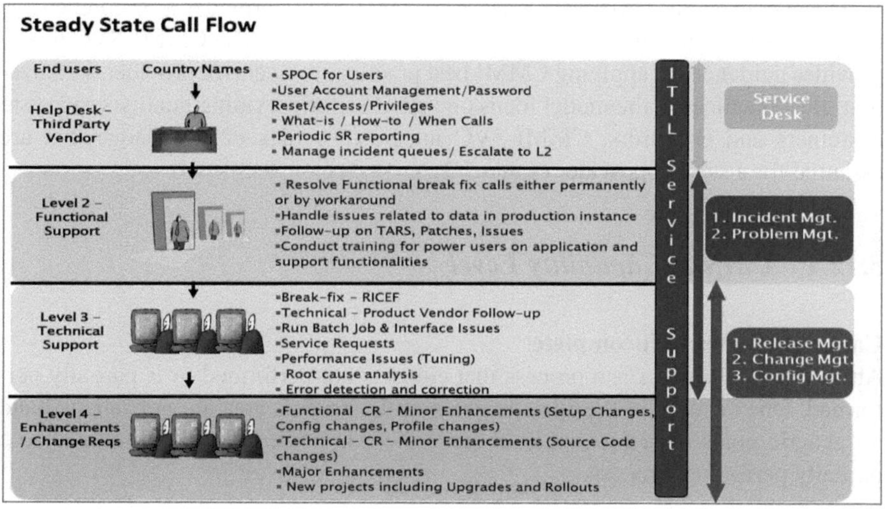

Fig. 3.18 ITIL service operation, www.itil.org

Service Level	Critical	Urgent	Normal	Low
Definition	•System not available •Threaten Business Continuity	•High impact on business operations or part of business operations	•Temporary impact to user •Query, Application of patches etc	•Little or no impact on Business and user •No rapid turn around required
Service Expectation	•Immediate Response and turnaround time	•High Response and turnaround time	•Moderate response and turn around time	•Taken up based on resource availability
Business Impact & Urgency	•Multiple Clients are affected •Mission critical application impacted •Manual workaround is not cost effective	•Few Clients are affected •Affecting particular function •Manual workaround does not exist	•Single client or individual work is affected •Medium priority application •Intermittent failures •Possible manual workaround exist	•Single client impact •Low priority application •No impact on work •Manual work around exist •Service request
Request Confirmation	•Email and Call to acknowledge •Email and call on resolution	•Email or Call to acknowledge •Email on resolution	•Email to acknowledge •Email on resolution	•Email to acknowledge •Email on resolution
Response Time	•45 Min	•4 hours	•8 business Hours	•2 business days
Resolution Time	•Work around in 4 hours, permanent fix in 1 business day	•Workaround in 1 business day, permanent fix in 2 business days	•5 business days	•Scheduled

Fig. 3.19 Service level definition

3.12 Capability Maturity Model Integration

CMMI (Capability Maturity Model Integration) models are collections of best practices that help organizations to improve their processes. These models are developed by product teams with members from industry, government, and the Software Engineering Institute (SEI). A Capability Maturity Model (CMM), including CMMI, is a simplified representation of the world. CMMs contain the essential elements of effective processes (CMMI, 2010).

This model, called CMMI for Services (CMMI-SVC), provides a comprehensive integrated set of guidelines for providing superior services. The CMMI-SVC model provides guidance for applying CMMI best practices in a service provider organization. Best practices in the model focus on activities for providing quality services to customers and end users. CMMI-SVC integrates bodies of knowledge that are essential for a service provider (Table 3.3).

3.12.1 CMMI: Capability Level

Capability Level 0: Incomplete

An *incomplete process* is a process that either is not performed or is partially performed. One or more of the specific goals of the process area are not satisfied and no generic goals exist for this level since there is no reason to institutionalize a partially performed process.

Capability Level 1: Performed

A capability level 1 process is characterized as a *performed process*. A performed process is a process that accomplishes the needed work to produce work products; the specific goals of the process area are satisfied.

Table 3.3 CMMI – Comparison of Capability and Maturity Levels, CMMI (2010)

Level	Capability levels	Maturity Levels
Level 0	Incomplete	
Level 1	Performed	Initial
Level 2	Managed	Managed
Level 3	Defined	Defined
Level 4		Quantitatively Managed
Level 5		Optimizing

Capability Level 2: Managed
A capability level 2 process is characterized as a *managed process*. A managed process is a performed process that is planned and executed in accordance with policy; employs skilled people having adequate resources to produce controlled outputs; involves relevant stakeholders; is monitored, controlled, and reviewed; and is evaluated for adherence to its process description.

Capability Level 3: Defined
A capability level 3 process is characterized as a *defined process*. A defined process is a managed process that is tailored from the organization's set of standard processes according to the organization's tailoring guidelines; has a maintained process description; and contributes process related assets to the organizational process assets.

3.12.2 CMMI: Maturity Level

A maturity level consists of related specific and generic practices for a predefined set of process areas that improve the organization's overall performance. The maturity level of an organization provides a way to characterize its performance. A maturity level is a defined evolutionary plateau for organizational process improvement. Each maturity level matures an important subset of the organization's processes, preparing it to move to the next maturity level.

Maturity Level 1: Initial
At maturity level 1, processes are usually ad hoc and chaotic. The organization usually does not provide a stable environment to support processes. Success in these organizations depends on the competence and heroics of the people in the organization and not on the use of proven processes. In spite of this chaos, maturity level 1 organizations provide services that often work, but they frequently exceed the budget and schedule documented in their plans.

Maturity Level 2: Managed
At maturity level 2, work groups establish the foundation for an organization to become an effective service provider by institutionalizing selected Project and Work Management, Support, and Service Establishment and Delivery processes. Work groups define a service strategy, create work plans, and monitor and control the work to ensure the service is delivered as planned. The service provider establishes agreements with customers and develops and manages customer and contractual

requirements. Configuration management and process and product quality assurance are institutionalized, and the service provider also develops the capability to measure and analyze process performance.

Maturity Level 3: Defined

At maturity level 3, service providers use defined processes for managing work. They embed tenets of project and work management and services best practices, such as service continuity and incident resolution and prevention, into the standard process set. The service provider verifies that selected work products meet their requirements and validates services to ensure they meet the needs of the customer and end user. These processes are well characterized and understood and are described in standards, procedures, tools, and methods.

Maturity Level 4: Quantitatively Managed

At maturity level 4, service providers establish quantitative objectives for quality and process performance and use them as criteria in managing processes. Quantitative objectives are based on the needs of the customer, end users, organization, and process implementers. Quality and process performance is understood in statistical terms and is managed throughout the life of processes.

Maturity Level 5: Optimizing

At maturity level 5, an organization continually improves its processes based on a quantitative understanding of its business objectives and performance needs. The organization uses a quantitative approach to understand the variation inherent in the process and the causes of process outcomes.

Maturity level 5 focuses on continually improving process performance through incremental and innovative process and technological improvements. The organization's quality and process performance objectives are established, continually revised to reflect changing business objectives and organizational performance, and used as criteria in managing process improvement.

A critical distinction between maturity levels 4 and 5 is the focus on managing and improving organizational performance. At maturity level 4, the organization and work groups focus on understanding and controlling performance at the sub process level and using the results to manage projects. At maturity level 5, the organization is concerned with overall organizational performance using data collected from multiple work groups. Analysis of the data identifies shortfalls or gaps in performance. These gaps are used to drive organizational process improvement that generates measurable improvement in performance.

3.12.3 CMMI: Services

Service Agreement

A *service agreement* is the foundation of the joint understanding between a service provider and customer of what to expect from their mutual relationship. The glossary defines a "service agreement" as a binding, written record of a promised exchange of value between a service provider and a customer.

Service Request
Even given a service agreement, customers and end users must be able to notify the service provider of their needs for specific instances of service delivery. In the CMMI-SVC model, these notifications are called "service requests," and they can be communicated in every conceivable way, including face-to-face encounters, phone calls, all varieties of written media, and even non-verbal signals.

Service Incident
Even with the best planning, monitoring, and delivery of services, unintended events can occur that are unwanted. Some instances of service delivery can have lower than expected or lower than acceptable degrees of performance or quality, or can be completely unsuccessful. The CMMI-SVC model refers to these difficulties as "service incidents." The glossary defines a "service incident" as an indication of an actual or potential interference with a service. The single word "incident" is used in place of "service incident" when the context makes the meaning clear.

3.13 Six Sigma

Six Sigma is a systematic approach for process improvements using analytical and statistical methods. It is assumed that each (business) process can be described as a mathematical function. Six Sigma is a statistical method based on the Normal Distribution (Gauss curve, bell curve). It is a probability distribution of the mean value μ in a large set of measures with the standard deviation σ (tqm 2014) (Fig. 3.20).

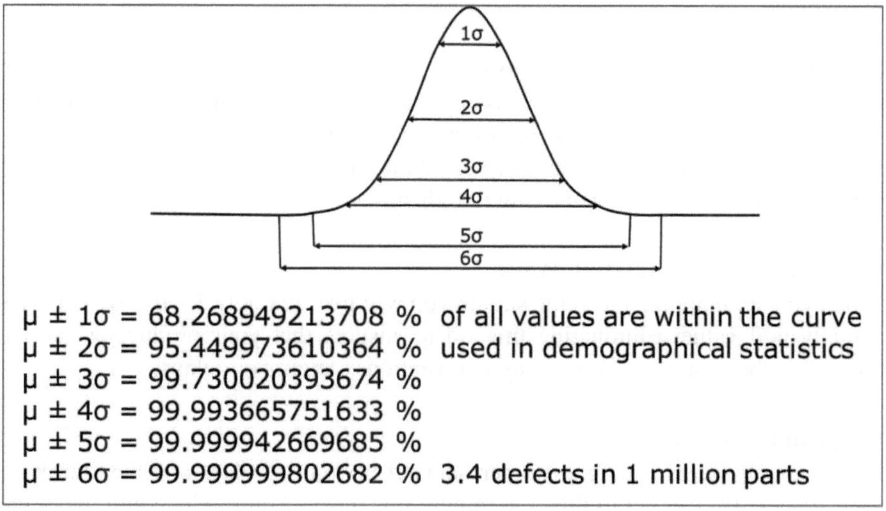

Fig. 3.20 Six Sigma

Six Sigma is a management philosophy to transform organizations to become more effective and efficient. It is a method to develop the future business leaders of an organization and uses two disciplined approaches:

DMAIC – Defining the problem, measuring important aspects, Analyzing the information flow, Improving and Controlling. It is used to develop/improve existing practice.

DMADV – Defining goals, Measuring Critical to Quality CTQs characteristics, Analyzing, designing details, Verifying. It is used to devise/design a defect-free procedure.

Six Sigma uses varied numerical and problem solving techniques and tools. It is being run by a trained and certified professional (Black Belt) and guided by a Master Black Belt.

3.14 Lean IT

Lean IT is the extension of lean manufacturing and lean services principles to the development and management of information technology (IT) products and services. Its central concern, applied in the context of IT, is the elimination of waste, where waste is work that adds no value to a product or service (Wikipedia 2014).

There are five key Lean IT principles (http://techexcel.com):

Identify Customer and Specify Value

Only a small fraction of the total time and effort in any organization actually adds value for the end customer. By clearly defining the values for specific products and/or services from the customer's perspective, all the waste can be eliminated.

Identify and Map the Value Stream

A value stream is the activities across all areas of an organization involved in delivering a product or service. This represents the end-to-end process that delivers the value to the customer. Once you have set out the customer requirement, the next step is to identify how you are delivering it to them.

Create Flow by Eliminating Waste

When you are mapping the value stream you will find that only 5–50 % of activities actually add value. Eliminating this waste ensures that your product or service "flows" to the customer without any interruptions, detours or delays.

Respond to Customer Pull

Pull is about understanding customer demand on your services and then tailoring your process to respond to this. Essentially this means you produce only what the customer wants, when the customer wants it.

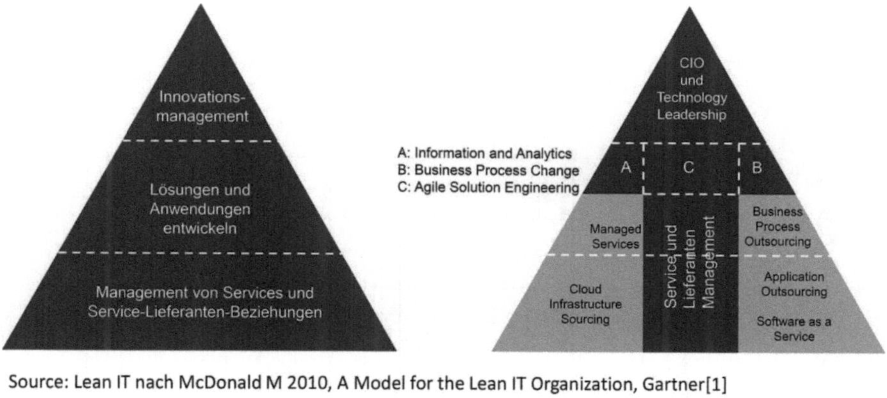

Fig. 3.21 Lean IT, source: McDonald M 2010, A Model for the Lean IT Organization, Gartner

Pursue Perfection
By creating flow and pull that link together, you will find more and more layers of waste become visible. This process continues towards perfection, where every asset and every action adds value for the end customer (Fig. 3.21).

3.15 Decisions: Paired Comparison Method and Scoring Model

Login to kdibis as described in Sect. 2.7. In the cockpit click *Global Sourcing Initiative*.

Paired comparison method and scoring model (Fig. 3.22). The result will be the decision for a single or a multi vendor model and in case of a single vendor which one.

3.16 Decisions: Global Sourcing Priorities

Login to kdibis as described in Sect. 2.7. In the cockpit click *Global Sourcing Initiative*.

Global sourcing priorities (Fig. 3.23). Students will rank twelve criteria and mark the impact of each decision as high or low. The results will be mapped against industry best practices and will have impact on the market shares of the four competitors.

3.17 Assigned Reading

Chapter 8.4 Global Sourcing: Shifting the Focus from Cost Saving to a Strategic Setup

Paired Comparison | Scoring Model

		Improve efficiency to invest in innovation	Increase productivity for applications maintenance services	Increased service and cost flexibility	Reduce overall IT operating costs and deliver savings from Day 1 onwards	Payment conditions to support NSN cash flow	Balance risk and reward sharing between NSN and the supplier	Contract period guideline 3-5 years	Commit to deliver effectively across a multi-supplier environment	Engage the highest quality supplier personnel	Support a robust and flexible governance organization	Strategic suppliers help NSN to drive its IT transformation	Leverage the expertise and economies of scale of the supplier			Gdigservices		Idktech	
	Criteria	C1	C2	C3	C4	C5	C6	C7	C8	C9	C10	C11	C12	Value	Weight %	Score	Weighted Score	Score	Weighted Score
C1	Improve efficiency to invest in innovation															5		8	
C2	Increase productivity for applications maintenance services															7		7	
C3	Increased service and cost flexibility															7		6	
C4	Reduce overall IT operating costs and deliver savings from Day 1 onwards															9		5	
C5	Payment conditions to support NSN cash flow															6		10	
C6	Balance risk and reward sharing between NSN and the supplier															8		9	
C7	Contract period guideline 3-5 years															9		8	
C8	Commit to deliver effectively across a multi-supplier environment															10		6	
C9	Engage the highest quality supplier personnel															5		9	
C10	Support a robust and flexible governance organization															6		7	
C11	Strategic suppliers help NSN to drive its IT transformation															7		7	
C12	Leverage the expertise and economies of scale of the supplier															8		5	
	Total																		

Fig. 3.22 Decisions – paired comparison method and scoring method

Global Sourcing Priorities: 1 = very important, 12 = not important - Impact high/low

Improve efficiency to invest in innovation	Select	Impact: ○high ○low
Increase productivity for applications maintenance services	Select	Impact: ○high ○low
Leverage the expertise and economies of scale of the supplier	Select	Impact: ○high ○low
Increased service and cost flexibility	Select	Impact: ○high ○low
Reduce overall IT operating costs and deliver savings from day 1 onwards	Select	Impact: ○high ○low
Payment conditions to support cash flow	Select	Impact: ○high ○low
Balance risk and reward sharing between company and the supplier	Select	Impact: ○high ○low
Contract period guideline 3-5 years	Select	Impact: ○high ○low
Commit to deliver effectively across a multi-supplier environment	Select	Impact: ○high ○low
Engage the highest quality supplier personnel	Select	Impact: ○high ○low
Support a robust and flexible governance organization	Select	Impact: ○high ○low
Strategic suppliers help to drive IT transformation	Select	Impact: ○high ○low

Fig. 3.23 Decisions – global sourcing priorities

References

Agerfalk PJ, Fitzgerald B (2008) Outsourcing to an unknown workforce: exploring opensourcing as a global sourcing strategy. MIS Q 32(2):385–409

CMMI 2010, Version 1.3, CMMI Product Team, Carnegie Mellon University

Cognizant 2012, https://www.cognizant.com/cognizant-2-0, accessed 10 September 2016

Bucksteeg M (2012), Itil 2011 – der Überblick, Addison-Wesley Verlag

Davis GB, Ein-Dor P, King WR, Torkzadeh R (2004) Information technology offshoring: prospects, challenges, educational requirements, and curriculum implications. In: Agarwal R, Kirsch LJ, DeGross JI (eds) Proceedings of the 25th international conference on information systems, Washington, DC, pp 1027–1038 Erdmann V, Koppel O (2009) Ingenieurarbeitsmarkt 2008/09 –Fachkraefteluecke, Demografie und Ingenieure 50Plus. VDI/IW. Available via http://www.iwkoeln.de/en/studien/gutachten/beitrag/6371

Gronwald K (2012), Global Sourcing: Shifting the Focus from Cost Saving to a Strategic Set-up, in Baeumer U, Kreutter P, Messner W (Eds.), Globalization of Professional Services, Springer

ISO/IEC20000 2012, ISI 20000 White Paper, APMG-International, High Wycombe. http://www.apmg-international.com. Accessed 6 January 2015

ITIL Glossary 2011, https://www.axelos.com/glossaries-of-terms.aspx. Accessed 15 January 2015

Miroudot S, Lanz R, Ragoussis A (2009) Trade in Intermediate Goods and Services, OECD Trade Policy Working Papers, No 93, OECD Publishing

McDonald M 2010, A Model for the Lean IT Organization, Gartner. http://blogs.gartner.com/mark_mcdonald/2010/06/25/a-model-for-the-lean-it-organization. Accessed 16 November 2014

Peeters C, Lewin A, Manning S, Massini S (2010) Shifting firm boundaries in global services sourcing: transaction costs, emerging capabilities and experience-based learning. Summer conference 2010 on opening up innovation: strategy, organization and technology, Imperial College London Business School, 16–18 June 2010

tqm 2014, Six Sigma, tqm.com Total quality Management. http://www.tqm.com/beratung/six-sigma. Accessed 16 November 2014

Chapter 4
The Challenges of Working with Emerging Economies

Abstract The discussion about emerging economies focuses on the identification of risk assessment parameters including the educational challenge and case studies about global sourcing risks.

4.1 How to Identify Emerging Economies

The term emerging economy was first used by economists at the International Finance Corporation (IFC) in 1981, when the group was promoting the first fund investments in developing countries (Khanna and Palepu 2010).

There are a variety of opinions about what characterizes an emerging economy depending on the focus of the respective persons or groups. The most common is the GDP growth rate which outpaced those of more developed economies in the last decade due to the opening of these large economies to global capital, technology, and talent (Khanna and Palepu 2010). Headline of the Financial Times from March 31, 2016: *Faster growing India confirmed as most dynamic emerging market* (Mallet, 2016). Absolute GDP comparison ranked Germany 4th in the world with $3.36 trillion and India 8th largest economy in the world with $2.07 trillion in 2013 (FindTheData 2016). Does that imply that India has become an emerged economy? Obviously not.

The main goal of this course is a thorough risk assessment for outsourcing IT and business services to India-based service providers. There are four key factors which have significant impact on global collaboration:

- Speed
- Social Change
- Historical inheritance
- Cultural gaps

K. Gronwald, *Global Communication and Collaboration*,
DOI 10.1007/978-3-662-53150-1_4

Additional risk factors have been identified as follows:

- GDP
- Educated labor pool
- Emerging markets as competitors
- Financial stability
- Unsecure intellectual property rights
- Corruption
- Gap between rich and poor
- Educational system
- Bureaucratic issues

We need to identify and separate those parameters which differ emerging economies from developed ones and more generic cultural distances (see Sect. 5.4).

4.2 The Gini Index

The Gini Index measures the extent of income distribution within a country. A value of 0 implies perfect equality, conversely, a value of 100 implies perfect inequality (Fig. 4.1). The income inequality cannot directly be correlated with emerging economies. Comparing the United States, Switzerland, Germany, and India, the United States has the highest inequality since 1985. Even Switzerland had a higher inequality until 2000 than India. While the income pattern in most countries is a pyramid, income distribution in India has changed to a diamond (Fig. 4.2).

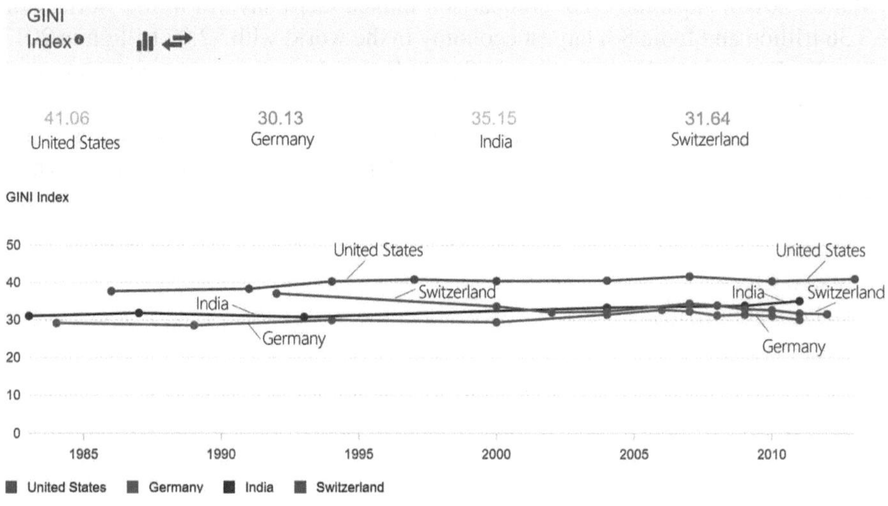

Fig. 4.1 The Gini Index, Source: FindTheData (2016)

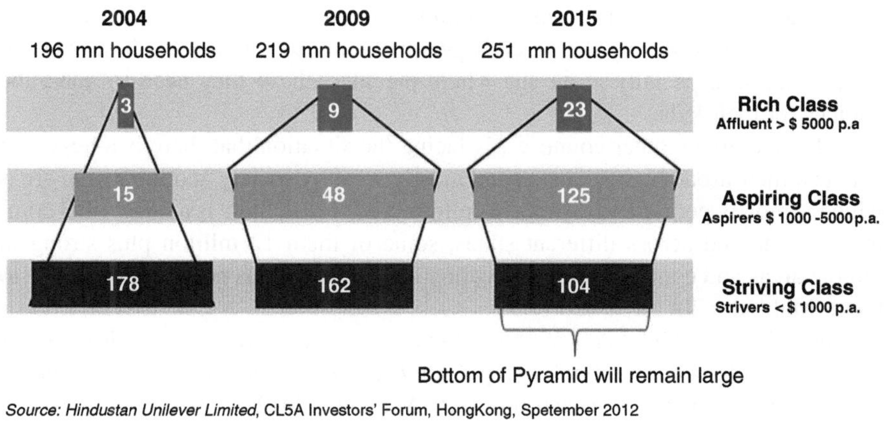

Fig. 4.2 Income distribution India, Source: Hindustan Unilever Limited, CLSA Investors' Forum, Hong Kong, September 2012

4.3 The Educational Challenge

The World Bank has described India as an "underperformer" in secondary education. I consider this a polite statement, because "secondary education" as we know e.g. from Switzerland and Germany does not really exist. The World Bank will invest $ 500 mn into India's secondary education system addressing issues of access, equity and quality efficiency (Deccan Herald 2009).

The quality of India's public education system characterizes one of the major challenges of an emerging economy (Azim Premji Foundation 2012):

- 35 % of children in grade 1 cannot recognize numbers 1–9.
- Almost 50 % children in grade 5 cannot read a grade 2 level text.
- A central issue is that no real learning happens; classes are "rote driven" with undue focus on memorization rather than conceptual understanding and application.

Another typical problem of India as an emerging economy is equity:

- Girls and socially disadvantaged backgrounds are 20 % lower in literacy – and similarly disadvantaged on all parameters.

Quote from Azim Premji Foundation: "The gap between poverty and wealth is closely related to education and tradition" (Azim Premji Foundation 2012).

The focus is on "tradition". Normally interpreted as "tradition which prevents progress". In the case of the dual vocational professional system, it is about "tradition which is worth to be revived". I will take India as an example, but it might be comparable to other societies, not only in emerging economies. More and more parents consider the highest goal of an educational model that their children go the baccalaureate path right from the beginning and ending with their PHD or MBA before 25, more fulfilling the parent's personal ambitions rather the best ones for their children, especially at an age where parents believe they need to make the choices for their kids.

India, like many other countries, is facing the situation that there is a huge gap between their urban high educated and mostly wealthy society and their rural areas which is mostly poorer and diverse in culture. Additional, there is a huge tribal community scattered across different states, some of them 12 million plus strong in remote areas and conflict zones. Educating their children has never been priority to them (Mahindra 2012).

Quote from a farm laborer of one of India's indigenous tribes about his daughter who goes to elementary school: *the girl can become a doctor, an engineer, a president or prime minister, or even a scientist.* (Mahindra 2012).

Why not become a nurse, a carpenter, a potter, … and after grooming to a master in her discipline become a doctor, an engineer, a president or prime minister – or even a scientist?

Quote from a leading Indian diplomat during a discussion about how to export the German dual vocational education system to India: *A master craftsmanship is an art, like writing your name on a rice corn, so plumbing cannot be a master craftsmanship* (Gronwald 2015).

These quotes unite India's mind set through all social ranks from a farm laborer to a highly educated diplomat and creates one severe cultural gap when talking about collaboration between developed economies and India, because *the main goal of a dual vocational professional education is exactly about making plumbing a master craftsmanship, based on the master-apprentice relationship organized in craft guilds* (Gronwald 2015).

The biggest challenge for these societies is to create a powerful educated labor force in non industrial crafts (in rural areas) based on the pillars of a dual vocational professional system, the master-apprentice relationship organized in craft guilds.

While Germany has declared the master craftsman certificate equal to a bachelor degree (Rundbrief 2012), a craft like carpenter, potter or plumber does not have any value in India's society – anymore.

We normally consider the *historical inheritance* of emerging economies as a burden. In this case, India has lost a historical inheritance just a little more than a century ago which would be essential to level with *developed* countries.

Coomaraswamy (1909) wrote in his book: "… and so we get a beautiful and affectionate relation between the apprentice and the master, which is impossible in the case of the busy professor who attends a class at a Technical School for a few hours a week, and at other times, when engaged on real work, and dealing with real problems, has no connection with the pupils at all … that supposing the aim be to train up a generation of skilled and capable craftsmen, it were better to appoint living master craftsmen as the permanent servants of the community, endowed with an inalienable salary, or better, a house, …and that they themselves should keep apprentices ... such a system would do more to produce skilled craftsmen, and to produce good work, than would twice the money spent on Technical Schools."

Today India only knows engineers and entrepreneurs.

4.4 Global Sourcing Risk Assessment

4.4.1 The Infosys Case (GadgetsNow 2010)

Over the years Deutsche Bank India had outsourced a significant amount of back office processes in various areas to the India-based IT service provider Infosys. More than 650 Business Process Outsourcing (BPO) executives worked at Infosys for Deutsche Bank.

In 2010 Deutsche Bank recognized that they had outsourced significant key competencies to Infosys and decided to back source about 150 people which were working in critical processes related to clients' trade and derivatives to its own captive center in Bangalore.

Following the bank's decision, Infosys sent an official communique to the 150 employees giving them the option to leave the company to be with Deutsche Network Services for much higher salaries (up to 50 %).

4.4.2 The Satyam Case

Satyam Computer was 1987 by Ramalinga Raju and his brother in Hyderabad. End of 2008 Satyam was the fourth largest India-based outsourcing company with 55,000 employees and a revenue of more than $ 2 billion (Balachandran 2015).

In January 2009 the head of Indian outsourcing company Satyam Computer Services (Ramalinga Raju) resigned, disclosing that profits had been falsely inflated for years and sending its shares plunging nearly 80 % (Reuters 2009).

Raju faked 13,000 employees and invested their virtual salaries into real estate.

Reuters called this *India's biggest corporate scandal* that *threatens future foreign investment flows into Asia's third-largest economy and casts a cloud over growth in its once-booming outsourcing sector* (Reuters 2009).

Raju committed that about $1 billion or 94 % of cash on Satyam's book was fictious. Just one month earlier Bernard Madoff, the former NASDAQ Chairman and founder of the Wall Street firm Bernard L. Madoff Investment Securities LLC was arrested over charges he swindled clients out of billions of dollars (Reuters 2009).

While Raju's fraud caused a national crisis with India's government stepping in directly and there was fear that this could have impact on the entire IT industry in India, Madoff's much bigger fraud did not cause a national crisis in the U.S.

Obviously emerging countries like India and developed countries are measured with different scales.

Just a couple of days after the disclosure of the Satyam fraud, the competition started chasing Satyam customers. While the non-Indian competition used arguments like *you cannot trust the Indians*, Indian competitors concentrated on discrediting Satyam as a company. That did not work as expected. Most customers pledged their support, as long as people met delivery commitments, as long as the operational effectiveness was in place, as long as people continued to deliver, as long as people continued to meet their expectations (NDTV 2009).

Satyam had an excellent reputation for delivery quality. That did not change. The Indian quality of target oriented mindset and delivery excellence and a good personal relationship to their counterparts across the globe, saved Satyam, even when they were not paid for months.

Tech Mahindra, owned by the Mahindra Group, and Satyam merged to form India's fifth largest IT exports company. The merged entity was called Mahindra Satyam and renamed to Tech Mahindra in 2012.

4.5 Emerging Economies and Innovation

Multiple corporate success stories have meanwhile proven that innovation in emerging markets is possible if the science and technology capabilities are utilized in the right way (Neumann 2012). Prahalad (2004) and Mashelkar (2011) highlighted specifically the opportunities arising in emerging markets from innovation. Others like Govindarajan et al. (2009) went even a step ahead and argued that innovation from emerging markets can reversely change the mature markets as well.

4.6 Decisions – Emerging Economy Risks

Login to kdibis as described in Sect. 2.7. In the cockpit click *Emerging Economies*.

Decisions are to be made about the priorities of emerging economy risks (Fig. 4.3). The results will be mapped against industry best practices and will have impact on the market shares of the four competitors. Students will rank fourteen criteria and mark the impact of each decision as high or low.

4.7 Assigned Reading

Section 8.6 Advancing Intercultural Competencies for Global Collaboration.

Emerging Economy Risks: 01 = very important, 14 = not important - Impact high/low

Relevance of still using the term Emerging Economy	Select	Impact: ○ high ○ low
Speed of economic growth	Select	Impact: ○ high ○ low
GDP	Select	Impact: ○ high ○ low
Large, low-cost and educated labor pools	Select	Impact: ○ high ○ low
Emerging markets as competitors	Select	Impact: ○ high ○ low
Speed of social change	Select	Impact: ○ high ○ low
Historical inheritance	Select	Impact: ○ high ○ low
Cultural gaps	Select	Impact: ○ high ○ low
Financial stability	Select	Impact: ○ high ○ low
Unsecure intellectual property rights	Select	Impact: ○ high ○ low
Corruption	Select	Impact: ○ high ○ low
Gap between rich and poor	Select	Impact: ○ high ○ low
Educational system	Select	Impact: ○ high ○ low
Bureaucratic issues	Select	Impact: ○ high ○ low

Fig. 4.3 Emerging economy risks

References

Azim Premji Foundation (2012), http://www.azimpremjifoundation.org, accessed 16 September 2016

Balachandran M (2015), The Satyam scandal: How India's biggest corporate fraud unfolded, http://qz.com/379877/the-satyam-scandal-how-indias-biggest-corporate-fraud-unfolded/, accessed 10. Feb. 2016

Coomaraswamy A (1909), The Indian Craftsman, Probsthain & Co., 41, Great Russell St., London, w.C., reprinted 2004 by Munshiram Manoharlal Publishers Pvt. Ltd., New Delhi

Deccan Herald (2009), India an 'under-performer' in secondary education, says World Bank report, http://www.deccanherald.com/content/29136/india-performer-secondary-education-says.html. Accessed 10 February 2016

FindTheData (2016), http://country-facts.findthedata.com/compare/1-29-122-180/United-States-vs-Germany-vs-India-vs-Switzerland. Accessed 10 September 2016

GadgetsNow (2010), http://www.gadgetsnow.com/articleshowprint/6483790.cms. Viewed 9th September, 2016

Govindarajan V, Trimble C, Immelt JR (2009) How GE is disrupting itself. Harvard Business Review. Available via http://hbr.org/2009/10/how-ge-is-disrupting-itself/ar/1

Gronwald K (2015), Globalization of Education Challenges and Issues, https://www.researchgate.net/publication/280802202_Globalization_of_Education. Accessed 16 September 2016

Khanna T. and Palepu K.G. (2010), Winning in Emerging Markets: A Road Map for Strategy and Execution, Harvard Business Press

Mahapatra S (2012), Guild, The Institutional Economic Base of Ancient India, International Journal of Social Science & Interdisciplinary Research Vol.1 Issue 9, September 2012, ISSN 2277 3630

Mahindra (2012), Mahindra Rise: One Opportunity – The Varsha Watti Story, https://www.youtube.com/watch?v=bFZqBsuHqC0. Accessed 15 September 2016

Mallet V. (2016), Faster growing India confirmed as most dynamic emerging market, Financial Times, https://www.ft.com/content/06b63142-2748-11e6-8ba3-cdd781d02d89. Accessed: 9 September 2016

Mashelkar R (2011) Re-inventing India. Sahyadri Prakashan, Pune

NDTV (2009), https://www.youtube.com/watch?v=eoFHUkUfLXY, accessed 10 September 2016

Neumann C (2012) Successful People Strategies for Innovation in Global Delivery and Virtual Teams, Baeumer U et al. (eds.), Globalization of Professional Services, Springer
Prahalad CK (2004) The fortune at the bottom of the pyramid. Prentice Hall, Upper Saddle River, NJ
Reuters (2009), Accounting scandal at Satyam could be India's Enron, http://www.reuters.com/article/us-satyam-idUSTRE50616H20090107, accessed 10. Feb. 2016
Rundbrief (2012), http://www.bundesregierung.de/Content/DE/PeriodischerBericht/RundbriefAusbildung/2012/02/2012-02-09-rundbrief-1-2012.html?docId=495494. Accessed 10 February 2016

Chapter 5
Intercultural Competencies

Abstract The development of intercultural competencies begins with theories of international cooperation, international business, and globalization. It finalizes with an in-depth discussion about how to manage cultural differences and implement those concepts in global teams.

5.1 Environment of International Cooperation

Globalization is not a rite of passage, and culture appears to be the most neglected and underestimated source of challenge in global professional services. Academic research on national culture and cultural differences has identified dimensions with an effect on the functioning not only of societies and individuals, but also of organizations and project teams. Once cultural differences are recognized and understood, there is a better chance of building bridges across cultural gaps instead of seeking to achieve feigned homogeneity (Messner and Schaefer 2012).

5.1.1 The Traditional Approach: International Trade, Foreign Direct Investment and Firm Internationalization (Morgan and Katsikeas 1997)

International Trade

The importance of international trade to a nation's economic welfare and development has been heavily documented in the economics literature since Adam Smith's (1776) pioneering inquiry into the nature and causes of the wealth of nations.

The rationale underlying this relationship suggests that economies need to export goods and services in order to generate revenue to finance imported goods and services which cannot be produced indigenously (Coutts and Godley 1992; McCombie and Thirlwall 1992).

Probably one of the broadest indicators of a nation's economic strength can be gauged from its gross domestic product (GDP), as this measure is an estimate of the value of goods and services produced by an economy in a given period (Tayeb 1992).

K. Gronwald, *Global Communication and Collaboration*,
DOI 10.1007/978-3-662-53150-1_5

	India	Germany
GDP (purchasing power parity)	$4.046 trillion (2010) $3.736 trillion (2009) $3.478 trillion (2008)	$2.951 trillion (2010) $2.857 trillion (2009) $2.998 trillion (2008)
GDP growth rate	**No 7 ww 8.3% (2010) 7.4% (2009) 7.4% (2008)**	**No 109 ww 3.3% (2010) -4.7% (2009) 1% (2008)**
GDP Agriculture GDP Industry **GDP Services**	16.1% 28.6% **55.3%**	0.8% 27.9% **71.3%**
Industrial production growth rate	9.7% (no 17 ww)	9.0% (no19 ww)
Exports	$201bn (no 22 ww)	$1.34 trillion (no 3 ww)
Imports	$327bn (no 13 ww)	$1.12 trillion (no 4 ww)

Fig. 5.1 Demographic GDP, source: The CIA Factbook, http://www.cia.gov/library/publications/the-world-factbook

The export-led growth thesis predicts export growth will cause economy-wide productivity gains in the form of enhanced levels of GDP (Fig. 5.1).

Foreign Direct Investments

The market imperfections theory states that firms constantly seek market opportunities and their decision to invest overseas is explained as a strategy to capitalize on certain capabilities not shared by competitors in foreign countries (Hymer 1970).

The capabilities or advantages of firms are explained by market imperfections for products and factors of production. That is, the theory of perfect competition dictates that firms produce homogeneous products and enjoy the same level of access to factors of production. However, the reality of imperfect competition, which is reflected in industrial organization theory (Porter 1985), determines that firms gain different types of competitive advantages and each to varying degrees.

Firm Internationalization

Piercy (1981) and Turnbull (1985) describe internationalization as the outward movement of a firm's operations. However, this expression could be embellished on to describe internationalization as "…the process of increasing involvement in international operations" (Welch and Luostarinen 1988, p. 36). Welch and Luostarinen (1988) have comprehensively reviewed this literature and concluded that "…there is a wide range of potential paths any firm might take in internationalization" (p. 43).

It has been contended that the literature concerned with internationalization, from an export development perspective, is probably one of the most advanced and mature areas of knowledge in international business (Haar and Ortiz-Buonafina 1995).

Firm Internationalization: Uppsala internationalization Model

Much of the extant literature on internationalization has been inspired by the work of Scandinavian researchers who are collectively referred to as the Uppsala School (e.g. Johanson and Vahlne 1977; Johanson and Wiedersheim-Paul 1975).

This literature generally suggests that the process of internationalization is founded on an evolutionary and sequential build-up of foreign commitments over time.

They identified four steps within this process which were distinguished by those firms with: no regular export activities; export activities via independent representatives or agents; the establishment of an overseas subsidiary; and overseas production/manufacturing units.

The contention implicit within this model is that the firm proceeds along the internationalization path in the form of logical steps, based on its gradual acquisition and use of intelligence from foreign markets and operations, which determine successively greater levels of commitment to those overseas destinations.

Firm Internationalization: Innovation-Related Internationalization
An extensive volume of research has examined the way in which firms progress along the internationalization continuum and suggests that a sequence of discrete stages exists which proxy the "stop and go" (Dalli 1994, p. 92), stepwise process exemplifying the evolution of international involvement.

Implicit between each set of stages is the notion that fairly stable periods exist in which firms consolidate and generate an appropriate resource base to respond to fortuitous environmental conditions which allow them to proceed to the next internationalization stage.

5.1.2 Global, Transnational, International and Multinational Companies (Hines 2007)

In the world of eCommerce and virtual business, it becomes more helpful to categorize a company by its intention or strategic focus, rather than kits actual operations (Fig. 5.2).

Fig. 5.2 Plot of International Business Strategies adapted from Charles Hill

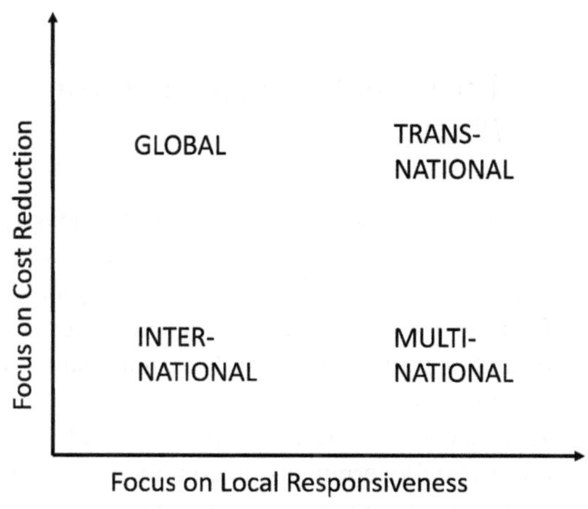

International Companies
have no foreign direct investments (FDI) and make their product or service only in their home country. In other words, they're exporters and importers. They have no staff, warehouses, or sales offices in foreign countries. The best examples of international companies, in the strict sense, are exotic retail shops that sell imported products, or small local manufacturers that export to neighboring countries.

Multinational Companies
cross the FDI threshold. They invest directly in foreign assets, whether it's a lease contract on a building to house service operations, a plant on foreign soil, or a foreign marketing campaign. Generally, though. Multinational companies, however, have FDI only in a limited number of countries, and they do not attempt to homogenize their product offering throughout the countries they operate in -- they focus much more on being responsive to local preferences than a global company would.

Global Companies
have investments in dozens of countries but maintain a strong headquarters in one, usually their home country. Their mantra is economies of scale, and they'll homogenize products as much as the market will allow in order to keep costs low. Their marketing campaigns often span the globe with one message (albeit in different languages) in an attempt to smooth out differences in local tastes and preferences.

Transnational Companies
are often very complex and extremely difficult to manage. They invest directly in dozens of countries and experience strong pressures both for cost reduction and local responsiveness. These companies may have a global headquarters, but they also distribute decision-making power to various national headquarters, and they have dedicated R&D activities for different national markets.

International Contractor INC
is an extension of the Transnational Firm to not only owner related associations (Brosse and Behrmann 1992).

5.2 Theory in International Business (Grosse and Behrman 1992)

International business is the study of business activities that cross national borders and, therefore, is fundamentally concerned with the firms that undertake that business and the national Governments that regulate them.

Empirical studies have distinguished international from domestic business strategies and operations, but they have not resulted in an international theory of cross-national business behavior.

Any theory of international business must be a theory of policies and activities of business and Governments, in conflict and cooperation.

A framework for constructing such a theory can be built on existing bargaining theory.

Primarily in political economy (Gilpin 1975), but also in business fields (Moran 1974; Gladwin and Walter 1980; Behrmann and Grosse 1990), the theory of inter-organization bargaining has been used to characterize and analyze business and government negotiation, policy-making and behavior.

In addition to the matters presented above which comprise the subject of IB negotiations, the activities of IB include the transfer of people and information within or between firms across national borders and also a variety of government policies that are stimulated by pressures from labor unions, local businesses or other interest groups.

The rules of the game for business operations are established by Governments (or by state or local units with tacit approval of the central Government). This means that firms whose operations cross national boundaries must necessarily assess and manage differences in legal, regulatory and institutional environments in each country.

The firms face some need to negotiate under and comply with actual or potential rules that differ in the two or more countries.

Country Risk
is the probability distribution that country-specific, governmental acts will adversely alter the value of the international firm.

A Government may limit financial activities of affiliates operating locally that wish to undertake transactions with foreign entities (for example, profit remittance, foreign borrowing or foreign investing, payment of royalties to the parent firm).

That risk is an unavoidable feature of the environment for a non-international firm in its own country.

The International Contractor, on the other hand, has the ability both to diversify country-specific risk by operating in more than one country and also to manage it via intrafirm, international activities or through negotiations with the Government.

5.3 Generation "D" as Synonym for the Future International Manager (Gooderham et al. 2013)

Unlike generation x and generation y, generation d(igital) is not determined by age. It's the group of people who are completely at ease with the digital revolution and consume online information regularly, whether they're 8 or 80 (netlingo 2016).

There is a preference shift for working in organizations that offer opportunities for autonomy, creativity and socially stimulating atmosphere. Bonuses and status have become of less importance.

Traditionally, HRM has involved systematic efforts to acquire, nurture and retain the carriers of knowledge resource which are crucial to company's goals. This was accomplished largely through rewards, salaries, benefits and bonuses.

Generation D work style and needs for creative activities has changed them more into 'artists' than 'corporate men'.

Parallel to the emerge of Generation D is the decline in the opportunity for vertical mobility to managerial positions due to flatter organizational forms. For companies in general the challenge is to create meaningful lateral career opportunities.

MNCs have a comparative advantage due to their large and geographically dispersed organizations that yield a wide range of lateral job moves for their employees. As such, MNCs can potentially offer much greater scope for career development than their domestic counterparts. For Employees it requires a higher degree of mobility.

Shift from command-and-control structures and working modes to modes that involve motivating highly competent employees to actively engage in knowledge creation and knowledge sharing. No longer financial capital, technology or other physical capital are the primary determinants of organizational success and failure. The concept of social capital, i.e. networks, common mind-sets and mutual trust is increasingly important to create synergies across their operations. The competitiveness of MNCs is dependent on creating knowledge synergies through cross-border knowledge sharing. Learning to develop, utilize and promote social capital will be key future tasks for international managers (Bogsnes 2009).

Social networking technologies have transformed the potential for achieving connectivity and therefore for developing social capital within complex global organizations. IBM's internal Beehive Web site helps employees to connect and brainstorm with peers they meet on interdepartmental projects or meetings. However, international managers must develop the ability to nurture virtual teams in a strategically selective way. Yet less than one-third of the more than 300 global executives surveyed and interviewed by McKinsey believed that their companies were getting the most out of information and communication technology (Gibbs et al. 2012).

The relationships with customers are undergoing radical change. Making things or producing services in small batches tailored to a customer is becoming routine.

Delivering customized goods and services requires a pronounced degree of agility.

MNCs need to be able to handle fluid networks, temporary projects, evolving and geographically distant centers of excellence and virtual organizations. The agility required of employees means the abandonment of rigid, hierarchical work structures in favor of more fluid, organic structures (Marsh 2012).

5.4 The Cage Distance Framework (Ghemawat 2001)

Cultural distance is a function of differences in values and communication styles that are rooted in culture (demographic or organizational). **Distance** is created when individuals or groups perceive that their values and communication styles differ from others (Igi Global 2016).

Ghemawat (2001) identified four dimensions of Distances:

- Cultural Distance
- Administrative and Political Distance
- Geographic Distance
- Economic Distance

	Cultural Distance	Administrative Distance	Geographic Distance	Economic Distance
Attributes creating distance	Different languages Different ethnicities; lack of connective ethnic or social networks Different religions Different social norms	Absence of colonial ties Absence of shared monetary or political association Political hostility Government policies Institutional weakness	Physical remoteness Lack of a common border Lack of sea or river access Size of country Weak transportation or communication links Differences in climates	Differences in consumer incomes Differences in costs and quality of: • natural resources • financial resources • human resources • infrastructure • intermediate inputs • information or knowledge
Industries or products affected by distance	Products have high linguistic content (TV) Products affect cultural or national identity of consumers (foods) Product features vary in terms of: • size (cars) • standards (electrical appliances) • packaging Products carry countryspecific quality associations (wines)	Government involvement is high in industries that are: • producers of staple goods (electricity) • producers of other "entitlements" (drugs) • large employers (farming) • large suppliers to government (mass transportation) • national champions (aerospace) • vital to national security (telecommunications) • exploiters of natural resources (oil, mining) • subject to high sunk costs (infrastructure)	Products have a low value-to-weight or bulk ratio (cement) Products are fragile or perishable (glass, fruit) Communications and connectivity are important (financial services) Local supervision and operational requirements are high (many services)	Dature of demand varies with income level (cars) Economies of standardization or scale are important (mobile phones) Labor and other factor cost differences are salient (garments) Distribution or business systems are different (insurance) Companies need to be responsive and agile (home appliances)

Mannaz

Fig. 5.3 CAGE Distance framework, source: http://www.slideshare.net/dxbugs/the-cage-framework

For each dimension a set of parameters have impact on Distance between countries and affect industries or products (Fig. 5.3).

5.5 About Globalization: People's Voice (Jim 1999)

5.5.1 Globalization: Positive Aspects

- International trade keeps prices low and quality high. Anytime a country in the past has tried to be self sufficient and not partake in the global markets, they find that their businesses become inefficient due to a lack of competition, prices rise, their products lack innovation, and they end up with hyperinflation.
- Globalization can bring wealth to some of the world's poor. For example, much of southeast Asia was terribly poor a few decades ago; thanks to globalization and international trade many of these countries have experienced annual growth in the double digits and many of those people are now much better off than their parents were a generation ago.
- Globalization can help bring world peace. As every country on the planet becomes more interconnected with every other country, there is a serious incentive for all of the involved to keep the peace. Thomas Friedman, in his book "The Lexus and

the Olive Tree", goes so far as to discuss the "Golden Arches" theory of world peace--he says that no countries that have McDonald's have ever or will ever attack each other.

- Globalization could help protect the environment. Some people have pointed out that in the past a nation like China could have produced as much pollution as they would have like to, but today if China wants to engage in the global marketplace the rest of their trading partners could potentially put pressure on them to clean up their act.

5.5.2 Globalization: Negative Aspects

- Globalization has led to greater disparity in wealth within many countries. Back to southeast Asia, the people of those countries did experience a tremendous amount of growth over the past couple of decades, but it wasn't experienced equally by all of their people. The poor have seen a moderate rise in incomes while the wealthy have seen incredible rises in their incomes.
- The creation of what is essentially a single large global market entails certain dangers. Previously, if a nation made financial mistakes and their markets collapsed, it had little affect on the rest of the world. Now, if Mexico, Korea, Brazil, Thailand, or any other emerging nation finds itself in financial collapse they have the potential to bring down most of the world with them. Consider the widespread economic downturns experienced across the globe today due to the American banking crisis.
- Globalization does hurt some workers in each country. For example, the US used to make most of the TVs sold in our stores. Now, the US buys all of its TVs from abroad. When NAFTA opened trade with Mexico, our TV factories closed their US plants and moved to Mexico, where they could find cheaper labor. On the flip side, Mexican farmers have been hurt by imports of American food. With all of our large farming machinery, local Mexican farmers can't compete with large American farmers, and they are being put out of business.
- Diseases can spread more easily now due to the vast numbers of people crossing international borders. Think of the Avian Flu scare from the last few years--someone could contract a disease in Asia and be in the US within a few hours and spreading a disease that previously would have killed them before they could reach another country in which to spread it.
- Globalization is also leading to a homogenization of the world's cultures. As nations open up their borders to free trade, they also have to accept many foreign companies coming into their country and doing business there. The most noticeable companies are McDonald's, KFC, Starbucks, Walmart, and other American cultural icons. Some people fear that in time there will cease to be exciting foreign cultures every nation will be filled with McDonald's, Starbucks, and Walmart.

5.6 Globalization: China's Big Mac Attack (Watson 2000)

No amount of stealth advertising or brilliant promotions could have done the trick alone. The fast-food industry did not create a market where none existed; it responded to an opportunity presented by the collapse of an outdated Confucian family system. The deeper one digs into the personal lives of consumers anywhere, the more complex matters become. People are not the automatons many theorists make them out to be. Consumers have most assuredly not been stripped of their cultural heritage, nor have they become the uncomprehending dupes of transnational corporations.

In 2000, McDonald's had more than 25,000 outlets in 119 countries. Most of the corporation's revenues now come from operations outside the United States, and a new restaurant opens somewhere in the world every 17 hours.

McDonald's makes heroic efforts to ensure that its food looks, feels, and tastes the same everywhere. A Big Mac in Beijing tastes virtually identical to a Big Mac in Boston. Menus vary only when the local market is deemed mature enough to expand beyond burgers and fries. Consumers can enjoy Spicy Wings (red-pepper-laced chicken) in Beijing, kosher Big Macs (minus the cheese) in Jerusalem, vegetable McNuggets in New Delhi, or a McHuevo (a burger with fried egg) in Montevideo.

Nonetheless, wherever McDonald's takes root, the core product -- at least during the initial phase of operation -- is not really the food but the experience of eating in a cheerful, air-conditioned, child-friendly restaurant that offers the revolutionary innovation of clean toilets. Critics claim that the rapid spread of McDonald's and its fast-food rivals undermines indigenous cuisines and helps create a homogeneous, global culture. Beijing and Hong Kong thus make excellent test cases since they are the dual epicenters of China's haute cuisine (with apologies to Hunan, Sichuan, and Shanghai loyalists). If McDonald's can make inroads in these two markets, it must surely be an unstoppable force that levels cultures. But the truth of this parable of globalization is subtler than that.

How did McDonald's do it? How did a hamburger chain become so prominent in a cultural zone dominated by rice, noodles, fish, and pork? In China, adult consumers often report that they find the taste of fried beef patties strange and unappealing. Why, then, do they come back to McDonald's? And more to the point, why do they encourage their children to eat there?

When Daniel Ng, an American-trained engineer, opened Hong Kong's first McDonald's in 1975, his local food-industry competitors dismissed the venture as a nonstarter: *Selling hamburgers to Cantonese? You must be joking!* Ng credits his boldness to the fact that he did not have an M.B.A. and had never taken a course in business theory. During the early years of his franchise, Ng promoted McDonald's as an outpost of American culture, offering authentic hamburgers to young people eager to forget that they lived in a tiny colony on the rim of Maoist China. The signs outside his first restaurants were in English; the Chinese characters for McDonald's (Cantonese Mak-dong-lou, Mandarin Mai-dang-lao) did not appear until the business was safely established. Over a period of 20 years, McDonald's gradually became a mainstay of Hong Kong's middle-class culture.

Today the restaurants are packed wall-to-wall with busy commuters, students, and retirees who treat them as homes away from home. A 1997 survey I conducted among Hong Kong university students revealed that few were even aware of the company's American origins. For Hong Kong youth, McDonald's is a familiar institution that offers comfort foods that they have eaten since early childhood.

Most Chinese newlyweds are choosing to create their own homes, thereby separating themselves from parents and in-laws. The traditional system of living with the groom's parents is dying out fast, even in the Chinese countryside. Recent research in Shanghai and Dalian (and Taipei) shows that professional couples prefer to live near the wife's mother, often in the same apartment complex. The crucial consideration is household labor, child care, cooking, shopping, washing, and cleaning. With both husband and wife working full time, someone has to do it, and the wife's mother is considered more reliable (and less trouble) than the husband's mother, who would expect her daughter-in-law to be subservient.

McDonald's opened in Beijing in 1992, a time when changes in family values were matched by a sustained economic boom. The startup date also coincided with a public "fever" for all things American sports, clothing, films, food, and so on.

American-style birthday parties became key to the company's expansion strategy. Prior to the arrival of McDonald's, festivities marking youngsters' specific birth dates were unknown in most of East Asia. In Hong Kong, for instance, lunar-calendar dates of birth were recorded for use in later life to help match prospective marriage partners' horoscopes or choose an auspicious burial date. Until the late 1970s and early 1980s, most people paid little attention to their calendar birth date if they remembered it at all. McDonald's and its rivals now promote the birthday party complete with cake, candles, and silly hats in television advertising aimed directly at kids. Given that most people in these cities live in tiny, overcrowded flats, the local Kentucky Fried Chicken or McDonald's is a convenient and welcoming place for family celebrations.

For the first time in Chinese history, children matter not simply as future providers but as full-scale consumers who command respect in today's economy. Until the 1980s, kids rarely ate outside the home. When they did, they were expected to eat what was put in front of them. The idea that children might actually order their own food would have shocked most adults.

McDonald's could not have succeeded in East Asia without appealing to new generations of consumer's children from 3 to 13 and their harried, stressed-out parents. Between 3:00 and 5:30 p.m. on Hong Kong weekdays, McDonald's restaurants are invaded by armies of young people in school uniforms. They buy a few fries, pour them out on a tray for communal snacking, and sit for at least an hour gossiping, studying, and flirting.

During the midmorning hours, the restaurants are packed with white-haired retirees who stay even longer, drinking tea or coffee (free refills for senior citizens) and lingering over pancake breakfasts. Many sit alone, reading newspapers provided by the management. Both retirees and students are attracted by the roomy tables, good light, and air-conditioning, a combination not easily found in Hong Kong, Beijing, or Shanghai. In effect, local citizens have appropriated private property and converted it into public space.

Meanwhile, China faces yet another family revolution, this one caused by the graying of the population. In 1998, 10% of China's people were over 60; by 2020, the figure is expected to rise to approximately 16%. In 2025, there will be 274 million people over 60 in China, more than the entire 1998 U.S. population. Tens of thousands of retirees roam Hong Kong's air-conditioned shopping malls, congregate in the handful of overcrowded parks, and turn their local McDonald's during the midmorning hours into a substitute for the public gardens, opera theaters, and ancestral halls that sheltered their parents. What stands out at McDonald's is the isolation among Hong Kong elders as they try to entertain themselves.

5.7 Manage Generic Cultural Differences

5.7.1 The Process of Management (Littrell 2008)

It is impossible for culture not to impact domestic business operations since every country has its own culture and every company is situated within a country. Because we are so immersed in our own cultures as individuals, it is easy to forget that how we conduct business and make plans is just as culturally bound as how others conduct business in their own countries. Our domestic culture dictates how our domestic companies operate, so it is nearly universally concluded by academics and practitioners that it is impossible to separate culture from business.

The question should therefore ask, "How does domestic culture impact domestic business operations", and "how is the domestic culture in another country different than mine?"

5.7.2 The Problem of Planning (Littrell 2008)

Planning is the process of setting goals, developing strategies, and outlining tasks and schedules to accomplish the goals. Project planning is a discipline for stating how to complete a project within a certain timeframe, usually with defined stages, and with designated resources:

- Setting measurable objectives
- Identifying deliverables
- Planning the schedule
- Making supporting plans

As the global and local societal and business environments change, strategy and planning must change, but culture remains the same, or changes much more slowly than other environmental influences.

Members of a culture respond to the values dictated by their culture.

When using culture as an analytic or predictive variable, the practitioner must remember that the major theories of cultural dimensions are compilations of measures of individual values, usually expressed by the mean, the average score, of a dimension.

In order to see why particular behaviors, prevail in a given culture, we need to better understand how generalized values are linked to specific actions.

5.7.3 Monochronic and Polychronic Time (Hall E and Hall M 1990)

Monochronic Time (M-time)
is one-thing-at-a-time, following a linear form. Time flows from past to present to future. Monochronic cultures stress a high degree of scheduling, and an elaborate code of behavior built around promptness in meeting obligations and appointments. Germany, Switzerland, U.S.

Polychronic (P-time)
cultures are opposite, human relationships and interactions are valued over "arbitrary" schedules and appointments. Many things may occur at once since many people are involved in everything, and interruptions are frequent. P-time, many-things-at-a-time, is common in Mediterranean and European Colonial-Iberian-Indian cultures.

5.7.4 Time Orientation (Hall E and Hall M 1990)

The USA, New Zealand, and Germany
The pace of life is fast, emphasis on clock time, traditionally monochronic but moving toward polychronic due to pace and complexity of business demands; emphasis is on time; sensitive to time; schedule revolves around the clock (Table 5.1).

Japan, China, Hong Kong
The pace of life is fast. Traditionally Asian countries have operated on event time; however, economic development and interactions with North American and Northern European Cultures have led to a clock time orientation, generally, monochronic in business operations.

Brazil and Argentina
The pace of life is slower. Emphasis is on people; time insensitive; schedule evolves from events; not overly keen to specify definite schedules; business and social activities often mix.

Table 5.1 Patterns between cultures with different time use systems (Hall E and Hall M 1990)

Patterns Between Cultures With Different Time Use Systems (Hall E and Hall M 1990)	
Members of monochronic cultures tend to be low context and:	Members of polychronic cultures tend to be high context and:
do one thing at a time	do many things at once
concentrate on the job	are highly distractible and subject to attend to interruptions before the issue at hand
take time commitments (deadline, schedules) seriously	focus on an objective to be achieved, but may not be concerned about creating plans to achieve it
are low-context and need information	are highly-context and already have information
are committed to the job	are committed to people and human relationships
adhere to plans	change plans often and easily
are concerned about not disturbing others; follow rules of privacy and consideration	are more concerned with those who are closely related (family, friends, close business associates) then with privacy
show great respect for private property; seldom borrow or lend	borrow and lend things often and easily
emphasize promptness	base promptness on the relationship
are accustomed to short-term relationships	have a strong tendency to build lifetime relationships

5.7.5 High and Low-Context Cultures (Hall E and Hall M 1990)

High and low context culture refers to the fact that when people communicate, they make assumptions as to how much the listener knows about the subject under discussion.

In low-context communication, the assumption is that the listener knows very little and must be told practically everything.

In high-context communication the listener is already "in context" and does not need to be given much background information. Chinese, Japanese, Arabs, and Mediterranean peoples, who develop extensive information networks among family, friends, colleagues and clients and who are involved in close personal relationships, tend to be high-context.

Low-context people include Americans, Germans, Swiss, Scandinavians, and other northern Europeans. Low-context people compartmentalize their personal relationships, their work, and many aspects of day-to-day life. Consequently, each time they interact with others they need detailed background information (Table 5.2).

5.8 Decisions: Intercultural Competencies

Login to kdibis as described in Sect. 2.7. In the cockpit click *Intercultural Competence*.

Students will rank six job preferences and mark the impact of each decision as high or low (Fig. 5.4). The results will be mapped against the results of international studies and will have impact on the market shares of the four competitors.

Table 5.2

Patterns Between Cultures With Different Combinations of Values (Hall E and Hall M 1990)	
Low-Context, Monochronic, Individualistic	High-Context, Polychronic, Collective
What is said is more important than how or where it is said	What is said and how or where it is said are significant in interpreting what is meant
Mastery over nature	Harmony with nature
Personal control over the environment	Fate controls
Doing	Being
Future orientation	Past or present orientation
Change is improvement	Tradition is valued
Time dominates	Focus on relationship
Human equality	Hierarchy/rank/status important
Youth is valued	Elders respected and valued
Self-help valued	Birthright inheritance
Individualism, privacy valued	Group welfare important
Competition important	Cooperation important
Informal	Formal
Directness/openness/honesty valued	Indirectness/ritual/face valued
Practicality/efficiency valued	Idealism/theory important
Materialist	Spiritualist/detachment from world

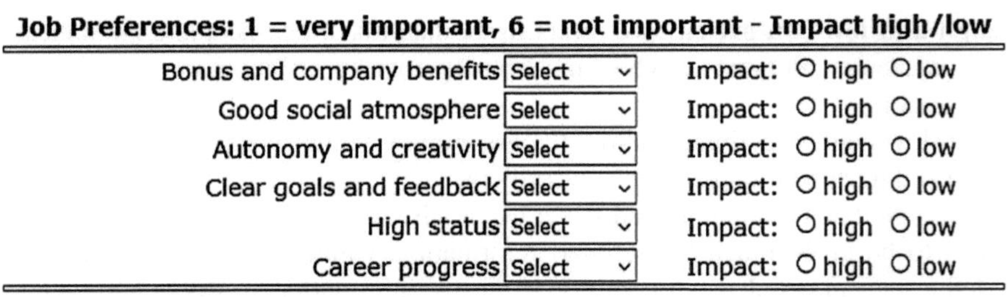

Job Preferences: 1 = very important, 6 = not important - Impact high/low

Bonus and company benefits	Select	Impact: O high O low
Good social atmosphere	Select	Impact: O high O low
Autonomy and creativity	Select	Impact: O high O low
Clear goals and feedback	Select	Impact: O high O low
High status	Select	Impact: O high O low
Career progress	Select	Impact: O high O low

Fig. 5.4 Intercultural competencies

5.9 Assigned Reading

Section 8.1 Lionel Messi's shoes: 'The greatest insult in Egyptian history?'
Section 8.2 Airbus Industries
Section 8.3 CRM Contributes to a Scary Halloween for Hershey

References

Behrmann, J. N. and Grosse R. (1990). International Business and Governments. Columbia, South Carolina: University of South Carolina Press

Bogsnes, B. (2009), Implementing Beyond Budgeting, Hoboken, NJ: Wiley.

Coutts, K. and Godley, W. (1992), Does Britain's balance of payments matter anymore?, in Michie, J. (Ed.), The Economic Legacy 1979-1992, Academic Press, London, pp. 60-7
Dalli, D. (1994), The exporting process: the evolution of small and medium sized firms toward internationalization, in Axinn, C.N. (Ed.), Advances in International Marketing, JAI Press, Greenwich, CT, pp. 85-110
Ghemawat P (2001), Redefining Global Strategy: Crossing Borders in a World Where Differences Still Matter, Harvard Business School Publishing, Boston, Massachusetts
Gibbs, T. Heywood S. and Weiss L. (2012), Technology as friend or foe? McKinsey Quarterly, June,http://www.mckinsey.com/business-functions/organization/our-insights/organizing-for-an-emerging-world
Gilpin, R. (1975). U.S. Power and the Multinational Corporation. New York: Basic Books
Gladwin, T. and Walter I. (1980). Multinationals Under Fire. Wiley
Gooderham, N., Grogaard, B., Nordhaug, O. (2013), International Management Theory and Practice, Edward Elgar
Grosse R., Behrman J.N. (1992), Theory in international business", Transnational Corporations, vol 1/no. 1, United Nations Conference on Trade and Development (UNCTAD)
Haar, J. and Ortiz-Buonafina, M. (1995), The internationalization process and marketing activities: the case of Brazilian export firms, Journal of Business Research, Vol. 32, pp. 175-81
Hall E. and Hall M. (1990), Understanding Cultural Differences, Consortium Book Sales & Dist
Hines, A. (2007), Get Your International Business Terms Right, CBS Moneywatch, CBS Interactive, http://www.cbsnews.com/news/get-your-international-business-terms-right. Viewed 6th September, 2016
Hofstede G (2016), http://www.clearlycultural.com/geert-hofstede-cultural-dimensions
Hymer, S. (1970), The efficiency (contradictions) of multinational corporations, American Economic Review, Vol. 60, pp. 441-8
Igi Global (2016), http://www.igi-global.com/dictionary/cultural-distance/6381. Viewed 6th September 2016
Jim in Japan (1999), What are the arguments for and against globalization? Yahoo! Answers, https://answers.yahoo.com/question/index?qid=20081111114744AAv7Gi8, accessed 15 September 2016
Johanson, J. and Vahlne, J.E. (1977), The internationalization process of the firm, Journal of International Business Studies, Vol. 8, Spring/Summer, pp. 23-32
Johanson, J. and Wiedersheim-Paul, F. (1975), The internationalization of the firm – four Swedish cases, Journal of Management Studies, Vol. 12 No. 3, pp. 305-22
Littrell R (2008), Managing Culturally Diverse Stakeholders in International Projects: The Problem of Planning, Rio´s International Journal on Sciences of Industrial and Systems Engineering and Management, Vol. 2, No. III, pp. 1-24. http://www.rij.eng.uerj.br/scientific/2008. Viewed 9th September 2016
Marsh, P. (2012), The New Industrial Revolution: Consumers, Globalization and the End of Mass Production, Yale University Press
McCombie, J.S.L. and Thirlwall, A. (1992), The re-emergence of the balance of payments constraint, in Michie, J. (Ed.), The Economic Legacy 1979-1982, Academic Press, London, pp. 68-74
Messner W, Schaefer N (2012), Advancing Intercultural Competencies for Global Collaboration, in Baeumer U, Kreutter P, Messner W (Eds.), Globalization of Professional Services, Springer
Morgan R, Katsikeas S (1997), Theories of international trade, foreign direct investment and firm internationalization: a critique", Management Decision 35/1 68-78, MCB University Press
Netlingo (2016), generation-d, http://www.netlingo.com/word/generation-d.php. Accessed 9 September 2016
Piercy, N.F. (1981), Company internationalization: active and reactive exporting, European Journal of Marketing, Vol. 15 No. 3, pp. 24-40
Porter, M.E. (1985), Competitive Advantage: Creating and Sustaining Superior Performance, Free Press, New York, NY
Smith, A. (1776), An Inquiry into the Nature and Causes of the Wealth of Nations, edited by E. Cannan (1961) and reprinted by Methuen, London

Tayeb, M. (1992), The Global Business Environment, Sage, London
Turnbull, P.W. (1985), Internationalization of the firm: a stages process or not?, paper presented at a conference on Export Expansion and Market Entry Modes, Dalhousie University, Halifax, October
Watson J 2000, China's Big Mac Attack, Council on Foreign Relations, Inc. http://www.foreignaffairs.com/articles/56052/james-l-watson/chinas-big-mac-attack, accessed 25 September 2016
Welch, L.S. and Luostarinen, R. (1988), Internationalization: evolution of a concept, Journal of General Management, Vol. 14 No. 2, pp. 34-55

Chapter 6
International Project Management

Abstract International project management includes the discussion of stakeholder management, why projects fail, about project success and stakeholder engagement approaches. Virtual team challenges, management and successes. Innovation in global delivery and virtual team and the assessment of virtual team best practices completes this chapter.

6.1 Stakeholder Management

A stakeholder is any group or individual who can affect or is affected by the achievement of the organization's objectives. Stakeholder theory is about a business, its about strategy and it says if a group can affect you then you need to deal with it. What's important is understanding how the value creation process works in a business. And in business A in the automobile industry in India, the value creation process may be different than in business B a web-based start-up in Silicon Valley (Freeman 1984).

6.1.1 Why Projects Fail

The Chaos Reports by the Standish Group have been published every year since 1994 and are a snapshot of the state of the software development industry (The Standish Group 2015).

Results 2015:

- 29 % of all projects succeeded (delivered on time, on budget, with required features and functions).
- 52 % were challenged (late, over budget, and/or with less than the required features and functions).
- 19 % failed (cancelled prior to completion or delivered and never used)".

These results do not vary considerably with type of project or industry sector.

K. Gronwald, *Global Communication and Collaboration*,
DOI 10.1007/978-3-662-53150-1_6

It is also of significance to note that the results do not appear to have changed significantly over the past 25 years despite a complete industry having emerged and £millions being spent on the subject of project management (Oliver 2014).

The key factors enabling project success or contributing to project failure are

1. Stakeholder management factors
2. Executive Sponsorship factors
3. Clarity of mission, objective and benefit
4. Accuracy of definition and planning including understanding of risk
5. Skills and experience factors
6. Communication factors
7. Team factors
8. Leadership
9. Resource factors
10. Change factors

6.1.2 Project Success

Project success is

- Meeting the project technical specification and/or project mission to be performed.
- Attaining high levels of satisfaction from the project stakeholders.
- Technical performance is integrally associated with perceived success of a project, whereas cost and schedule performance are somewhat less intimately associated with perceived success.
- In the long run what really matters is whether the stakeholders are satisfied.
- Positive schedule and cost performance mean little in the face of a poorly performing end product.

6.2 Stakeholder Engagement Approaches (stakeholdermap.com 2016)

Stakeholder engagement is the process used by an organization to engage relevant stakeholders for a purpose to achieve accepted outcomes (AccountAbility 2008).

Partnership
Shared accountability and responsibility. Two-way engagement joint learning, decision making and actions.

Participation
Part of the team, engaged in delivering tasks or with responsibility for a particular area/activity. Two-way engagement within limits of responsibility.

Consultation
Involved, but not responsible and not necessarily able to influence outside of consultation boundaries. Limited two-way engagement: organization asks questions, stakeholders answer.

Push Communications
One-way engagement. Organisation may broadcast information to all stakeholders or target particular stakeholder groups using various channels e.g. email, letter, webcasts, podcasts, videos, leaflets.

Pull Communications
One-way engagement. Information is made available, and stakeholders choose whether to engage with it e.g. web-pages, or construction hoardings.

6.3 Virtual Teams

As companies continue to expand globally, the number of people working in teams with colleagues and managers separated from them by many miles (and often different time zones), is growing. This virtual team strategy has many advantages, but it presents its own set of managerial challenges; working online is less formalized, and companies frequently lack clear policies on how to manage virtually (Reiche 2013).

Advances in communications and information technology create new opportunities for organizations to build and manage virtual teams. Such teams are composed of employees with unique skills, located at a distance from each other, who must collaborate to accomplish important organizational tasks (Kirkman et al. 2002).

While work teams were used in the U.S. as early as the 1960s, the widespread use of teams and quality circles began in the Total Quality Management movement of the 1980s. In the late 1980s and early 1990s, many companies implemented self-managing or empowered work teams. To cut bureaucracy, reduce cycle time, and improve service, line-level employees took on decision-making and problem-solving responsibilities traditionally reserved for management. By the mid-1990s, increasing numbers of companies such as Goodyear, Motorola, Texas Instruments, and General Electric had begun exporting the team concept to their foreign affiliates in Asia, Europe, and Latin America to integrate global human resource practices (Kirkman et al. 2001). Now, due to communication technology improvements and continued globalization, virtual teams have increased rapidly worldwide (Fig. 6.1).

Virtual teams are groups of people who work interdependently with shared purpose across space, time, and organization boundaries using technology to communicate and collaborate (Lipnack and Stamps 2000) Virtual team members may be located across a country or across the world, rarely meet face-to-face, and include members from different cultures (Maznevski and Chudoba 2000). Many virtual teams are cross-functional and emphasize solving customer problems or generating

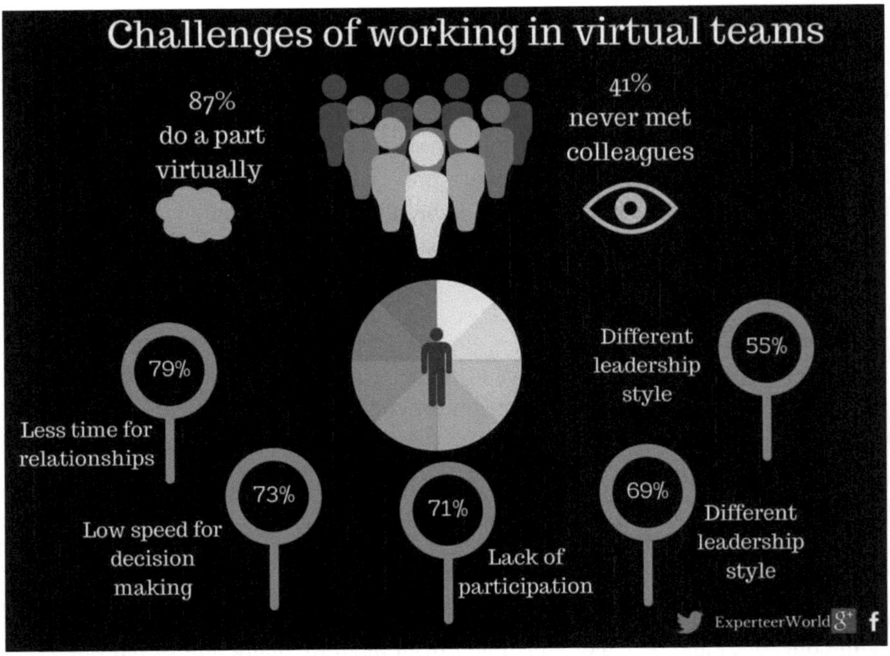

Fig. 6.1 Challenges of working in virtual teams, Source: experteer Magazine (2014)

new work processes (Chase 1999). Virtual work allows organizations to combine the best expertise regardless of geographic location (Gibson and Cohen 2003) (Fig. 6.2).

6.3.1 Five Challenges to Virtual Team Success (Kirkman et al. 2002)

Challenge 1: Building trust within virtual teams
Building trust requires rapid responses to electronic communications from team members, reliable performance, and consistent follow-through.

Unlike face-to-face teams, where trust develops based on social bonds formed by informal chats around the water cooler, impromptu meetings, or after-work gatherings, virtual team members establish trust based on predictable performance.

Challenge 2: Maximizing process gains and minimizing process losses on virtual teams
A critical priority for virtual team leaders is helping their virtual teams maximize process gains and minimize process losses.

Training begins with teambuilding and continues with efforts to help virtual teams create charters and mission statements, clarify goals, and develop operating norms.

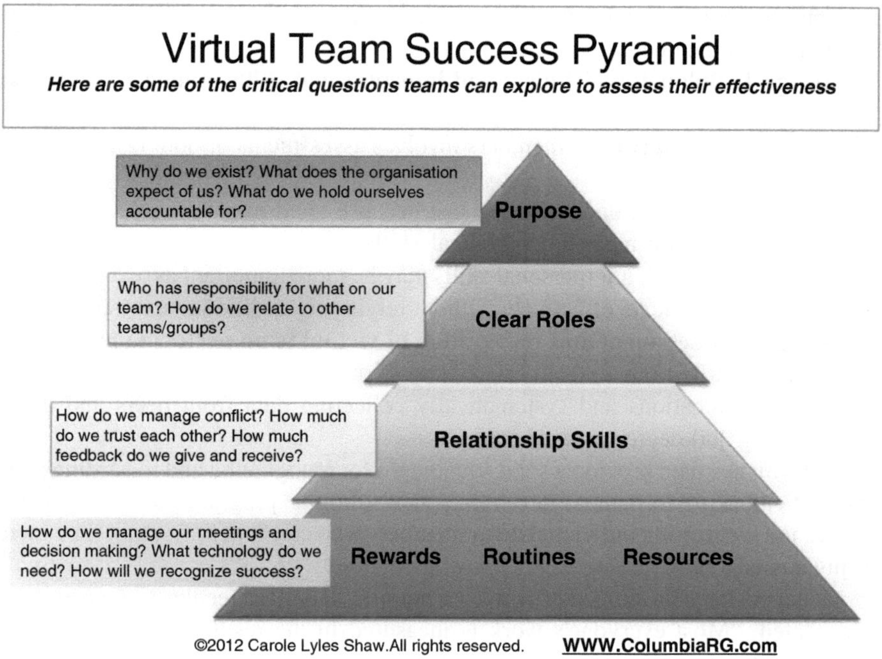

Fig. 6.2 Virtual team success pyramid, source: Shaw (2012)

Sustaining virtual team effectiveness requires an ongoing virtual training program to build new skills in meetings management, problem solving, decision-making, and other team processes.

Comprehensive training efforts allow virtual teams to create synergy by bridging barriers of time and space and collaborating effectively.

Moreover, stereotyping, gossip, politics, and conflict are often minimized in virtual teams.

Challenge 3: Overcoming feelings of isolation and detachment associated with virtual teamwork

General managers admitted that it took some time to recognize how to deal with virtual team member isolation.

Initially, these managers interpreted minimal communication as a signal that all was well.

Over time, however, managers recognized that some virtual team members needed more frequent and some almost daily communication.

Experience with isolated virtual team members is that feelings of detachment and alienation, while possible, can be overcome with careful attention to social needs.

Psychological testing identifies members with strong social needs, realistic job previews shape expectations of prospective employees, increased client contact and teambuilding meet social needs, and virtual team leaders proactively reach out to far-flung team members.

Challenge 4: Balancing technical and interpersonal skills among virtual team members

The selection of virtual team members involves assessments of both task and interpersonal skills.

Contrary to conventional wisdom, just because team members seldom interact face-to-face does not mean interpersonal skills will be less important than task-relevant skills. Indeed, interpersonal skills may be more important as team members attempt to communicate effectively without relying on traditional non-verbal cues.

Challenge 5: Assessment and recognition of virtual team performance

Individual contributions to team effectiveness can be assessed by monitoring electronic communications and systematically collecting data from peers and direct reports using 360-degree assessments.

Performance data provide a solid foundation for recognizing and rewarding team and individual performance, developing new training programs to assist virtual teams, and identifying individual team members who can benefit from off-line mentoring and coaching.

Managers have developed effective techniques to deliver feedback. As one manager stated, "Most everyone's work is measured in the results they produce and through statistics, and it can all be pulled out systematically for each individual."

In the virtual workplace, team members can be judged more on what they actually do rather than on what they appear to be doing.

6.3.2 Managing Virtual Teams (Reiche 2013)

Be Available

It can be isolating working virtually. Don't make team members feel you are absent; be in regular contact to talk not just about their day-to-day duties, but beyond that to general queries about their day, mood and social life.

Organize Regular meetings with Both Individuals and the Whole Team

This should be done both online – through IT technology such as videoconferencing, social media or Skype – and face-to-face, at least once or twice a year. Even if companies are cutting costs, it's a cost well spent on building relationships.

Encourage Informal Conversations

Humans are social animals, and people tend to assume the worst if they don't know what others are up to. To help build relationships and trust between members, encourage your team to share their feelings and chat informally whenever they can.

Rotate

To further break down barriers between team members, try to ensure at least one team member spends a short period of time in another location.

Be Creative with Team Bonding
For example, after your team achieves a particular goal, organize a virtual reward ceremony. Send a small present to all team members and get everyone to open it at the same time during a video call (Fig. 6.3).

Treat Time Zones Fairly

With teams spread around the world, you may have a very short window to meet some members or the whole team. Rotate every week the times for meetings to make sure one member is not always waking up early for meetings and that another is not going home too late.

Prioritize Cultural Sensitivity
Being culturally aware in a virtual environment, where people are based around the world, is even more important than in face to face settings. It´s crucial you have an awareness of the cultural differences in your team and promote cultural training for all members. For example – Susan sends short and "very direct" emails to other team members. If they don't know that's part of her culture, others may feel uncomfortable and feel she's treating them poorly.

Invest in Socializing Pre-existing Teams
If you inherit a strong pre-existing sub team (everyone knows each other and works excellently together) – bear in mind that these teams may create even more barriers if they begin working virtually with other, unfamiliar, team members. People in strong pre-existing teams are more reluctant to share information as they have a method that ´works´. Invest in building relationships between the whole team or, recruit someone new in every location and start from scratch.

Look for Shared Understanding When Recruiting
If recruiting, look for people that have worked internationally and who share previous experiences and similarities. Not necessarily in terms of culture, but in terms of shared training activities, having worked on similar projects, education background etc.

Fig. 6.3 Team Bonding, source: Wipro Technologies (2004)

The aim is to have some diversity but to make it easy to build trust with some point of contact.

Manage Expectations

Team members might be expecting certain global opportunities (like moving to headquarters at some stage). How do you motivate your team? What happens if the team goes well? You need to deal with this along with HR – so you should know from the beginning what you can offer them.

6.3.3 Making Virtual Teams Work (Watkins 2013)

Get the Team Together Physically Early-on

It may seem paradoxical to say in a post on virtual teams, but face-to-face communication is still better than virtual when it comes to building relationships and fostering trust, an essential foundation for effective team work.

If you can't do it, it's not the end of the world (focus on doing some virtual team building).

But if you can get the team together, use the time to help team members get to know each other better, personally and professionally, as well to create a shared vision and a set of guiding principles for how the team will work.

Schedule the in-person meeting early on, and reconnect regularly (semi-annually or annually) if possible.

Clarify Tasks and Processes, Not Just Goals and Roles

All new leaders need to align their team on goals, roles and responsibilities in the first 90 days.

With virtual teams, however, coordination is inherently more of a challenge because people are not co-located.

So it's important to focus more attention on the details of task design and the processes that will be used to complete them.

Simplify the work to the greatest extent possible, ideally so tasks are assigned to sub-groups of two or three team members.

And make sure that there is clarity about work process, with specifics about who does what and when.

Then periodically do "after-action reviews" to evaluate how things are going and identify process adjustments and training needs.

Commit to a Communication Charter

Communication on virtual teams is often less frequent, and always is less rich than face-to-face interaction, which provides more contextual cues and information about emotional states – such as engagement or lack thereof.

The only way to avoid the pitfalls is to be extremely clear and disciplined about how the team will communicate.

Create a charter that establishes norms of behavior when participating in virtual meetings, such as limiting background noise and side conversations, talking clearly and at a reasonable pace, listening attentively and not dominating the conversation, and so on.

The charter also should include guidelines on which communication modes to use in which circumstances, for example when to reply via email versus picking up the phone versus taking the time to create and share a document.

Leverage the Best Communication Technologies

Developments in collaborative technologies – ranging from shared workspaces to multi-point video conferencing – unquestionably are making virtual teaming easier.

However, selecting the "best" technologies does not necessarily mean going with the newest or most feature-laden.

It's essential not to sacrifice reliability in a quest to be on the cutting edge.

If the team has to struggle to get connected or wastes time making elements of the collaboration suite work, it undermines the whole endeavor.

So err on the side of robustness.

Also be willing to sacrifice some features in the name of having everyone on the same systems.

Otherwise, you risk creating second-class team members and undermining effectiveness.

Build a Team with Rhythm

When some or all the members of a team are working separately, it's all-too-easy to get disconnected from the normal rhythms of work life.

One antidote is to be disciplined in creating and enforcing rhythms in virtual team work.

This means, for example, having regular meetings, ideally same day and time each week.

It also means establishing and sharing meeting agenda in advance, having clear agreements on communication protocols, and starting and finishing on time.

If you have team members working in different time zones, don't place all the time-zone burden on some team members; rather, establish a regular rotation of meeting times to spread the load equitably.

Agree on a Shared Language

Virtual teams often also are cross-cultural teams, and this magnifies the communication challenges – especially when members think they are speaking the same language, but actually are not.

The playwright George Bernard Shaw famously described Americans and the British as "two nations divided by a common language."

His quip captures the challenge of sustaining shared understanding across cultures.

When the domain of team work is technical, then the languages of science and engineering often provide a solid foundation for effective communication.

However, when teams work on tasks involving more ambiguity, for example generating ideas or solving problems, the potential for divergent interpretations is a real danger (see for example this Anglo-Dutch translation guide).

Take the time to explicitly negotiate agreement on shared interpretations of important words and phrases, for example, when we say "yes," we mean… and when we say "no" we mean…and post this in the shared workspace.

Create a "Virtual Water Cooler"

The image of co-workers gathering around a water cooler is a metaphor for informal interactions that share information and reinforce social bonds.

Absent explicit efforts to create a "virtual water cooler," team meetings tend to become very task-focused; this means important information may not be shared and team cohesion may weaken.

One simple way to avoid this: start each meeting with a check-in, having each member take a couple of minutes to discuss what they are doing, what's going well and what's challenging.

Regular virtual team-building exercises are another way to inject a bit more fun into the proceedings.

Also enterprise collaboration platforms increasingly are combining shared workspaces with social networking features that can help team members to feel more connected.

Clarify and Track Commitments

In a classic HBR article "Management Time, Who's got the Monkey?" William Oncken and Donald L. Wass use the who-has-the-monkey-on-their-back metaphor to exhort leaders to push accountability down to their teams.

When teams work remotely, however, it's inherently more difficult to do this, because there is no easy way to observe engagement and productivity.

As above, this can be partly addressed by carefully designing tasks and having regular status meetings.

Beyond that, it helps to be explicit in getting team members to commit to define intermediate milestones and track their progress.

One useful tool: a "deliverables dashboard" that is visible to all team members on whatever collaborative hub they are using.

If you create this, though, take care not to end up practicing virtual micromanagement.

There is a fine line between appropriate tracking of commitments and overbearing (and demotivating) oversight.

Foster Shared Leadership

Defining deliverables and tracking commitments provides "push" to keep team members focused and productive; shared leadership provides crucial "pull."

Find ways to involve others in leading the team.

Examples include: assigning responsibility for special projects, such as identifying and sharing best practices; or getting members to coach others in their areas of expertise; or assigning them as mentors to help on-board new team members; or asking them to run a virtual team-building exercise.

By sharing leadership, you will not only increase engagement, but will also take some of the burden off your shoulders.

Don't Forget the 1:1 s

Leaders' one-to-one performance management and coaching interactions with their team members are a fundamental part of making any team work.

Make these interactions a regular part of the virtual team rhythm, using them not only to check status and provide feedback, but to keep members connected to the vision and to highlight their part of "the story" of what you are doing together.

6.4 Innovation in Global Delivery and Virtual Teams (Neumann 2012)

No Content

6.5 Decisions: Virtual Team Best Practices

Login to kdibis as described in Sect. 2.7. In the cockpit click *International Project Management.*

Decisions are to be made about the priorities of virtual team priorities (Fig. 6.4). Students will rank eighteen criteria and mark the impact of each decision as high or low. The results will be mapped against industry best practices and will have impact on the market shares of the four competitors.

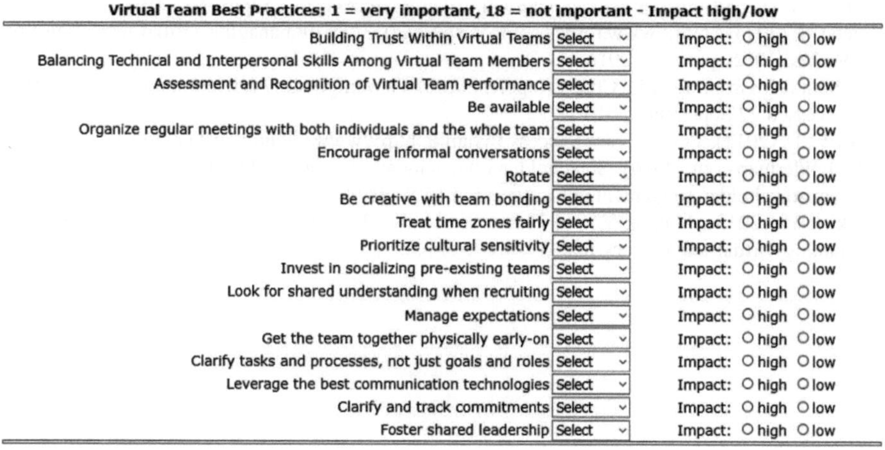

Virtual Team Best Practices: 1 = very important, 18 = not important - Impact high/low

Building Trust Within Virtual Teams	Select	Impact: ○ high ○ low
Balancing Technical and Interpersonal Skills Among Virtual Team Members	Select	Impact: ○ high ○ low
Assessment and Recognition of Virtual Team Performance	Select	Impact: ○ high ○ low
Be available	Select	Impact: ○ high ○ low
Organize regular meetings with both individuals and the whole team	Select	Impact: ○ high ○ low
Encourage informal conversations	Select	Impact: ○ high ○ low
Rotate	Select	Impact: ○ high ○ low
Be creative with team bonding	Select	Impact: ○ high ○ low
Treat time zones fairly	Select	Impact: ○ high ○ low
Prioritize cultural sensitivity	Select	Impact: ○ high ○ low
Invest in socializing pre-existing teams	Select	Impact: ○ high ○ low
Look for shared understanding when recruiting	Select	Impact: ○ high ○ low
Manage expectations	Select	Impact: ○ high ○ low
Get the team together physically early-on	Select	Impact: ○ high ○ low
Clarify tasks and processes, not just goals and roles	Select	Impact: ○ high ○ low
Leverage the best communication technologies	Select	Impact: ○ high ○ low
Clarify and track commitments	Select	Impact: ○ high ○ low
Foster shared leadership	Select	Impact: ○ high ○ low

Fig. 6.4 Virtual team best practices

6.6 Assigned Reading

Section 8.5 Successful People Strategies for Innovation in Global Delivery and Virtual Teams

References

AccountAbility (2008), http://www.accountability.org

Chase N (1999), Learning to lead a virtual team. Quality, 38(9): 76.; and Geber, B. 1995. Virtual teams. Training, 32(4): 36–40; and Bell, B. S., & Kozlowski, S. W. J. 2002. A typology of virtual teams: Im-plications for effective leadership. Group & Organization Management, 27(1): 14–49

Experteer Magazine (2014), What are the challenges of working in virtual teams? https://us.experteer.com/magazine/what-are-the-challenges-of-working-in-virtual-teams. Accessed: 16 September 2016

Freeman, R. E. (1984), Strategic Management: A Stakeholder Approach. Boston: Pitman

Gibson, C, Cohen, S (2003). Virtual teams that work: Creating the conditions for virtual team effectiveness. San Francisco: Jossey-Bass

Kirkman B, Gibson C, & Shapiro (2001) "Exporting" teams: Enhancing the implementation and effectiveness of work teams in global affiliates. Organizational Dynamics, 30(1): 12–29

Kirkman B et al. (2002) Five challenges to virtual team success: Lessons from Sabre, Inc., Academy of Management Executive; Aug 2002, Vol. 16 Issue 3, p 67-79, 13p, 1 chart, 4 bw

Lipnack J, Stamps J (2000), Virtual teams: People working across boundaries with technology. 2nd ed. New York: Wiley. See also, Duarte, D. L, & Snyder, N. T. 2001. Mastering virtual teams. 2nd ed. San Francisco: Jossey-Bass

Maznevski M, Chudoba K (2000). Bridging space over time: Global virtual-team dynamics and effectiveness. Organization Science, 11(5): 473–492; and Montoya-Weiss, M. M., Massey, A. P., & Song, M. 2001. Getting it together: Temporal coordination and conflict management in global virtual teams. Academy of Management Journal, 44(6): 1251–1262, for issues involving virtual teams composed of members from different countries

Oliver M. (2014), Stakeholder Management - Why projects fail, Performance Coaching International, http://www.performancecoachinginternational.com. Accessed 23 September 2016

Reiche S (2013), http://www.forbes.com/sites/iese/2013/06/20/managing-virtual-teams-ten-tips. Viewed 10th September, 2016

The Standish Group (2015), Chaos Report, https://www.infoq.com/articles/standish-chaos-2015. Accessed 22 September 2016

Shaw C. L. (2012), Virtual Team Success Pyramid, http://www.ColumbiaRG.com

Stakeholdermap.com (2016), Stakeholder Engagement approaches, http://www.stakeholdermap.com/stakeholder-engagment.html. Accessed 16 September 2016

Watkins M. (2013), Making Virtual Teams Work: Ten Basic Principles. https://hbr.org/2013/06/making-virtual-teams-work-ten

Chapter 7
Conflict Management in International Projects

Abstract The management of culture has become increasingly important to many organizations and business disciplines, particularly multicultural and international project management. Cultural differences often result in varying degrees of conflict and require careful consideration.

7.1 Hofstede's Dimensions of National Culture (Hofstede 2001)

Through the publication of his scholarly book Culture's Consequences (1980, new edition 2001), Geert Hofstede (1928) became the founder of comparative intercultural research.

He is recognized internationally for having developed the first empirical model of *dimensions* of national culture, thus establishing a new paradigm for taking account of cultural elements in international economics, communication and cooperation.

Later, he also developed a model for organizational cultures.

Culture is the collective programming of the mind distinguishing the members of one group or category of people from others.

Management is getting things done through other people. Or more specifically: coordinating the efforts of people towards common goals.

The other people involved may be subordinates, clients, customers, suppliers, authorities, or the public in general (Stakeholder).

Important is that management is always about people.

The values that distinguished country cultures from each other could be statistically categorized into four to six groups.

- Power Distance (PDI)
- Masculinity versus Femininity (MAS)
- Uncertainty Avoidance (UAI)
- Long-Term Orientation (LTO) vs. short term orientation
- Indulgence versus restraint (IVR)

K. Gronwald, *Global Communication and Collaboration*,
DOI 10.1007/978-3-662-53150-1_7

Power Distance (PDI)
Power distance is the extent to which the less powerful members of organizations and institutions (like the family) accept and expect that power is distributed unequally.

Individualism Versus Collectivism (IDV)
The degree to which individuals are integrated into groups.

In individualistic societies, the stress is put on personal achievements and individual rights.

People are expected to stand up for themselves and their immediate family, and to choose their own affiliations.

In contrast, in collectivist societies, individuals act predominantly as members of a lifelong and cohesive group or organization (note: "The word collectivism in this sense has no political meaning: it refers to the group, not to the state").

People have large extended families, which are used as a protection in exchange for unquestioning loyalty.

Masculinity Versus Femininity (MAS)
The distribution of emotional roles between the genders.

Masculine cultures' values are competitiveness, assertiveness, materialism, ambition and power, whereas feminine cultures place more value on relationships and quality of life.

In masculine cultures, the differences between gender roles are more dramatic and less fluid than in feminine cultures where men and women have the same values emphasizing modesty and caring.

As a result of the taboo on sexuality in many cultures, particularly masculine ones, and because of the obvious gender generalizations implied by Hofstede's terminology, this dimension is often renamed by users of Hofstede's work, e.g. to Quantity of Life vs. Quality of Life.

Uncertainty Avoidance (UAI)
A society's tolerance for uncertainty and ambiguity.

It reflects the extent to which members of a society attempt to cope with anxiety by minimizing uncertainty.

People in cultures with high uncertainty avoidance tend to be more emotional. They try to minimize the occurrence of unknown and unusual circumstances and to proceed with careful changes step by step planning and by implementing rules, laws and regulations.

In contrast, low uncertainty avoidance cultures accept and feel comfortable in unstructured situations or changeable environments and try to have as few rules as possible.

People in these cultures tend to be more pragmatic, they are more tolerant of change.

Long-Term Orientation (LTO) Versus Short Term Orientation
First called "Confucian dynamism", it describes societies' time horizon.

Long term oriented societies attach more importance to the future.

They foster pragmatic values oriented towards rewards, including persistence, saving and capacity for adaptation.

In short term oriented societies, values promoted are related to the past and the present, including steadiness, respect for tradition, preservation of one's face, reciprocation and fulfilling social obligations.

Indulgence Versus Restraint (IVR)
The extent to which member in society try to control their desires and impulses.

Whereas indulgent societies have a tendency to allow relatively free gratification of basic and natural human desires related to enjoying life and having fun, restrained societies have a conviction that such gratification needs to be curbed and regulated by strict norms.

7.2 Differences Between Cultures on the Value Dimensions (Hofstede 2016)

Power Distance Index
shows very high scores for Latin and Asian countries, African areas and the Arab world. On the other hand, Anglo and Germanic countries have a lower power distance (only 11 for Austria and 18 for Denmark). For example, the United States has a 40 on the cultural scale of Hofstede's analysis. Compared to Guatemala where the power distance is very high (95) and Israel where it is very low (13), the United States is in the middle. In Europe, power distance tends to be lower in northern countries and higher in southern and east-ern parts: for example, 68 in Poland and 57 for Spain vs. 31 for Sweden and 35 for the United Kingdom.

Regarding the **individualism index**, there is a clear gap between developed and Western countries on one hand, and less developed and eastern countries on the other. North America and Europe can be considered as individualistic with relatively high scores: for ex-ample, 80 for Canada and Hungary. In contrast, Asia, Africa and Latin America have strong collectivistic values: Colombia scores only 13 points on the IDV scale, and Indonesia 14. The greatest contrast can be drawn comparing two extreme countries on this dimension: 6 points for Guatemala vs. 91 points score for the United States. Japan and the Arab world have middle values on this dimension.

Uncertainty Avoidance
scores are the highest in Latin American countries, Southern and Eastern Europe countries including German speaking countries, and Japan. They are lower for Anglo, Nordic, and Chinese culture countries. However, few countries have very low UAI. For example, Germany has a high UAI (65) and Belgium even more (94) compared to Sweden (29) or Denmark (23) despite their geographical proximity.

Masculinity
is extremely low in Nordic countries: Norway scores 8 and Sweden only 5. In contrast, Masculinity is very high in Japan (95), and in European countries like Hungary, Austria and Switzerland influenced by German culture. In the Anglo world, masculinity scores are relatively high with 66 for the United Kingdom for example. Latin countries present contrasting scores: for example, Venezuela has a 73-point score whereas Chile's is only 28. In the USA as well as in other masculine cultures such as Britain and Ireland, there is a feeling that conflicts should be resolved by a good fight.

High **long term orientation** scores are typically found in East Asia, with China having 118, Hong Kong 96 and Japan 88. They are moderate in Eastern and Western Europe, and low in the Anglo countries, the Muslim world, Africa and in Latin America.

Indulgence Scores
are highest in Latin America, parts of Africa, the Anglo world and Nordic Europe; restraint is mostly found in East Asia, Eastern Europe and the Muslim world.

7.3 Thomas & Kilman's Conflict Management Styles (Thomas and Kilmann 2015)

Because no two individuals have exactly the same expectations and desires, conflict is a natural part of our interactions with others. Two basic dimensions (assertiveness, cooperativeness) of behavior define five different modes for responding to conflict situations (Fig. 7.1):

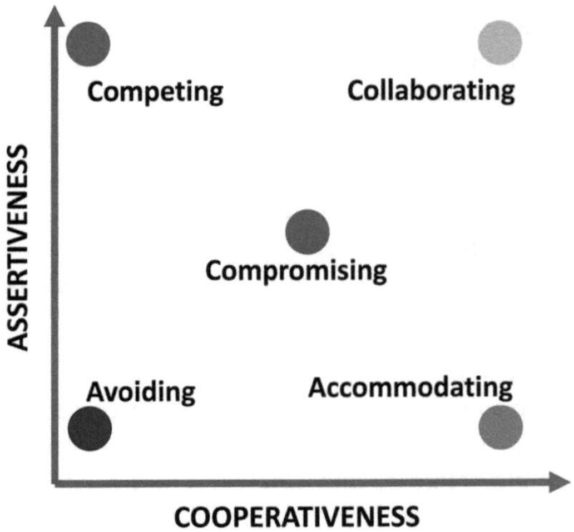

Fig. 7.1 Conflict management styles, Source: (Thomas and Kilmann 2015)

Competing
is assertive and uncooperative – an individual pursues his own concerns at the other person's expense. This is a power-oriented mode in which you use whatever power seems appropriate to win your own position – your ability to argue, your rank, or economic sanctions. Competing means "standing up for your rights," defending a position which you believe is correct, or simply trying to win.

Accommodating
is unassertive and cooperative – the complete opposite of competing. When accommodating, the individual neglects his own concerns to satisfy the concerns of the other person; there is an element of self-sacrifice in this mode. Accommodating might take the form of selfless generosity or charity, obeying another person's order when you would prefer not to, or yielding to another's point of view.

Avoiding
is unassertive and uncooperative – the person neither pursues his own concerns nor those of the other individual. Thus he does not deal with the conflict. Avoiding might take the form of diplomatically sidestepping an issue, postponing an issue until a better time, or simply withdrawing from a threatening situation.

Collaborating
is both assertive and cooperative – the complete opposite of avoiding. Collaborating involves an attempt to work with others to find some solution that fully satisfies their concerns. It means digging into an issue to pinpoint the underlying needs and wants of the two individuals. Collaborating between two persons might take the form of exploring a disagreement to learn from each other's insights or trying to find a creative solution to an interpersonal problem.

Compromising
is moderate in both assertiveness and cooperativeness. The objective is to find some expedient, mutually acceptable solution that partially satisfies both parties. It falls intermediate between competing and accommodating. Compromising gives up more than competing but less than accommodating. Likewise, it addresses an issue more directly than avoiding, but does not explore it in as much depth as collaborating. In some situations, compromising might mean splitting the difference between the two positions, exchanging concessions, or seeking a quick middle-ground solution.

Each of us is capable of using all five conflict-handling modes. None of us can be characterized as having a single style of dealing with conflict. But certain people use some modes better than others and, therefore, tend to rely on those modes more heavily than others – whether because of temperament or practice. Your conflict behavior in the workplace is therefore a result of both your personal predispositions and the requirements of the situation in which you find yourself.

7.4 Culture and Conflict Management (Mohammed et al. 2008)

The management of culture has become increasingly important to many organizations and business disciplines, particularly multicultural and international project management. Cultural differences often result in varying degrees of conflict and require careful consideration.

The term business culture has become increasingly used since its introduction in the 1980's and its importance and effect upon all manner of organizations has achieved considerable significance especially as those organizations have engaged in more international exploits (Pheng and Yuquan, 2000). While internationalization of business provides opportunity in terms of economies of scale and growth for example, it also presents special managerial difficulties. Failing to handle the diversity and complexity of host cultures and their integration with existing or intended organizational culture can be catastrophic. Poor employee motivation, low staff retention, marketing ineffectiveness and loss of competitive advantage are the potential results. On the other hand, successful cultural management can foster innovative practices, organizational knowledge creation and become a potential source of competitive advantage (Hoecklin 1996; Evans et al. 1991; Hofstede 1985).

A study surveyed 116 Project Managers in a multinational telecom organization in 15 countries around the globe using the Thomas-Kilmann Conflict Mode Method (Thomas and Kilmann 2015) to determine their approach toward managing conflict.

Indian, French and UK Project Managers' conflict management style are correlated with Hofstede's description of their cultural characteristics. There are significant links between the cultural dimensions of Individualism and Masculinity with the propensity for Project Managers to adopt a Competitive style of conflict management. Uncertainty Avoidance correlates with a tendency for Project Managers to adopt an Avoiding approach to conflict management. Other relationships are found between Hofstede's cultural dimensions and conflict management styles in Project Managers.

7.4.1 Competitor

Individuals pursue their own goals at the expense of others (Fig. 7.2).

7.4.2 Accommodator

Individuals support others in the pursuit of their goals (Fig. 7.3).

7.4.3 Avoider

Individuals neglect their own goals and those of others (Fig. 7.4).

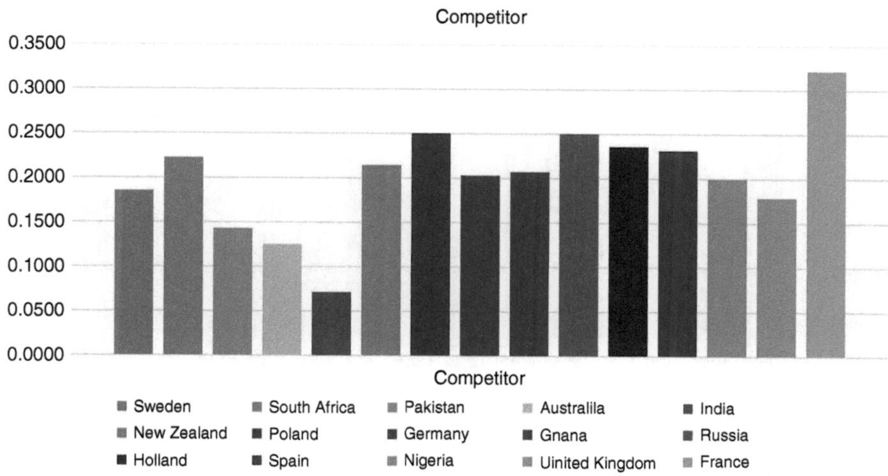

Fig. 7.2 Conflict management style ranking – Competitor

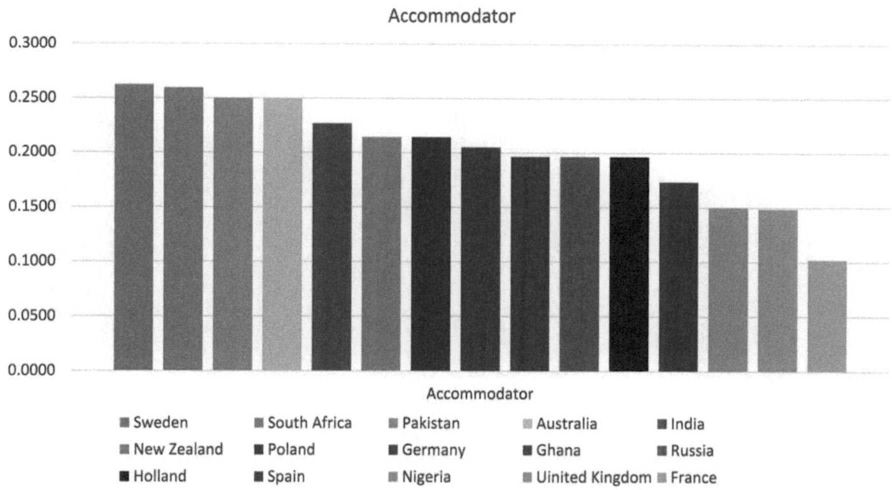

Fig. 7.3 Conflict management style ranking – Accommodator

7.4.4 Collaborator

Individuals attempt to find ways for themselves and others to achieve their goals (Fig. 7.5).

7.4.5 Compromiser

Individuals attempt to partially fulfil their own goals and those of others (Fig. 7.6).

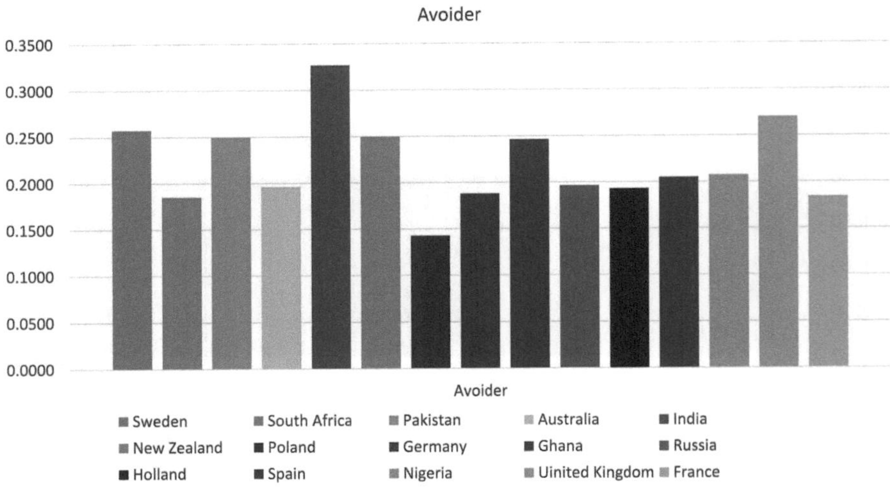

Fig. 7.4 Conflict management style ranking – Avoider

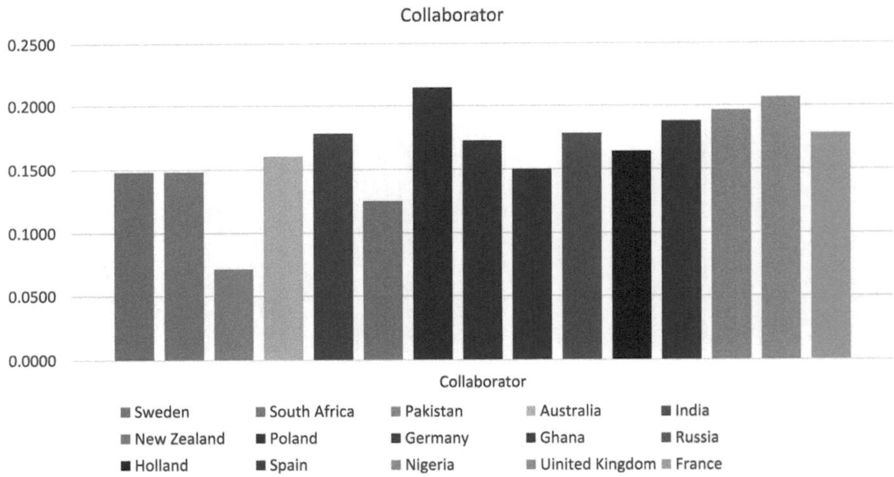

Fig. 7.5 Conflict management style ranking – Collaborator

7.4.6 Conflict Management Style Ranking Total Average

Conflict management style ranking total average (Fig. 7.7)

7.5 Decisions: Conflict management style ranking

Login to kdibis as described in Sect. 2.7. In the cockpit click *Conflict Management in International Projects*.

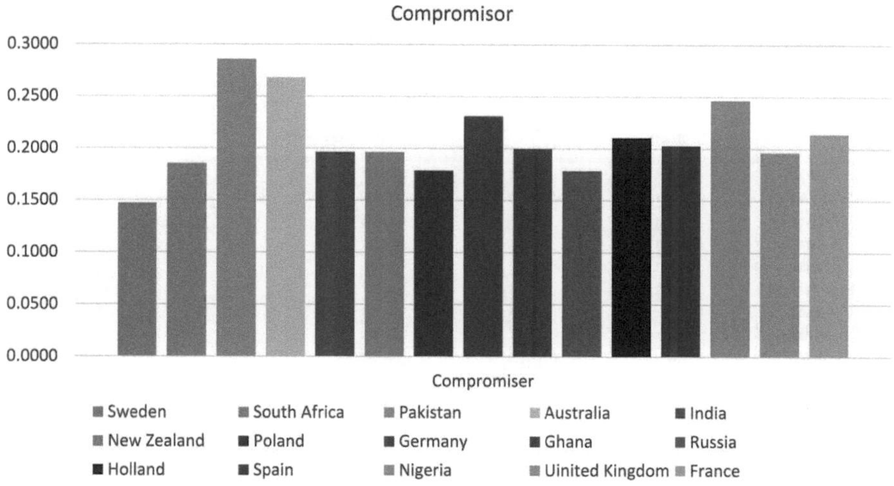

Fig. 7.6 Conflict management style ranking – Compromiser

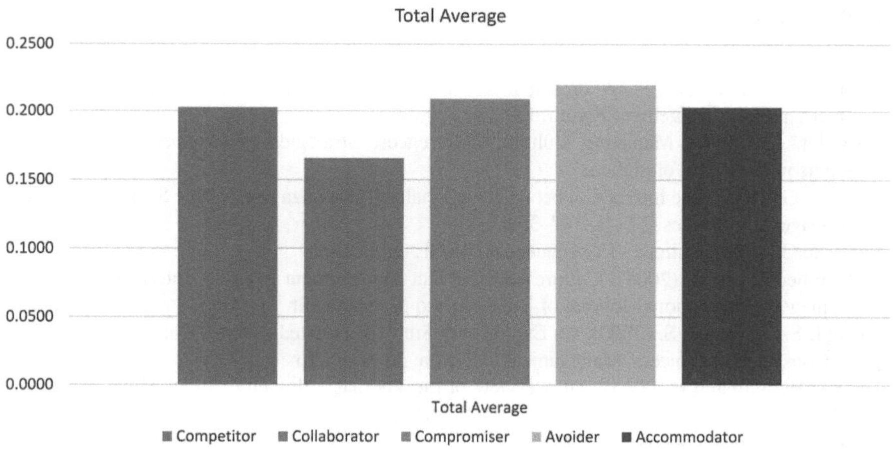

Fig. 7.7 Conflict management style ranking total average

Students will rank five conflict management styles for fifteen countries (Fig. 7.8). The decisions will be compared with the results of a survey and will have impact on the market shares of the four competitors.

7.6 Assigned Reading

Section 8.6 Advancing Intercultural Competencies for Global Collaboration

Conflict Management Style Ranking: 1 = very important, 5 = not important - Impact high/low

Country	Competitor	Collaborator	Compromiser	Avoider	Accommodator
	Individuals pursue their own goals at the expense of others.	Individuals attempt to find ways for themselves and others to achieve their goals.	Individuals attempt to partially fulfill their own goals and those of others.	Individuals neglect their own goals and those of others.	Individuals support others in the pursuit of their goals.
Sweden	Select	Select	Select	Select	Select
South Africa	Select	Select	Select	Select	Select
Pakistan	Select	Select	Select	Select	Select
Australia	Select	Select	Select	Select	Select
India	Select	Select	Select	Select	Select
New Zealand	Select	Select	Select	Select	Select
Poland	Select	Select	Select	Select	Select
Germany	Select	Select	Select	Select	Select
Ghana	Select	Select	Select	Select	Select
Russia	Select	Select	Select	Select	Select
Holland	Select	Select	Select	Select	Select
Spain	Select	Select	Select	Select	Select
Nigeria	Select	Select	Select	Select	Select
United Kingdom	Select	Select	Select	Select	Select
France	Select	Select	Select	Select	Select

Fig. 7.8 Conflict management style ranking

References

Evans W A et al. (1991), A cross-cultural comparison of managerial styles, Asia Pacific, International Management Forum, 15 (3/4), 28–32

Hoecklin, L. (1996), Managing Cultural Differences: Strategies of Competitive Advantage, Addison-Wesley, Wokingham

Hofstede G (1985), The Interaction between National and Organizational Value System. Journal of Management Studies, 22 (4), 347–357

Hofstede G (2001), Culture's Consequences, SAGE Publications

Mohammed U. et al. (2008), Culture and Conflict Management Style of International Project Managers, International Journal of Business and Management

Pheng L.S., & Yuquan S. (2000). An Exploratory Study of Hofstede's Cross Cultural Dimensions in Construction Projects. Management Decision. 20 (1), 1–16

Thomas W, Kilmann R (2015), An overview of the Thomas-Kilmann Conflict Mode Instrument TKI, http://www.kilmanndiagnostics.com/overview-thomas-kilmann-conflict-mode-instrument-tki. Accessed: 16 September 2016

Part III
Course Material

Abstract

Part III contains complementary course material like case studies, game company profiles, and papers.

Chapter 8
Papers and Cases

Abstract This chapter includes complementary reading material as detailed background information to specific topics which can be used for an in-depth analysis by instructors and students. Reference to these articles is given at the end of each corresponding chapter.

8.1 Lionel Messi's shoes: 'The greatest insult in Egyptian history?' (CNN 2016)

Lionel Messi's shoes: 'The greatest insult in Egyptian history?'

It started out innocently enough. The beloved Argentinian football player Lionel Messi offered a pair of his used football boots as a donation during an Egyptian television program on the private network MBC Masr – a private network.

"One of the things he does is give charity all over the world and these will be among the donations he gives," Egyptian presenter Mona El-Sharkawy says as she sits across from the celebrity with the red and white boots held up to the camera.

"And he gave these to our program because we will start an auction for them. Messi, Thank you very very much."

But quickly the goodwill gesture turned into a great offense against the Egyptian people.

"We (Egyptians) have never been so humiliated during our seven thousand years of civilization," Said Hasasin, a controversial parliament member and TV presenter responded during his program Sunday, "I will hit you with the shoes, Messi," he said, as he held up his own shoes, and mockingly said he would donate his leather lace-ups to Argentina.

CNN's attempts to contact Messi through his club team Barcelona have so far proved unsuccessful.

The controversy centers on the significance of shoes in Arab culture. Considered one of the lowliest of items, because it literally touches the ground, many Egyptians find it a dirty and inappropriate object.

To call someone a "gazma," the Arabic word for shoe, is a great insult. And if a family elder catches sight of your soles, say if you have your feet up, you are sure to pay the price.

K. Gronwald, *Global Communication and Collaboration*,
DOI 10.1007/978-3-662-53150-1_8

Even Egypt's Football Association spokesman Azmy Megahed chimed in on the issue, saying: "Our poor don't need him. Shoes work for him…I am confused, if he intends to humiliate us, then I say he better put these shoes on his head and on the heads of the people supporting him. Give your shoes to your country, Argentina is full of poverty."

In Egyptian culture, if your shoe is left overturned at someone's doorway, it's a great snub. If you walk into someone's home with your shoes, it's a disgrace. If, as happens in nearly every Egyptian soap opera, someone lifts their shoe as if to hit you, they intend to add insult to injury.

The two common articles on everyone's feet are simply one of the strongest offenses in the Middle East.

The affront was so great that El-Sharkawy had to defend her program publicly on Monday by arguing that donations were not necessarily intended for Egypt's poor.

"Messi did not even mention Egypt and I did not say the proceeds would go to Egypt," the anchor said in what appeared to be an attempt to recall the scandal, "I am so surprised that people are accusing us of things that weren't even said."

But not all were so quick to make a villain of the 28-year old Messi. A fellow footballer rushed to his defense on social media.

"The most precious thing the writer owns is his pen and the most precious thing the footballer owns is his shoes," famed Egyptian striker Ahmed "Mido" Hossam wrote on Twitter, "I hope we stop the false accusations."

8.2 Airbus Industries (Airbus 2015)

Airbus Industries

Airbus has developed its own transportation system to airlift the large, pre-assembled sections of its jetliners from their production locations to final assembly lines in Toulouse and Hamburg. This service is performed by a fleet of five A300-600ST Super Transporters.

These modified A300-600 s, nicknamed the 'Beluga', have a bulbous main-deck cargo cabin which enables the loading of complete fuselage sections and wings of single-aisle, long-range and future A350 XWB aircraft (47 metric tons, 900 nautical miles).

The A380's size means its fuselage and wing sections are shipped via a surface transportation network that includes specially-commissioned roll-on roll-off ships to carry these sections from production sites in France, Germany, Spain and the United Kingdom to the French city of Bordeaux. From there, sections are transported by barge along the Garonne River to the Toulouse final assembly line.

As for other Airbus aircraft programs, production of the A380 takes place in different sites across Europe. Each site produces completely equipped sections, which are transported to final assembly.

Most A380 sections are transported to Toulouse by sea, river and road. A number of smaller components, such as the vertical fin produced in Stade or the nose section produced in Meaulte, France, carried in Airbus' Beluga fleet.

Airbus Industries: A Worldwide Network of Design Offices and Engineering Centers

The design office at Airbus' headquarters in Toulouse, France gathers such top-level competencies as architecture integration, general design, structural design and computation, integration tests and systems, and propulsion.

Five additional Airbus design offices and engineering centers are located throughout Europe, with sites operating in **Spain, the UK, Russia and Germany** – the latter of which includes two facilities in **Hamburg** and **Bremen**.

Airbus' Filton, UK location focuses on design, engineering and support for Airbus wings, fuel systems and landing gear integration, with additional teams working on systems, structures and aerodynamics projects.

In **Spain, the company's Getafe facility** handles composites design, development and manufacture, as well as the design and manufacturing of tooling.

The Engineering Centre **Airbus Russia (ECAR) is a joint venture facility with the Russian industrial group Kaskol.** ECAR design teams support Airbus engineers in Hamburg and Toulouse, focusing primarily on fuselage structure, stress and systems installation, as well as the design of cabin interiors and freight compartments.

As part of its pledge to support the development of **India's** aviation sector, Airbus in 2007 opened its **Bangalore** engineering center, which cooperates closely with the company's other engineering sites around the world, as well as with the country's growing aerospace industry.

As a **100 % Airbus-owned subsidiary**, the **Airbus Engineering Centre India Pvt. Ltd. (AECI)** focuses on the development of advanced capabilities in the areas of modelling and simulation, covering such areas as flight management systems, computational fluid dynamics (CFD), as well as digital simulation and visualization.

The Bangalore facility's cooperation with other Airbus sites include the development of a simulated A380 flight management system that allows system engineers to provide mature specifications for suppliers of flight management systems, which are key elements in such modern jetliners as Airbus' twenty-first century flagship.

Inauguration of the **Airbus (Beijing)** Engineering Centre (ABEC) in 2005 marked a new phase in the decades-long industrial partnership between China and Airbus, with the goal of making **China** a **full risk-sharing partner** of up to a 5 % airframe work share on a new-generation Airbus aircraft. This strategy has since been applied to the A350 XWB.

The Beijing-based facility is a **joint venture** between Airbus and China's two largest aviation companies – China Aviation Industry Corporation I (AVICI) and China Aviation Industry Corporation II (AVICII), and its core activities center on specific design packages for new aircraft programs.

Airbus' first **North American** design and engineering facility was opened in **Wichita**, Kansas during 2002. Beginning with an initial staff of 40 people, this location – which is involved in wing design for the A380 and other long-range Airbus aircraft – employed more than 300 highly-skilled engineers as of October 2011, with additional growth anticipated during the following years.

In 2010, the location was expanded with a second engineering center to focus on wing work for Airbus aircraft, as well as to house a team of in-service repair engineers specializing in critical support for customers around the world.

Southeast of Wichita in the U.S. is the Airbus Americas Engineering facility in **Mobile, Alabama**, which is responsible for various interior elements of the next-generation widebody A350 XWB jetliner – including design and engineering work for its cabin, crew rest areas, lavatories and galleys.

Airbus Industries: Production Sites

France: Toulouse's responsibilities include engineering (general design, systems and integration tests, definition of the structure and more), structure testing and a materials processes development center, systems organization, A400M design and development, flight tests, the Beluga hangar and one of Airbus' three delivery centers. It also hosts final assembly lines for the A320, A350 XWB and A330 – including the cabin furnishing and painting – as well as the A380's final assembly and preparation for flight.

The **Saint-Nazaire** plant specializes in structural assembly, equipping and testing of front and central fuselage sections for the entire Airbus family. It receives sub-assemblies to be fitted for the forward fuselage for the A320 Family, the forward and central fuselage for the A330 and A380 families, and the nose fuselage for the A400M and A350 XWB. Saint-Nazaire is also in charge of equipping and testing these sections before delivering them to Airbus final assembly lines.

Nantes specializes in the manufacturing and assembly of the center wing boxes for all Airbus aircraft, and is a leader in the manufacture of Carbon Fibre Reinforced Plastic structural parts, such as the A350 XWB keel beam. Nantes also is responsible for manufacturing the radomes for the entire Airbus family, the ailerons for the A330 and A380 families and air inlets for the A350 XWB, A380 families and A320neo.

UK: Located in **North Wales**, Airbus' **Broughton** site assembles wings for the entire family of aircraft commercial aircraft, producing over 1,000 wings per year. Its activities include wing skin milling, stringer manufacture, full wing equipping and wing box assembly.

Filton is the other **UK**-based site for Airbus, with its engineering and research & technology groups responsible for wing design, landing gear and fuel systems design and testing; manufacturing of components and the assembly of the A400M wings.

Getafe, located in central **Spain**, specializes in aeronautical component engineering, design, production and assembly. The plant is the delivery center for final assembly lines in Toulouse and Hamburg for all the programs with the exception of the A380 – a role it shares with the **Puerto Real** plant in **Cádiz**.

Located in the **south of Spain, Puerto Real** specializes in automated assembly of movable surfaces (rudders and spars) for all Airbus jetliner programs. It also is responsible for final equipment and delivery to the final assembly line of large, complex structural components – such as the horizontal tail plane and belly fairing of the A380 fuselage and produce the horizontal tail plane boxes of the A350 XWB.

8.3 CRM Contributes to a Scary Halloween for Hershey (techtarget 2004)

CRM Contributes to a Scary Halloween for Hershey
Candy producers record 40 % of their annual sales between October and December. Halloween, the biggest candy-consuming holiday, accounts for about $2 billion in sales.7 For a candy producer, missing Halloween is like a toy company missing Christmas. Unfortunately, in 1999, that's just what happened to Hershey, the nation's largest candy maker.8 Just before the big candy season, shelves at warehouses and retailers lay empty of treats such as Hershey bars, Reese's Peanut Butter Cups, Kisses, Kit-Kats, and Rolos. Though inventory was plentiful, orders had not arrived and distributors could not fully supply their retailers.

Hershey announced in September that it would miss its third quarter earnings forecasts due to problems with new customer order and delivery systems that had been recently rolled out. The new enterprise resource planning (ERP) and CRM processes and technology implemented earlier in the year had affected Hershey's ability to take orders and deliver product. The $112 million system aimed to modernize business practices and provide front-to-back automation from order-taking to truck-loading, but Hershey lost market share as problems allowed rivals to benefit during the season. Mars and Nestlé both reported unusual spurts of late orders as the Halloween season grew nearer. The most frustrating aspect of the situation is that Hershey had plenty of candy on hand to fill all its orders. It just couldn't deliver the orders to customers.

By December 1999, the company announced it would miss already lowered earnings targets. It stated that lower demand in the last few months of the year was in part a consequence of the earlier fulfillment and service issues. Hershey had embarked on the project in 1996 to better coordinate deliveries with its retailers, allowing it to keep its inventory costs under control. The company also needed to address Y2K problems with its legacy systems. CRM, ERP, and supply chain management systems were implemented, along with 5,000 personal computers and a complex network of servers. The intention was to integrate these software and hardware components in order to let the 1,200-person sales force shepherd orders step-by-step through the distribution process. Sales could also better coordinate with other departments to handle every issue from order placement to final delivery. The system was also designed to help Hershey measure promotional campaigns and set prices, plus help run the company's accounting operations, track ingredients, and schedule production and truck loading.

Hershey realized that the business process changes involved with such a transformation were highly intricate. However, despite the size and complexity of the undertaking, the firm decided on an aggressive implementation plan that entailed a large piece of the new infrastructure going live at the same time. Unfortunately, the project ran behind schedule and wasn't ready until July 1999 when the Halloween orders had already begun to come in. Problems in getting customer orders into the system and transmitting the correct details of those orders to warehouses for shipping began immediately. By August, the company was 15 days behind in filling orders, and in September, order turnaround time was twice as long as usual.

In recent years, Hershey sales growth had exceeded its rivals, and the company was expecting 4–6 % growth that year. However, sales instead slipped and the company admitted that problems with the new system alone had reduced sales by $100 million during the period.

8.4 Global Sourcing: Shifting the Focus from Cost Saving to a Strategic Set-up (Gronwald 2012)

Global Sourcing: Shifting the Focus from Cost Saving to a Strategic Set-up

Abstract The common understanding of global sourcing as a procurement centric task of companies to resolve shortage of talents in the context of established offshoring and outsourcing models will be reviewed for product sourcing and service sourcing separately. Understanding offshoring as a location-specific delivery model and outsourcing, on the other hand, having significant impact on the governance, delivery system and the companies' organization (onsite or offshore), global sourcing is seen as a combination of both. Discussing various offshoring and outsourcing failures at the beginning of the twenty-first century has impact on future global sourcing strategies. As a result, we will introduce the concept of "outsourcing of global sourcing" as part of a service provider's delivery model. Indian service providers have developed a unique system of education, processes and tool-based delivery systems which are mostly standardized across the industry. High attrition in the industry requires a focus on knowledge retention rather than people retention. This attrition and rotation of highly skilled and experienced talents enables small start-ups now to inherit the principles and processes of the big ones and implement global sourcing as business model for SMEs worldwide. This gives once again India a competitive advantage in the professional services market.

1. **Introduction**

There have been various definitions in the literature of offshoring, outsourcing and global sourcing, changing over the period of time. We will therefore restrict the discussion on papers published 2008 or later. Only in the recent years, India-based service providers have matured as global service providers while companies have become more outsourcing ready. Global sourcing as a procurement model has been discussed in various ways during the last couple of years with a clear focus on impact on the companies' organization. This article introduces a new concept of outsourcing of global sourcing passing it to the service provider as part of their delivery model focused on India-based service providers who are best suited for this concept as a result of their cultural, organizational and business model.

2. **Offshoring and Outsourcing**

Although there has been quite a common understanding among various authors about the distinction between offshoring and outsourcing, in daily business they are often used "almost as synonyms" (Agerfalk and Fitzgerald 2008). In order to be more precise, offshoring is linked to location, while outsourcing is about governance (see Davis et al. 2004) or ownership (see Miroudot et al. 2009). In other words, offshoring does not require an external service provider, while outsourcing can be done anywhere. In-house offshoring, without the involvement of an external service provider, captive centers, is dominating shared services still. According to these definitions, there is no difference between offshore and nearshore, both are the same: delivering services from a foreign country. The selection criteria for the location of an offshore center are linked to costs, logistics, availability of resources, taxes, legal restrictions, political stability, etc., but they do not have impact on the governance or delivery model needed for running an offshore center; the same rules apply to any location.

Outsourcing, on the other hand, does have significant impact on the governance, delivery system and the firm's organization (onsite or captive). Thus, the basic question when it comes to sourcing models is not so much where, but what, why and how.

There are some observations which are misleading the discussion about the right souring model in-side a firm and between a firm as a customer and an outsourcing vendor.

- Many sourcing discussions still are about nearshore versus offshore, although there is no difference between them. Both represent one and the same sourcing model: a location outside the firm's premises in a foreign country (but not necessarily outside the firm's boundaries) (see Miroudot et al. 2009).
- Many research and statistics do not make any difference between what to offshore or out-source, "service functions" like IT and administration (cost factors) or "product functions" like R&D, engineering services, innovation or product development. But, this distinction has a significant impact on the right decision when it comes to outsourcing.
- According to Peeters et al. (2010), cost savings have been the main arguments for offshoring and outsourcing decisions on vendor and on customer's side with offshoring into low-cost countries and outsourcing discussions about labor arbitrage and rate cards. This implicitly suggests that service functions would be the major offshoring/outsourcing components tradition-ally and product functions have come into the discussion only recently. It is just the opposite. Although less than 10 % of the companies were going offshore until 1998–1999, two functions

have been dominating since the beginning: IT as cost factor, and innovation services (R&D, engineering, product design) as production factors (see Manning et al. 2008; Peeters et al. 2010). Innovation services were the leading offshored services between around 1993 and 1996. Between 1998 and 2000, when the offshoring wave started on a larger scale, IT became the dominating offshored service, but still followed by innovation services. I will focus on those two principal services, one a service function and other a product function for further discussions.

3. **The Offshoring Learning Curve and Outsourcing Readiness**

Between 2000 and 2009, IT was the fastest growing offshored service, expanding from 10 % to more than 45 % of companies with 40 % outsourced in 2000 and 70 % in 2009. While 50 % of the companies in UK and the USA already outsourced their services in 2000, less than 10 % did it in Germany. In 2009, almost 70 % of the companies in the UK, the USA, Germany, and Scandinavia were outsourcing their services (see Peeters et al. 2010).

Many companies went through an expensive outsourcing learning curve until around 2005 when most offshored captive or outsourced services were run as staff augmentation in a factory model with rate cards and where moving to cheap countries was dominating. Landis et al. (2005) observed significant differences between the matured product outsourcing and the outsourcing of service functions, like IT. This study is based on 25 large enterprises representing an outsourcing contract value of £26bn: "62 per cent realized that their outsourced IT required more management effort than expected, 57 per cent said they could not release internal resources for other projects, leading to larger than anticipated management overheads, 52 per cent ranked cost-related issues as the main risks, 81 per cent had limited or no transparency to a supplier's pricing and cost structure, resulting in increased chances of paying additional costs, 48 per cent did not have a standardized methodology to evaluate the business case for outsourcing." Savvas (2005), referring to Landis et al. (2005).

My personal experiences during these years suggest that many of those companies were neither outsourcing nor offshoring ready and especially the large Indian services providers were not really ready for the global services market.

Even today there are some general cultural flaws where Indian vendors do not meet the expectations of their meanwhile matured customers and prospects: the lack of strong program managers, the tendency of being reactive and not proactive as demanded these days and a lack of predictability based on a different work style (a significant challenge in countries such as Germany); and many "managed services" projects are still staff augmentation based, "people centric" not "team centric".

The key message from the study that managing outsourcing partners (or offshore centers) can in-crease internal costs more than that will be compensated by cost savings through outsourcing and offshoring can be extrapolated to multivendor environments and global sourcing strategies. The move from global sourcing as a procurement task to a vendor-specific delivery model will be discussed below in Sect. 5.

4. **Talent Development: The India Differentiator**

Indian outsourcing service providers (meanwhile large and small ones) have some significant cultural advantages for incorporating global sourcing as a delivery model with respect to other countries. Here where and to whom to outsource play an important role. India has become the global hub for R&D and innovation in engineering and IT services, not because it has better, cheaper or got more resources than the rest of the world, but because Indian enterprises develop their talents in a different manner and so perform better. When it comes to the discussion about the number of engineering graduates in India compared to the rest of the world, there is often the argument from outside India that "only 25 % of graduates are ready for work" (McKinsey). Indian companies, on the other hand, realized long ago that 0 % of the graduates are ready, especially in the IT industry. The large Indian enterprises have virtually become universities, employing hundreds of faculty (see Wadhwa 2008) and up to 15,000 students per year, which is 1 % of applicants as average industry standard. Since 2010, more and more top US graduates are applying at top Indian vendors due to the quality of postgraduate education. Most Indian vendors are members of the "American Society for Training & Development" (ASTD), the world's largest professional association dedicated to industry training and development. Mahindra Satyam won the 2007 Global Best Awards for their education from ASTD as first non-US company. All top Indian companies have been among the top 20 each year. Attrition is high during the first 2–3 years in this field, but this has turned out to have more advantages than disadvantages for India's services industry, including the small ones. Since the education standard is generally high and standardized between the companies, they end up training not just for themselves, but for the entire industry. With a team-oriented working culture, the focus of the system has to be more on "knowledge retention" than "people retention", one important factor to establish global sourcing delivery models. Global enterprises outside India have started to adopt this model and apply it for other emerging countries like Mexico and Romania (see Manning et al. 2008).

5. **Outsourcing of Global Sourcing: A Delivery Model**

The shortage of science and engineering talents in most industry nations has become main motivator for companies chasing these resources on a global scale. Germany alone has a shortage of around 35,000 engineers (Erdmann and Koppel 2009).

Today there are three main drivers for outsourcing and offshoring to countries such as India: cost savings, flexible capacity and gaining access to new technology (innovation) for both product and service sourcing. This defined "global sourcing of talent" (Manning et al. 2008) as procurement task which led to the current common understanding of being a company and not service provider driven activity. This model has an even greater impact on internal company organizations with the danger of failure (in service sourcing) than the previously offshoring adventures from 2003. Quoting Contractor et al. (2010): "...global strategy amounts to...the optimal disaggregation or slicing of the firm's value chain into as many constituent pieces as organizationally and economically feasible, followed by…decisions as how each slice should be allocated geographically ('offshoring') and organizationally ('outsourcing')". Miroudot et al. (2009) call this the process of "creative destruction" and associate it with outsourcing. They refer to the book "Capitalism, Socialism and Democracy" by Joseph Schumpeter, who introduced this term in 1942. It describes the process of transformation of an economy that accomplishes radical innovation.

While this concept has been established successfully as product sourcing in the automotive and aerospace industry which has integrated tier1 and tier2 suppliers into their value chain over a couple of decades, adopting this simply to services functions, like IT, will not work as proven already. There are examples of automotive companies which have done exactly that: replicate their product sourcing concept and outsource their IT services to many (50 plus) small- and mediumsized de-pendent-independent local service providers, many of them working on premise or very close to the company over the last decades. Offshoring these is impossible. Therefore, vendor consolidation programs have been initiated and some began using Indian service providers as tier1 suppliers (frontend) with the intention to have the local providers working as tier2 through the Indian front end, passing the sourcing tasks to the Indian vendor on a global scale.

We therefore introduce global sourcing as part of the service providers' delivery model (outsource global sourcing). Due to their homogenous training system across the services industry, resulting in similar centralized competency and delivery organizations with the same underlying quality and process systems (CMM5, Six Sigma, Lean, etc.), and similar tool support, Indian service providers are best prepared for this model.

Backbone is what has been evolved over the last 10–15 years as "global delivery model", used by all of the major Indian providers, and expanded into an "advanced shared competency delivery mod-el" as a competency-based delivery model which integrates support, maintenance and project execution. The fundamental concept is to provide services using virtualized delivery centers across the globe with a standard platform of tools and processes leveraging industry best practices. The model is capable of handling dynamics in work volume, and provides committed year-on-year productivity gains. It serves the major market demands of global sourcing: cost savings, flexible capacity and gaining access to new technology with a dedicated customer facing team and virtually zero bench, and is based on the principle of "knowledge retention" accepting attrition as part of the process.

Global sourcing is an organizational concept, not a technical problem. It is a delivery organization based on centralized competency towers as pillars: industry, processes, and technology, with standardized governance, service delivery, knowledge management/retention and issue resolution processes. A strong tool support for service level management, productivity management, demand management (demand planning, demand execution), capacity management, etc., is mandatory.

Landis et al. (2005) recommended that companies should replicate the service provider's principles, models, and organization and insource again. That did not happen obviously. Establishing these concepts needs significant investments over a long period of time. Offshoring into a captive center would require similar investments. Since service factors (IT) are cost factors, this would just in-crease the costs, unless the captive centers are converted to profit centers, which turns them into (half-) outsourcing provider. Most of those attempts failed, and that include opening the captive services to the market and turning it into a full service provider. Many of them have offshored and outsourced significant parts to Indian service providers in order to stay competitive.

For a professional service provider, these services are their core business, and that enables them to make these investments with a clear ROI: another good reason to pass global sourcing and delivery to a professional (Indian) service provider.

6. **Global Sourcing as Delivery Business Model for a Small Indian Start-Up Company**

The well-established Indian system of company training and education with a high attrition rate enables start-ups to build on systems and experienced resources from global service providers and in-corporate those high standards into their delivery models and focus successfully on the global SME market (25–1,000 employees) which is difficult to access for the large global players. Suyati Technologies is based in Kochi in the state of Kerala at the far south corner of India. They have created a global sourcing delivery model they call "Dedicated Global Team" (Mukund 2010) offering global sourcing as a delivery service. They will hire dedicated teams in India or anywhere else in the world based on customer requirements as Suyati's full employees for product sourcing, services or consulting. The key is to hire and retain talent by supporting the team with excellent processes, infra-structure, technical, HR and administrative services like any other large service provider.

7. **Conclusion**

With a clear understanding of offshoring and outsourcing and its historical development in the industry, global sourcing strategies as a procurement sourcing model have no significant differences to common staff augmentation models, only focusing more on talent than cheap resources. Implementing these as part of advanced delivery models of global service providers will take the risks from and pass advantages to the company. We could show that the India-based system is best suited due to educational, cultural and organizational principles. Even the high attrition could be used as advantage in a homogeneous environment for helping even small start-ups enabling them to develop high-quality standard delivery models which give them access to the global SME market. The reality looks a little different. Although the discussed advanced delivery models and infrastructures are in place, they have not been fully understood and executed. Many procurement managers, on the one side, and delivery managers, on the other side, have staff augmentation mindsets and many managed services project still are hidden staff augmentation projects. Discussing the next step of outsourcing global sourcing and incorporating it into the delivery models of service providers might help them to achieve finally globalization of professional services.

8.5 Successful People Strategies for Innovation in Global Delivery and Virtual Teams (Neumann 2012)

Successful People Strategies for Innovation in Global Delivery and Virtual Teams

Abstract While we often do not see great product innovation from countries that have traditionally a strong presence as global delivery destinations (China, India or Eastern Europe), a lot of innovation exists in the underlying processes, management models or as "hidden" innovation inside products we perceive coming from developed markets. At the same time, innovation will not happen without highly engaged people, glued together by a strong sense of urgency and common mission. Way too often, companies believe that through a set of global processes and policies they can create a functioning global delivery organization or a distributed R&D landscape and that local talent will unquestioningly follow them, as long as the pay cheque displays a high figure. Though the global firm needs global processes and a set of standardized policies and common values, it is by far not sufficient. A global people strategy including local values and true participation will open many avenues for the globally distributed centers to have a diverse set of policies. It does not only provide a better local fit, but also increases the employee engagement significantly. As a result, employees will be encouraged to actively work towards a better working environment, better products, and better services – and ultimately solve many of the challenges in their everyday work, through innovative solutions. This article describes proven people strategies to create a highly innovative global workforce.

1. **Introduction**

Recent studies suggest that there is not only a strong linkage between engaged employees of a company and the companies output and profitability, but also a significant increase in innovation, when employees of the firm are highly engaged see (Gallup 2010). As the evidence seems to be established, the next questions to ask specifically in a global delivery or R&D network are about the type of innovation we can expect and how to create highly engaged teams, who not only drive excellence in their delivery, but also think beyond the scope of their project and try to constantly find new solutions to daily challenges.

This article will use SAP as an example since it has succeeded in distributing its software development and global service offerings around the world since 1994. The journey started with an R&D center (SAP Labs) in Palo Alto, and this initial research & product development hub was soon followed by SAP Labs in ten more countries. Today, there is a network of 15 SAP labs in 12 countries. From those labs, SAP offers professional services to its customers, internal services for global lines of business, and creates software products in distributed teams. The creation of software products happens usually in one to three locations per product. Today every location is able to handle the full development life cycle of the created products. In other words, SAP has not followed the traditional route of splitting requirement analysis, blueprint, design, coding, quality assurance, and testing – but believes in doing all these steps within small teams in all locations.

In many ways, SAP's strategy with respect to the distribution of its services and product development is different from that of many other multinational companies, as it started very early with a relatively large number of hubs, which allowed certain "near-shoring" of talents and services, as well as attracting a much higher diversity of talent around the globe.

On the other hand, with the high number of centers (which in average have about 1,000 engineers), there are various challenges to solve:

- One has to have absolutely proven and scalable processes in place.
- One needs to constantly reduce the complexity of too many locations for one specific product.
- One needs quality leadership locally as well as globally, that is ready and willing to work un such a multicultural/multidimensional environment.
- One, most importantly, needs to constantly engage with all employees in all locations – from believing in the strategy to the excellence in their daily work.

Regardless of whether SAP created the Labs by herself as a real new setup from scratch (like in Palo Alto, Ireland, Hungary, and in all four BRIC countries) or integrated them as part of acquisitions (like in France, Canada, Bulgaria, Germany, or Israel), there are always four key dimensions that play a role when creating a new SAP Lab:

- Risks and cost scenarios (the typical hard factors of locations)
- Market potential
- Talent
- Innovation

Whereas the first three dimensions led many global IT companies to open service delivery centers or research hubs in the BRIC countries over the last 20 years, breakthrough innovation were often not expected from those locations.

On the other hand, multiple corporate success stories have meanwhile proven that innovation in emerging markets is possible if the science and technology capabilities are utilized in the right way. Leading researchers like Prahalad (2004) and Mashelkar (2011) highlighted specifically the opportunities arising in emerging markets from innovation. Others like Govindarajan et al. (2009) went even a step ahead and argued that innovation from emerging markets can reversely change the mature markets as well. In Fig. 8.1, Mashelkar (2011) tried to put all countries in one single diagram in a simple way.

The real success factor for SAP has been the empowerment of the employees in those centers far away from the decision makers in the headquarter, and their engagement level. We realized that the engagement level, which in the end defines the output and innovation, has to be constantly stimulated in order to remain high. Depending on the size of the organization and its life cycle, the approach has to be varied.

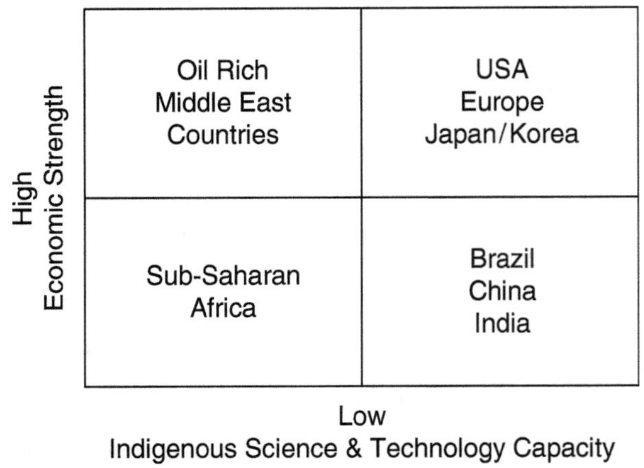

Fig. 8.1 Positioning of the developing world in the science and technology landscape

SAP managed to have consistently high levels of employee engagement in its offshore centers. China and India, for example, in 2011, had employee engagement values above global average, and also topped local benchmarks in local best employer studies.

At the same time, in many of the SAP Labs, the innovation index (which is a summary of different KPIs like patent applications, invention disclosures, and participation and success rates in innovation campaigns) is often higher than that in its headquarter in Walldorf, Germany.

So what is the secret behind the success in keeping such high levels of motivation and innovation?

- Global innovation programs which are available across the globe.
- Global people strategy which encourages local participation and inclusion.
- Integration and trust between local teams, local management, global management, and leadership.

2. **Global Innovation Programs and Local Participation**

The other important point is the type of innovation to look for: It may be unrealistic to expect the next breakthrough product innovation, which redefines the world market for those products, from an offshore R&D center or a global delivery hub. This is unlikely, as the mission of the teams in these multinational company settings is often narrowly defined, the exposure to the customer demand beyond the domestic market is low, and the expertise on methods and models to create intellectual property is often nonexistent.

Nevertheless, a lot of innovation happens either built-in as product components or as a completely new innovation in the area of processes or models. Kumar and Puranam (2012) argue that innovation from countries like India can be often "invisible," but nevertheless very relevant. There are four levels of invisible innovation in a pyramid model (see Fig. 8.2):

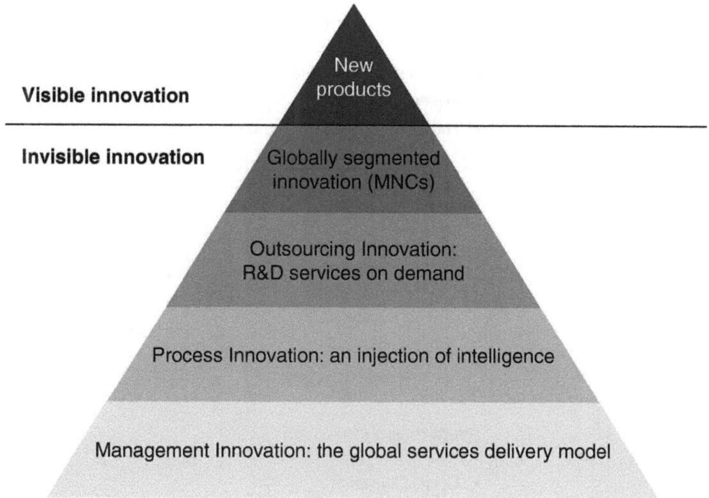

Fig. 8.2 Invisible innovation

1. Globally segmented innovation, by major multinational corporations (like GE, CISCO, and SAP). This describes horizontal segmentation of product development, e.g., complete product components or solutions coming from one country, whereas the final assembled product is still perceived by the consumer as an innovative product from another country (usually the multinational company's headquarters).
2. Outsourcing innovation. Whereas specifications of expected results are given by a client, the complete R&D to get to those results is outsourced. So whereas the intellectual property may still be owned by the client, the innovation to get there was done by the outsourcing firm.
3. Process innovation through injection of talent. This describes the phenomenon of overqualified personnel often working in large offshore or call centers which results in breakthrough process innovation, as the employees do not just fulfil a duty but want to utilize their skills and make the process more efficient.
4. Management innovation in the global delivery model, by large outsourcing firms, e.g., in India. This describes the highly efficient, scalable delivery systems, invented and fine-tuned by those firms, which make specifically IT projects possible on large scale with a very high success rate.

How to get people to actively participate in the innovation process? First and foremost, it is important to make all innovation systems in a company available at all its global centers, irrespective of whether those are core research hubs or captive product development centers of global delivery units. No one is less or more innovative than someone else as per a job description or location!

Irrespective of whether these are process-driven systems, intellectual property driven systems, market-driven systems, or event-driven systems (Fig. 8.3), most, if

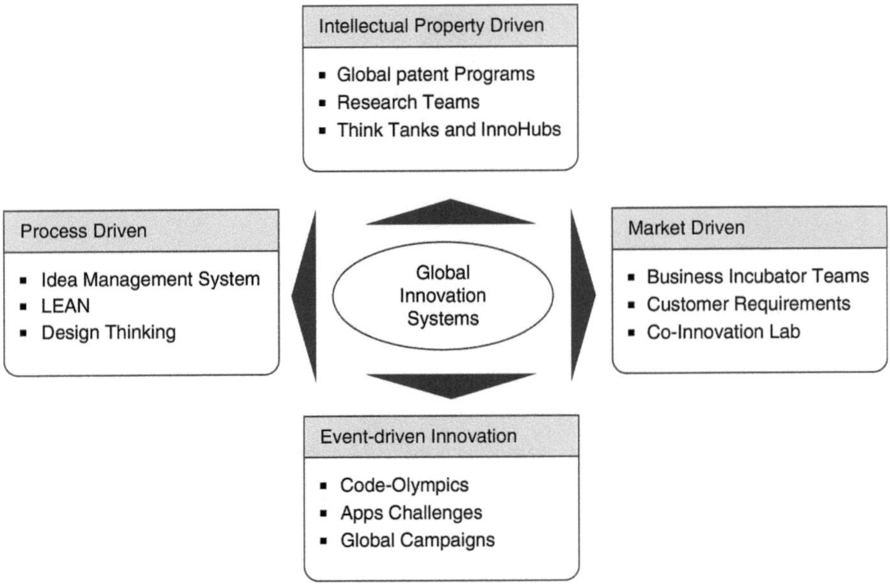

Fig. 8.3 Global innovation systems

not all of them, should be made available in all locations. Participation should be encouraged through local incentives and adjustments of these systems.

3. **Global People Strategy and Local Inclusion**

There are two important aspects for the global delivery firm or a global R&D network when it comes to the people strategy:

- The availability of people-related policies, benefits, and programs across the globe.
- The opportunity for the local teams not only to adjust global programs to make them a better fit, but also specifically being able to participate on a grassroot level creating complementary elements of such programs and policies, which globally no one would have thought about.

3.1. **Availability of Global Policies and Programs**

Most multinational companies have a global strategy when it comes to their people programs, but the main question is how much of that is reflected at the grassroot level. So having a great people development program in your headquarter which colleagues in Shanghai have never heard about, or having a global stock option program which is unavailable to colleagues in Bangalore, leads to a "them versus us" thinking and deep de-motivation; top management loses credibility very fast if injustice is even perceived in its slightest form.

In the context of a globally successful distributed service or R&D, there are some areas where a company has to ensure that as a matter of fairness and transparency, they should be similarly structured and the key elements made available for all employees globally. These are as follows:

- Compensation and benefits
- Career models
- Organizational design
- Pay for performance culture

But beyond those, a multinational company that relies on a global workforce which works as a team (like a professional services company) needs to put special emphasis on simplification of the programs, to allow local flavors and enrichment of the framework.

3.2. **The Localization Challenge**

It is obvious that not every global program can run everywhere in the same shape or fashion – this would neither be desirable nor wise. Often, companies speak of "global programs" in this respect. Examples of localization are as follows:

- Compensation structure: The compensation matrix should always follow the local market conditions and requirements.
- Benefit basket: Again, local elements must be taken care of, e.g., pension funds, health insurances (in India perhaps parents can be included), and transport to the company (a must in China, Brazil, and India).
- Career model: Though the principles should be the same globally (and certain career levels should match on a global scale), there could be the need locally for additional career levels (driven by the demand for more frequent promotions).
- Talent management: It is important to have a global standard regarding employees considered to be a part of a special talent pool. But the program itself can be quite different, as colleagues would have different expectations: Whereas in some cultures, no one would like to be publicly announced as "Top Talent" or "High Potential," in other cultures this is a matter of pride. The same is true for corporate awards, which could have a large impact in Asian countries, but a lesser impact in central Europe.
- People development: Again, in Europe, a development culture of "on the job" and "training as per job need" might be preferred, whereas in India colleagues are more interested to do formal courses (even with grades and certificates) and learn things beyond their current job responsibilities to increase their job market value. This has to be taken into consideration when people development programs are structured.

Even more important than creating this "global framework" is to present colleagues with the opportunities to actively participate in the creation of policies that may be relevant to them. This kind of participative role is usually taken care of in large European companies by the selected workers council. But in a typical offshore location, such systems do not exist, or they are often not effective.

Therefore, the management should create working teams of employees who take the ownership, on a continuous basis, for certain policies or day-to-day concerns. At

SAP Labs India, for example, this was started with three employee committees for food, transport, and social activities and later expanded to the so-called Ignite team, who work on most of the existing employee-impacting policies and programs. Obviously within a framework of "nonnegotiable" items (like pay hike), the senior management retains the right to veto.

Such engagement immediately creates an atmosphere of trust and inclusion. Besides, it makes the programs and policies usually much stronger, since neither the local management nor the global management would know about all the little difficulties the team members face every day. Areas that matter to colleagues and where policy proposals could be worked out by cross-level/cross-line teams are travel, family benefits, working time flexibility, vacation models, and the like.

4. **Integration and Trust**

A very important area, which is often forgotten in the daily focus on execution, is to create over time an atmosphere of mutual trust between globally distributed centers. Locations, managers, and employees alike must feel integrated into the global corporation and need to become a real part of the commonly shared culture.

"Integration" consists of three main elements:

- Direction (a shared strategy and vision)
- The right people in the right places (people who have autonomy, responsibility, and accountability)
- Relationship (negotiating differences, building strong teams and partnerships, understanding others, and leadership skills)
- Relationship is at the core of integration because without strong relationships amongst managers and employees, any attempt to reach a shared vision will fail as hierarchies and global lines have their limitations.

4.1. **Direction and Leadership**

A high-performing, innovative culture can only be created if the leadership in all locations is equipped with the right tools and skills, and displays the required level of passion. Besides, leaders are expected to provide direction to their employees. Beyond the well-known features of a good leader, in the multi-locational context, one needs culture-sensitive, globally savvy, and experienced leaders. Only then their direction will be understood and accepted. To build these skills, the following measures can be implemented:

- Make global competence mandatory for Global Leadership Positions (Rule: 2 years of experience in a location other than one's own nationality or a proven track record of different roles within a career).
- Create Global Leadership Associate Program (GLAP): Many leading global companies already have such programs (with long traditions of success) that keep track of promising leaders and assess their different roles and locations (out of their comfort zones); resolving today's repatriation issues by providing plans for all mobile managers that utilized their newly acquired global competence (Return on investment for SAP).

- Create awareness on the do's and don'ts of leading virtual teams by systematically introducing best practices on virtual management (e.g., trainings should be "must attend" for leaders of virtual teams).
- Develop constantly the next generation of leaders from across the globe.

Similar to leadership, innovation can hardly be fostered by brilliant individuals keeping their knowledge with them. Instead, a "high touch" development program focuses on elements like cultural sensitivity, virtual teamwork, and LEAN across borders. Beyond this it is important to invest in talents, for example, by presenting young talent with the opportunity to learn from seniors, specifically on international events. Another successful approach is to rotate the best: The best people should not only voluntarily rotate with other locations, but it should also become a mandatory exercise.

4.2. **The Right People at the Right Places**

The selection and continuous development of the right people at the right places are very important elements of a successful people strategy in a global context. Important decisions have to be taken for the senior positions on the following criteria:

- Local fit (understanding of local culture, language, and business rules?)
- Global network (how well is the person connected globally, e.g., with the headquarter?)
- Core skills resp. value-add (can the new manager bring new and additional skills to the new team or organization?)

Beyond the personal fit, if the environment does not suit the job expectations, there is a high probability of failure. Elements should include the following:

- Collaborative culture
- Decentralized decision making (e.g., giving competence and decision authority to LEAN teams in the different locations)
- Focusing on high performance by teams rather than by individuals (LEAN Principle)

4.3. **Relationship**

No technology can substitute the "human-touch" impact of a face-to-face meeting: Face-to-face meetings facilitate shared understanding which is beyond other means. Such relationships are especially important in high-context cultures (e.g., Brazil, China, India, and Korea), and a company needs to supply resources and time for these kind of interactions.

This could be done through:

- Creation of horizontal project groups for some of the projects that are highly visible in the company; such groups should span board areas (LoBs) and locations, and work on challenges which are perceived as a common threat or an opportunity.

- Creation of a program for the top 100 leaders of the firm, which gives selected managers the opportunity to socialize, learn, and work together on multiple occasions with a special focus on the customer and business.
- Creation of a "Young Volunteer Program." It is an opportunity for promising interns/students/young colleagues to spend a couple of weeks in a different location on a volunteer program (using low-cost options such as shared accommodations, self-funded flights, etc.). The people they meet and the common experiences that are shared leave them with an open-minded approach and at times create lifelong friendships and contacts.
- Offer similar access to technology and infrastructure wherever there is a significant employee presence. For instance, LEAN facilities (at SAP they are called "APP-Houses") offer a flexible environment for easy collaboration on-site. In addition, access to global communication systems should be there, like telepresence, use of webcams or virtual team software.
- Broadening the horizon of current and future Leaders. Single-location/single line careers lead to micromanagement ("I know it best," "Not invented here") and a lack of cultural understanding. The physical mobility of employees and leaders is key in helping to "get to know what you don't know" and in building strong personal relationships within global companies.

5. **Conclusion**

Technology advances, availability of talent on global scale, comparative cost advantages, and strong processes have certainly helped, over the last two decades, in making the global service delivery and globally distributed R&D a success. Nevertheless, most processes and the organizational design of multinational companies have been created to maximize efficiency and output. Cost, scale, quality, and speed are no longer differentiators between global service delivery firms and (within a multinational company) different captive centers.

The differentiator today is the additional value that a specific unit can deliver, which is determined by the innovative ideas and solutions people can apply to the problem of the client, irrespective of whether the customer is internal or external. For this to happen, those who deliver the service on a day-to-day basis must be highly motivated, engaged, and willing to work beyond the call of duty – individually as well as within the team.

The measures described above can help in making this happen, though these can only serve as an orientation and not as the ultimate recipe for success, which will vary depending on companies, cultural and strategic fit of measures, within its people strategy, which have to be ensured.

8.6 Advancing Intercultural Competencies for Global Collaboration (Messner and Schaefer 2012)

Advancing Intercultural Competencies for Global Collaboration

Abstract Globalization is not a rite of passage, and culture appears to be the most neglected and underestimated source of challenge in global professional services.

Academic research on national culture and cultural differences has identified dimensions with an effect on the functioning not only of societies and individuals, but also of organizations and project teams. Once cultural differences are recognized and understood, there is a better chance of building bridges across cultural gaps instead of seeking to achieve feigned homogeneity. Global managers need to develop a set of twelve affective, behavioral, and cognitive competencies for successful intercultural interaction. A targeted development of these key competencies requires a sound appraisal to identify individual strengths and limitations. They can be assessed and developed using ICCA™ (Intercultural Communication and Collaboration Appraisal) as a diagnosis framework. At its core, ICCA™ looks at the areas in which one's environment is "different" from the culture one is going to work with. And using the Q methodology as a psychometric measurement tool, it charts a path towards advancing intercultural competencies by studying the manager's subjective viewpoints.

1. **Introduction**

In the twenty-first century, successful professional services firms are organized across countries, continents, and cultures. Teams are set up and work is performed in places where employees with the right skills are available at the best price. It is a logic that dictates companies to focus on the best value and quality of their products or services (Fig. 8.4).

William J. Amelio, CEO of Lenovo, called it Worldsourcing. As per Amelio (2007), the label on the outside simply identifies the last stop on a complex global delivery journey; a minor glitch or sub-par standards can nearly destroy a brand.

Still, globalization is not a rite of passage. There are horror stories about failed endeavors to globalize service delivery, lack of quality, cultural clashes, data thefts, and companies moving things back home for these very reasons. Getting the processes and governance structures right for delivering consistent products or services from various parts on the globe (see Messner 2010) is really only one part of the

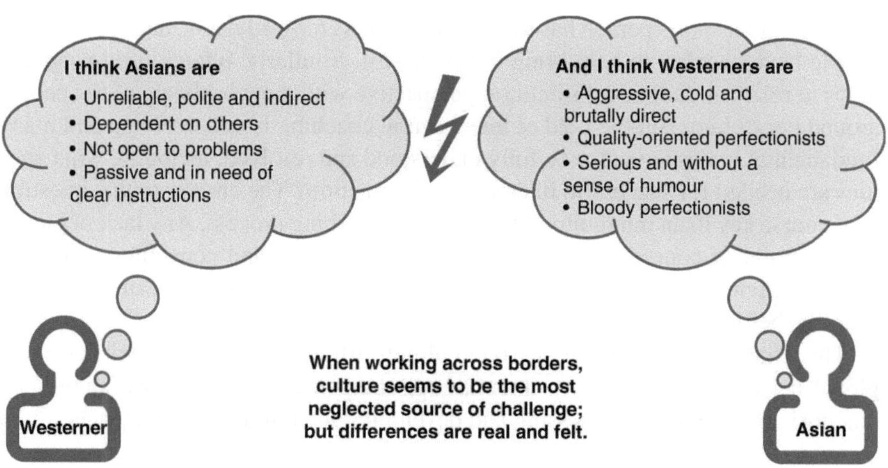

Fig. 8.4 Perceived cultural differences

game. And just as we are imagining that teams in different countries and cultures are all following the same standards towards a common goal, we notice many deep-seated misconceptions about the other culture in day-to-day interactions. Some get articulated; some don't and stay tucked away beneath the conscious mind.

It is beyond argument that in every cross-cultural alliance there is scope and potential for misunderstanding. While working across borders, culture seems to be the most neglected and underestimated source of challenge in selling in each other's country, in acquisitions, and in producing products or delivering professional services.

Cultural differences are real and felt. What people from one culture think about themselves and about members of another culture is often in stark contrast to how they are being seen from the other culture. Figure 8.1 shows common perceptions between Westerners and Asians. For example, while Westerners say that Asians are polite, indirect, dependent on others, and in a perceived way unreliable, Asians call Westerners cold, aggressive, direct and think that with all the perfectionism and punctuality they exhibit, they have forgotten about personal relationships.

Superficial aspects of culture, like English as a business language, office dress code, American-style fast food, and standardized processes and governance structures, can lead to believe that potential cultural differences can easily be navigated. But values and attitudes, which really drive differences between nations and cultures, are invisible at first glance, but impact the way how work is delivered the most.

There are two ways in which we react to differentness. One, we try to deny or wish differences away. Second, we worry about them as an obstacle to progress and success. In order to overcome this state of ethnocentricity, we need to be fully aware of our cultural differences and about our own competencies in dealing with them. But the truth is that, according to Bhawuk and Brislin (1992) becoming interculturally fluent in another culture can take three or more years of full-time exposure in the other culture. The other truth is that in today's fast moving age of worldsourcing, global business does not give anyone this much time. We need an instrument to help set us on the right path; alone we will never achieve our full potential.

Every great sports person has a coach, politicians have advisors, and top business people have coaches to help bring out their best. Similarly, intercultural coaching helps to relate an individual's cultural perspective with the worldview of the people around her or him. But the field of intercultural coaching is still evolving and many fundamental issues are yet to be fully understood and resolved, including what abilities are needed for successful intercultural interaction? The answer to this question is of course key to an intercultural training and coaching process. Any lack of clarity on this point of course means that the focus of training and coaching is likewise unclear, leaving the globally dispersed and culturally multi-faceted team in as bad a shape as before.

This chapter discusses the key intercultural differences and their relevance for global delivery, highlights key intercultural competencies, and it also suggests a diagnosis framework for assessing and developing intercultural competence.

2. **Culturally Driven Differences and Similarities**

Academic research on national culture and cultural differences started in the 1950s. Issues qualifying as common problems worldwide were identified and some first criteria for the identification of cultural differences proposed. Edward T. Hall highlighted that "Culture is man's medium; there is not one aspect of human life that is not touched and altered by culture. This means personality, how people express themselves [...], the way they think [...], how problems are solved [...]". And he further warned that "denying culture and obscuring the effects that it can have on human talents can be as destructive and potentially dangerous as denying evil" (Hall 1976).

But only in the 1980s, the first worldwide survey about values of people in different countries was conducted by the Dutch professor Geert Hofstede; he stresses that "culture is more often a source of conflict than of synergy. Cultural differences are a nuisance at best and often a disaster" (Hofstede 1967–2007). Between 1994 and 2004, the pioneering work of Hofstede was followed by House et al. (2004), Chhokar et al. (2007) and their GLOBE study of leadership and organizational behavior effectiveness. It identified cultural dimensions which have an effect on the functioning of societies, groups, businesses, and individuals.

- **Power distance** is the degree to which people expect and agree that power should be shared unequally.
- **Institutional collectivism** describes the degree to which the society encourages and rewards collective action, group loyalty is emphasized at the expense of individual goals, and whether being accepted by other people is important.
- **In-group collectivism** depicts the degree to which people express pride, loyalty, and interdependence in their families.
- **Assertiveness** is the reflection of beliefs as to whether people should be assertive, aggressive, confrontational, and tough in social relationships.
- **Future orientation** describes the orientation towards planning and sacrificing instant individual or collective gratification for long-term future rewards.
- **Uncertainty avoidance** is the extent to which ambiguous situations are threatening to individuals, to which rules and order are preferred, and to which uncertainty is tolerated in society.
- **Performance orientation** represents the degree to which an organization or a society encourages and rewards its members for performance improvement and excellence.
- **Gender egalitarianism** gives a picture of the extent to which an organization or a society minimizes gender role differences while promoting gender equality.
- **Humane orientation** describes if individuals in organizations or societies are encouraged or rewarded for being fair, altruistic, friendly, generous, caring, and in general kind to others.

The GLOBE study provides indices for these dimensions on a scale of 1–7 to compare current perceptions (as-is practices) with ideal perceptions (should-be values). In addition, these constructs are compared at a societal and organizational level.

Other models, such as proposed by Trompenaars and Hampden-Turner (1997) or Walker et al. (2004), share a large degree of practical commonality. But all these models show that people from different cultures think and act differently while being tasked with the same job. Once a global manager recognizes and understands these cultural differences, there is a better chance of "building bridges across the cultural gaps, and not seeking to achieve 'one size fits all' homogeneity in the team". Instead, "The global manager has to collaborate with the team in establishing 'cultural ground rules' for day-to-day work that focus on the common tasks and goals, rather than try to eliminate the individual cultural differences" (Raghavan 2008).

3. **Competencies for Effective Intercultural Collaboration**

The importance of communication to build bridges between cultures is well acknowledged. According to Spitzberg (1993), such intercultural communication will be competent when it accomplishes the objectives in a manner that is appropriate to the context and relationship.

Unfortunately, most existing models of intercultural competence are fairly fragmented with only a list of skills, abilities, and attitudes. While such lists appear to be useful on the surface, there is no sense of integration or coherence across lists.

In order to tell which competencies are most important for intercultural collaboration, we have derived intercultural skills from various academic publications (e.g., Bhawuk and Brislin (1992), Graf and Mertesacker (2010), Spitzberg (1993) to name but a few) and connected them with our own experience in the field. The resulting twelve essential intercultural competencies are shown in Fig. 8.5.

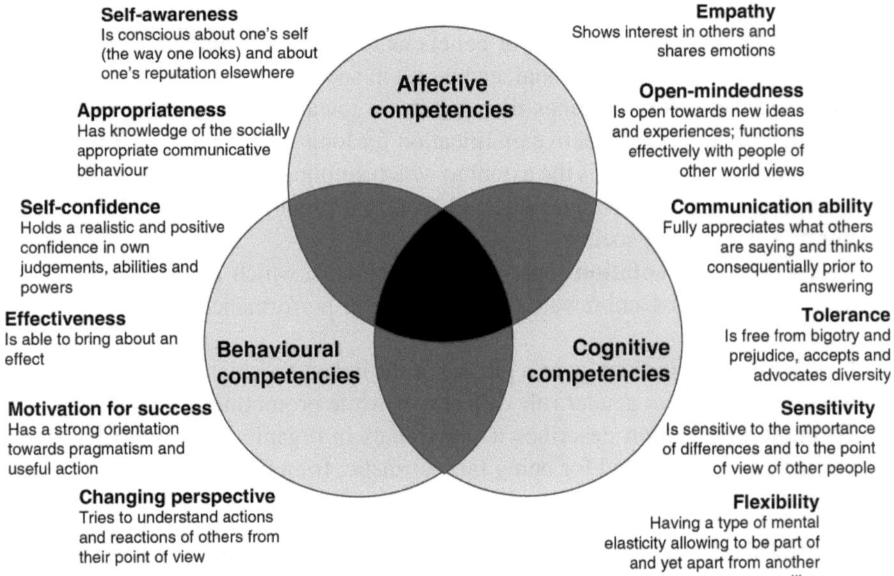

Fig. 8.5 Key intercultural competencies

By means of an international survey, we have then asked a group of 137 interculturalists and international managers to pinpoint the six most important competencies:

- Open-mindedness
- Changing perspectives
- Communication Ability
- Flexibility
- Tolerance
- Sensitivity

While the obvious approach was to count how often each competence was classified as important, a more comprehensive picture emerged when we also took the actual ranking into account. Some competencies were only selected by few of the survey participants, but when selected, they were ranked most prominently.

Therefore, we introduced a sounder weighting of the competency rank (the first most, the second most, the third most important competence, etc.) by using the mean of the rankings as the criteria of importance. In a subsequent step all competencies that were not considered for rank one to six by a survey participant were labelled with position seven. While this approach avoids the problem of a few, but prominent responses, it shrinks and under-rates the real difference between the competencies. Figure 8.3 shows the summary of the results of the survey in more detail.

4. **ICCA™: Intercultural Communication and Collaboration Appraisal**

Despite these varied constructs of intercultural competence, a study by Deardorff (2006) concludes that intercultural competence can indeed be measured. However, its multi-dimensional and multi-perspective nature needs to be taken into account. Numerous such external instruments now exist that claim to assess intercultural competencies. Notwithstanding, various surveys – such as Fantini (2009) and Graf and Mertesacker (2010) – conclude that most existing single instruments are usually inadequate for measuring all aspects of intercultural competence; some are predictive, others formative, normative, and/or summative.

In our research work, we have brought together applied skills with requisite psychological expert knowledge and developed ICCA™ (Intercultural Communication and Collaboration Appraisal) as a practical, reliable, and cross-culturally valid diagnostic instrument (Messner and Schaefer 2012). Using ICCA™, one can identify the areas in which one and one's environment is "different" from the culture one is going to work with. ICCA™ also provides concrete advice on how to develop which skills to become more appropriate and effective in intercultural collaboration. ICCA™ can be used for a wide variety of purposes, including:

- Individual assessment in intercultural coaching and counselling situations
- Group analysis in intercultural teambuilding efforts
- Selection of expatriates
- Needs assessment in an organization for training design
- Further academic research

The instrument is available as an online version and a paper and pencil version, for one-time individual self-appraisal and as a licensable version for trainers, coaches, and corporates. It is easy to complete and it generates an in-depth graphic profile. At its core, ICCA™ consists of four parts:

- Part 1: Cultural predisposition
- Part 2: Time personality
- Part 3: Competencies in intercultural collaboration
- Part 4: Organizational commitment

See Figs. 8.6 and 8.7.

4.1. **Part 1: Cultural Predisposition**

The increasing globalization of the professional services firm and connection of its project teams in its delivery centers across the globe does not mean that cultural differences are disappearing or diminishing. On the contrary, when cultures come into contact, they may converge on some aspects, but their idiosyncrasies will likely amplify. One of the challenges is acknowledging and appreciating cultural subtleties in different parts of the world. In order to work effectively with globally distributed teams, managers need to respond positively to practices and values that may be drastically different from what they are accustomed to.

By holding up a mirror, this part of ICCA™ permits the participant to embark on a journey of self-discovery and see the remarkable grip of unconscious culture. It builds upon the questionnaire items for the GLOBE dimensions as proposed in

Survey: Ranking the intercultural competencies by importance

Competency	Rank	Arithmetic mean	Standard deviation
Open-mindedness	1	3,28	1,992
Changing perspectives	2	4,59	2,013
Communication ability	3	4,60	2,115
Flexibility	4	4,79	2,098
Tolerance	5	4,80	2,235
Sensitivity	6	5,04	2,070
Empathy	7	5,20	2,050
Self-awareness	8	5,45	2,278
Appropriateness	9	6,13	1,537
Motivation for success	10	6,15	1,777
Self-confidence	11	6,30	1,516
Effectiveness	12	6,72	0,999

Fig. 8.6 Demographic information

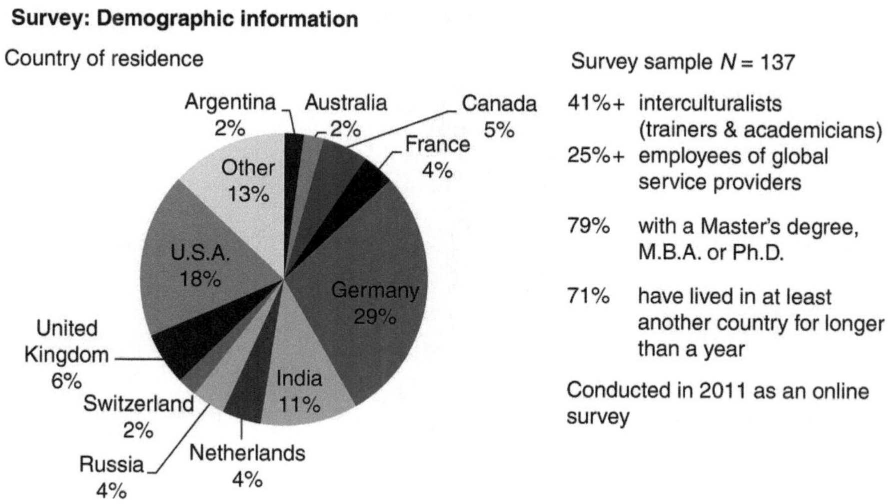

Fig. 8.7 Relative importance of intercultural competencies

House et al. (2004) and respondents rate the items on a 7-point Likert-type scale. With the help of diagrams shown in Fig. 8.8 and a verbatim description of how individuals on the different sides of the spectrum tend to behave, participants can make comparisons to determine similarities and differences among themselves and initiate ways to improve intercultural relationships.

4.2. **Part 2: Time Personality**

The concept of time personality has recently become increasingly relevant with discussions around work vs. personal time and home office concepts. But there is also an underlying cultural dimension of time personality, such as preferences and feelings towards combining activities or not.

Hall (1959) discovered that whole cultures, such as those encountered in the Middle East, Latin America, and Asia are polychronic. Polychronic time, as the term implies, is non-linear and cyclical, several things are happening at once. Completion of all transactions is more important than adherence to pre-set schedules. High context communication is the accepted and expected norm. On the other hand, monochronic time emphasizes schedules, segmentation, and promptness. It promotes linear thinking and low context communication styles. According to Hall (1976), a strong correlation between approaches to time and communication style exists. Individualistic and monochronic-oriented cultures follow a low context communication style, i.e., the mass of information is explicitly vested in the message. More collectivistic and polychronic-oriented cultures are high context, and they operate based on information which is already internalized with the other person; very little explicit information is transmitted as part of the actual communication.

While polychronicity depends on the boss to handle contingencies and stay on top of thing, monochronicity suffers from blindness to humanness of its members,

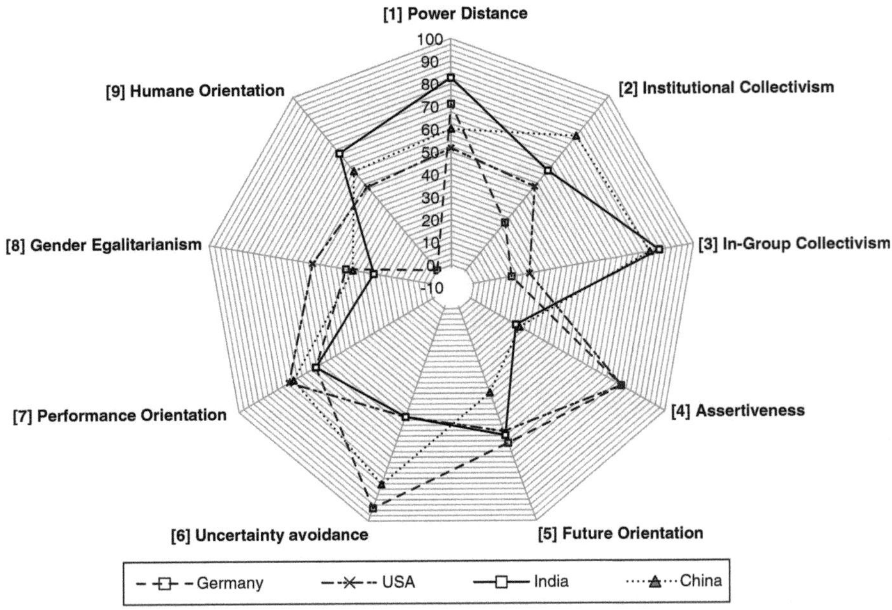

Fig. 8.8 Intercultural dimensions

making it look like inhumane to polychronic people. However, typical monochronic Westerners are also psychologically stressed in many ways when confronted with polychronic business partners.

Scientific attempts to measure aspects of time orientation started in the late 1970s and in the early 1990s; Kaufmann et al. (1991) introduced the PAI Scale resulting in a myriad of derived instruments. The concept of time personality was hypothesized by Francis-Smythe and Robertson (1999) and included behaviors, cognitions, and affect. Lindquist and Kaufman-Scarborough (2007) developed a more exacting reflective model independent of specific disciplines with PMTS (polychronic–monochronic tendency scale) as the resulting measurement scale. Besides behavioral measures, it includes measures for the preference, the liking, and the feeling of being comfortable with a type of behavior.

During the research leading to ICCA™ and based on feedback especially from non-native English speaking participants, the wording of the five items proposed by Lindquist and Kaufman-Scarborough (2007) was adapted to increase their intelligibility and general applicability. Two reverse-scored items were added and while they are not included in the calculation of the ICCA™ time personality value, they serve as a disruptive element for the participants in an otherwise unidirectional questionnaire.

The focus of this part of ICCA™ is to show the individual's tendency towards either monochronic or polychronic behavior and the degree of positive feeling about this position on the continuum. It is a reflective (latent) construct and hence the position on the scale is driven by a person's actual polychronic–monochronic tendency position. The time personality value calculated by ICCA™ thus enables to determine whether an individual matches the predominant time and communication style in another culture and it thereby allows forecasting the efficiency when working together within a specific cultural group.

4.3. **Part 3: Competencies in Intercultural Collaboration**

A targeted development of key competencies in intercultural collaboration requires a thorough appraisal to identify individual strengths and weaknesses. Such an expert appraisal is a questionnaire-based instrument to identify deficiencies in relevant competencies consisting of three parts: the questionnaire, the report, and suggestions for development.

All three parts can be found in ICCA™ as well. However, instead of using a standard Likert-type scale questionnaire, a prescribed symmetrical, unimodal distribution as shown in Fig. 8.9 is imposed on the participants to force them to carefully think about their relative intercultural communication strengths and limitations.

Items placed in the middle categories are psychologically less salient than extremely placed items in portraying a person's competencies. This so-called Q methodology was originally developed by Stephenson (1935, 1953), is now an established psychometric research method to study people's subjective viewpoints, and applied by Schaefer (2011) for the assessment and development of management key qualifications.

The critical incident methodology was chosen to derive items which aptly describe the intercultural competencies. The Q methodology has many advantages over the standard Likert-type questionnaires; it motivates participants better and already through the process of comparing and sorting items they are able to reach a deep introspection of their own behavior and competencies. Reviewing the layout with a coach can be the beginning of a high-quality intercultural coaching dialogue.

4.4. **Part 4: Organizational Commitment**

The last part of ICCA™ looks at the commitment to the organization. At a general level, it describes a psychological state that characterizes the relationship of an employee with the organization for which they work; and this psychological state has implications for an employee's decision to remain in the organization or to quit and find another job elsewhere. While human resource management has been researched plentiful in the Western hemisphere, only recently Jha (2011) has analyzed organizational commitment in the context of India's IT services industry as well.

Three factors of organizational commitment have been identified by Meyer and Allen (1991).

- The affective factor describes an individual's emotional attachment, identification with, and involvement in the organization and its goals. It results from and is induced by individual and organizational value congruency. Certain characteristics of the job, good performance, the feeling that the organization "cares" for

Fig. 8.9 Q methodology

its employees when making decisions, and the degree to which employees are involved in the goal setting and decision-making process are elements which help creating intrinsically rewarding situations.

- The normative factor reflects the sense of moral obligation to remain in an organization, an old-style value of loyalty and duty. This is measured by the extent to which an employee feels obliged to make personal sacrifices and not criticize the organization.
- The continuity factor exhibits the individual's awareness of the costs of leaving an organization. Non-transferable personal investment, such as close working relationships with other employees, community involvement, acquired job skills being unique to the organization, and monetary investments, such as contributions to pension funds or stock options, can make it look too costly for an employee to leave and seek employment somewhere else.

The analysis of organizational commitment as part of the ICCA™ is useful on two levels. First, a professional services company can study organizational commitment to understand the strengths of its employee base and overall the health of its organization. It should also know that it can actively influence the affective and normative factors by providing challenging jobs. Second, positive organizational commitment also supports an individual employee in passing quickly and unharmed through the phase of disillusionment which appears to be almost a given in intercultural encounters. Looking at the degree of affective, normative, and continuity commitment as pre-warning indicators, a skilled coach can enter into a high-quality coaching dialogue and thus help the employee not to fall too deep into the state of culture shock, but regain productivity as quickly as possible.

5. **Conclusion**

Cultural incidents are a legitimate cause for concern in globally distributed professional services delivery. But at the same time, they can become a motivation for learning about the other culture instead of turning against it. And in this process, one learns a great deal about one's own culture as well. At home, one is rarely ever prompted to reflect on the cultural self and own views. But once encountering another frame of reference, unusual behavior of colleagues is noticed just as one becomes aware of one's own behavior. Unusual behavior is observed as a difference to one's usual behavior, to what has so far been seen as the norm.

Developing the ability to see situations and behavior from multiple perspectives is a great benefit even if working in a mono-cultural environment. It allows identifying alternatives to the standard way of doing things. Thinking outside the box, reinventing the organizational setup, changing the paradigm – in professional services delivery one does it all the time.

With ICCA™ we have introduced a practical, reliable, and cross-culturally valid diagnosis framework for intercultural communication and collaboration appraisal, which is grounded in business reality and charts a path to progress intercultural competencies in a quality coaching dialogue. A sound assessment is an integral part of the intercultural coaching and education process; it provides an objective indicator to balance subjective views. When properly executed, ICCA™ not only provides solid information about the individual that can guide the coaching process, but can also enrich and transform the global collaboration experience. Nevertheless, none of the findings should be considered to be absolute; in the daily interplay of lives, things can often be completely different. The key is that the ICCA™ participant as benefactor will find some significant meaning in the process of becoming more effective and appropriate in global collaboration.

References

Agerfalk PJ, Fitzgerald B (2008) Outsourcing to an unknown workforce: exploring opensourcing as a global sourcing strategy. MIS Q 32(2):385–409

Contractor FJ, Kumar V, Kundu SK, Pedersen T (2010) Reconceptualizing the firm in a world of out-sourcing and offshoring: the organizational and geographical relocation of high-value company functions. J Manage Stud 47(8):1417–1433

Davis GB, Ein-Dor P, King WR, Torkzadeh R (2004) Information technology offshoring: prospects, challenges, educational requirements, and curriculum implications. In: Agarwal R,

Kirsch LJ, DeGross JI (eds) Proceedings of the 25th international conference on information systems, Washington, DC, pp 1027–1038
Erdmann V, Koppel O (2009) Ingenieurarbeitsmarkt 2008/09 –Fachkraefteluecke, Demografie und Ingenieure 50Plus. VDI/IW. Available via http://www.iwkoeln.de/en/studien/gutachten/beitrag/63712
Gallup (2010) Press Statement on the Gallup Study 2010. Dated 09 Feb 2011. Available on http://www.gallup.com
Govindarajan V, Trimble C, Immelt JR (2009) How GE is disrupting itself. Harvard Business Review. Available via http://hbr.org/2009/10/how-ge-is-disrupting-itself/ar/1
Kumar N, Puranam P (2012) India inside: the emerging innovation challenge to the West. Harvard Business Review, Boston, MA
Landis MK, Mishra S, Porello K (2005) Calling a change in the outsourcing market. Deloitte Consulting
Manning S, Massini S, Lewin AY (2008) A dynamic perspective on next-generation offshoring: the global sourcing of science and engineering talent. Acad Manage Perspect 22(3):35–54
Mashelkar R (2011) Re-inventing India. Sahyadri Prakashan, Pune
Miroudot S, Lanz R, Ragoussis A (2009) Trade in Intermediate Goods and Services, OECD Trade Policy Working Papers, No 93, OECD Publishing. Available via http://dx.doi.org/10.1787/5kmlcxtdlk8r-en. Accessed 3 Nov 2009
Mukund K (2010) Dedicated global team approach. Suyati Technologies, Kerala
Peeters C, Lewin A, Manning S, Massini S (2010) Shifting firm boundaries in global services sourcing: transaction costs, emerging capabilities and experience-based learning. Summer conference 2010 on opening up innovation: strategy, organization and technology, Imperial College London Business School, 16–18 June 2010. Available via http://www2.druid.dk/conferences/viewpaper.php?id¼501491&cf¼43. Accessed 20 Jan 2012
Prahalad CK (2004) The fortune at the bottom of the pyramid. Prentice Hall, Upper Saddle River, NJ
Savvas A (2005) Disappointed corporates bring outsourcing back in house, ComputerWeekly.com. Available via http://www.computerweekly.com/news/2240060870/Disappointedcorporates-bring-outsourcing-back-in-house. Accessed 25 Apr 2005
Wadhwa V (2008) A disciple becomes the guru should the United States learn from India? Harv Int Rev. Available via http://hir.harvard.edu/global-education/a-disciple-becomes-the-guru. Accessed 19 Dec 2008
Amelio WJ (2007) Worldsourcing replaces outsourcing. Available via BBC News Channel. http://news.bbc.co.uk/1/hi/business/7133283.stm. Accessed 28 Oct 2011
Bhawuk DPS, Brislin R (1992) The measurement of intercultural sensitivity using the concepts of individualism and collectivism. Int J Intercult Relat 16:413–436
Chhokar JS, Brodbeck FC, House RJ (2007) Culture and leadership across the world: the GLOBE book of in-depth studies of 25 societies. Lawrence Erlbaum Associates, Mahwah, NJ
Deardorff DK (2006) Identification and assessment of intercultural competence as a student outcome of internationalization. J Stud Int Educ 10:241–266
Fantini AE (2009) Assessing intercultural competence. Issues and tools. In: Deardorff DK (ed) The SAGE handbook of intercultural competence. Sage, Thousand Oaks, CA
Francis-Smythe J, Robertson I (1999) Time-related individual differences. Time Soc 8(2):273–292
Graf A, Mertesacker M (2010) Interkulturelle Kompetenz als globaler Erfolgsfaktor. Z Manag 5:3–27. doi:10.1007/S12354010011 5Z
Hall (1959) The silent language. Fawcett
Hall (1976) Beyond culture. Anchor Books, New York
Hofstede (1967–2007) Hofstede™ cultural dimensions. http://www.geert-hofstede.com. Accessed 26 Jan 2007
House RJ, Hanges PJ, Javidan M, Dorfman PW, Gupta V (2004) Culture, leadership, and organizations. The GLOBE study of 62 societies. Sage, Thousand Oaks, CA
Jha S (2011) Influence of psychological empowerment on affective, normative and continuance commitment. A study in the Indian IT industry. J Indian Bus Res 3(4):263–282

Kaufmann CF, Lane PM, Lindquist JD (1991) Exploring more than 24 hours a day: a preliminary investigation of polychronic time use. J Consum Res 18(3):392–401
Lindquist JD, Kaufman-Scarborough CJ (2007) The polychronic-monochronic tendency model. PMTS scale development and validation. Time Soc 16(2/3):269–301. doi:10.1177/0961463X07080270
Messner W (2010) Intelligent IT Offshoring to India. Roadmaps for Emerging Business Landscapes. Palgrave MacMillan, Houndmills
Messner W, Schaefer N (2012) The ICCA™ facilitator's manual. Intercultural communication and collaboration appraisal. Createspace, London
Meyer JP, Allen NJ (1991) A three-component conceptualization of organizational commitment. Hum Resour Manage Rev 1:61–89
Raghavan A (2008) Going global and taking charge: the road ahead for the Indian manager. Vikalpa 33(4):61–68
Schaefer N (2011) Diagnose und Entwicklung von Schluesselqualifikationen fuer Fuehrungskraefte. Das Diagnoseinstrument Q-Sort-Appraisal. Verlag Wissenschaft & Praxis, Sternenfels
Spitzberg BH (1993) A model of intercultural communication competence. In: Samovar LA, Porter RE (eds) Intercultural communication: a reader. Wadsworth Publishing, Boston, MA
Stephenson W (1935) Correlation persons instead of tests. Character Pers 4:17–24
Stephenson W (1953) The study of behavior: Q-technique and its methodology. University of Chicago Press, Chicago
Trompenaars F, Hampden-Turner F (1997) Riding the waves of culture: understanding cultural diversity in global business. McGraw-Hill, New York
Walker D, Walker T, Schmitz J (2004) Doing business internationally. Tata McGraw-Hill, New Delhi
Airbus Industries (2015), http://www.airbus.com. Viewed 10th March, 2015
CNN (2016), http://edition.cnn.com/2016/03/31/football/lionel-messi-egypt-shoes-insult. Viewed 31st March, 2016
Techtarget (2004), A Review of CRM Failures, http://media.techtarget.com/searchCRM/downloads/CRMUnpluggedch2.pdf. Viewed 9th September 2016

Chapter 9
Company Profiles

Abstract Chapter 9 includes the company profiles of Alpha Group, Green Group, Royal Group, Wild Horse Group.

9.1 Global Results

Global results of all four groups (Fig. 9.1).

9.2 Global and Regional Revenue Market Share

9.2.1 Global Revenue Market Share

Global market share by revenue (Fig. 9.2): Alpha Beer 27 %, Green Beer 17 %, Royal Beer 28 %, Wild Horse Beer 28 %.

9.2.2 Market Share Americas by Revenue

Market share Americas by revenue (Fig. 9.3): Alpha Beer 42 %, Green Beer 13 %, Royal Beer 16 %, Wild Horse Beer 29 %.

9.2.3 Market Share Europe by Revenue

Market share by revenue Europe (Fig. 9.4): Alpha Beer 13 %, Green Beer 24 %, Royal Beer 49 %, Wild Horse Beer 14 %.

9.2.4 Market Share Africa by Revenue

Market share Africa by revenue (Fig. 9.5): Alpha Beer 0 %, Green Beer 13 %, Royal Beer 24 %, Wild Horse Beer 63 %.

K. Gronwald, *Global Communication and Collaboration*,
DOI 10.1007/978-3-662-53150-1_9

Region	Alpha Beer			Green Beer			Royal Beer			Wild Horse Beer			Total		
	Volume 1000hl	Revenue Million$	EBITDA %	Volume 1000hl	Revenue Million$	EBITDA %	Volume 1000hl	Revenue Million$	EBITDA %	Volume 1000hl	Revenue Million$	EBITDA %	Volume 1000HL	Revenue Million$	EBITDA %
Americas	151125	15200	40%	47615	4850	39%	56000	5704	39%	82700	10450	32%	337440	36204	38%
Europe	42900	4012	27%	100400	7420	34%	112500	14915	19%	43600	4398	25%	299400	30745	26%
Africa	0	0	0%	31250	1500	20%	28863	2900	10%	48400	7462	6%	108513	11862	12%
Asia Pacific	88218	5555	24%	41400	2270	28%	19800	2695	11%	71200	3867	28%	220618	14387	23%
Total	282243	24767	30%	220665	16040	30%	217163	26214	20%	245900	26177	23%	965971	93198	26%

Fig. 9.1 Global results

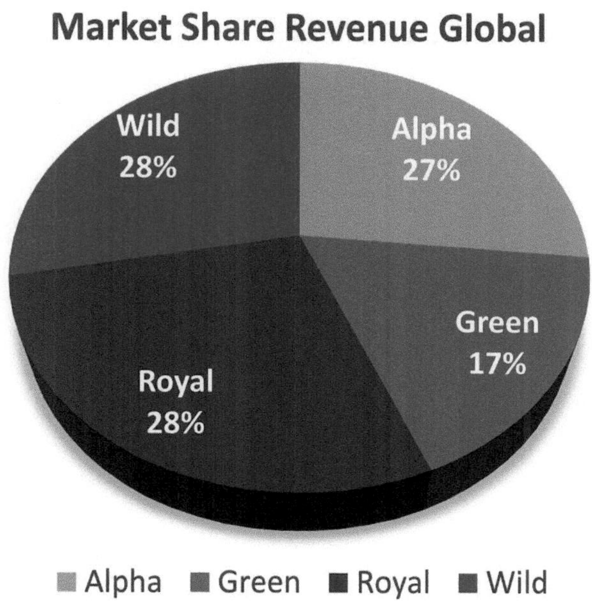

Fig. 9.2 Global revenue market share

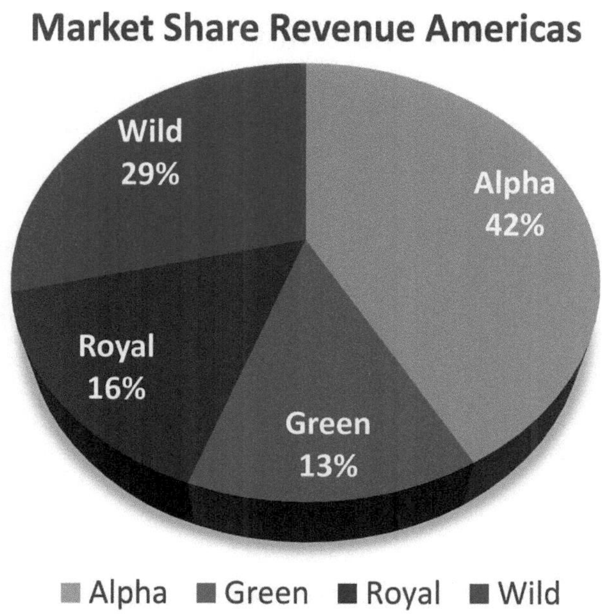

Fig. 9.3 Revenue market share Americas

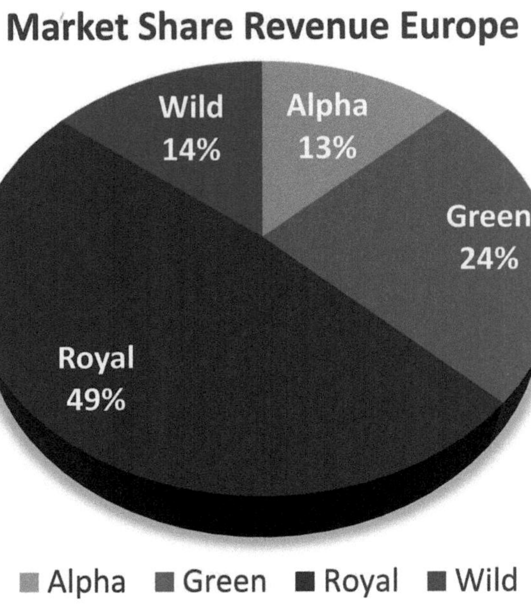

Fig. 9.4 Revenue market share Europe

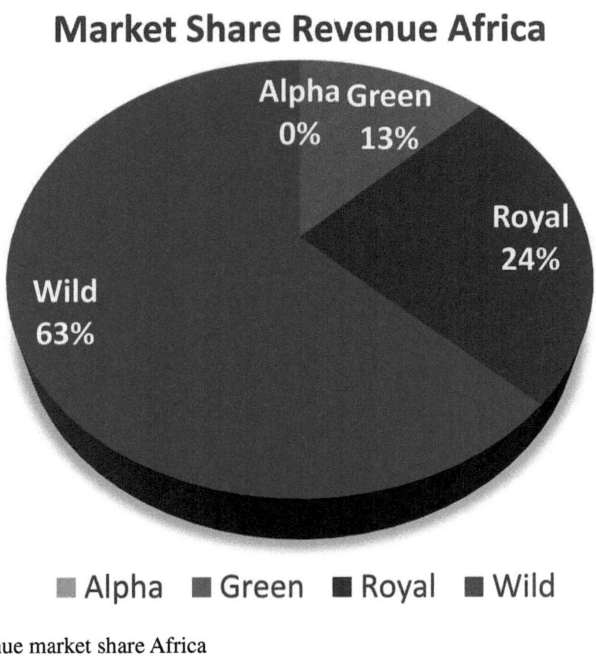

Fig. 9.5 Revenue market share Africa

9.2.5 Market Share Asia Pacific by Revenue

Market share Asia Pacific by revenue (Fig. 9.6): Alpha Beer 38 %, Green Beer 16 %, Royal Beer 19 %, Wild Horse Beer 27 %.

9.3 Global Volume Market Share

9.3.1 Global Market Share by Volume

Global market share by volume (Fig. 9.7): Alpha Beer 29 %, Green Beer 23 %, Royal Beer 23 %, Wild Horse Beer 25 %.

9.3.2 Market Share Americas by Volume

Market share Americas by volume (Fig. 9.8): Alpha Beer 45 %, Green Beer 14 %, Royal Beer 17 %, Wild Horse Beer 24 %.

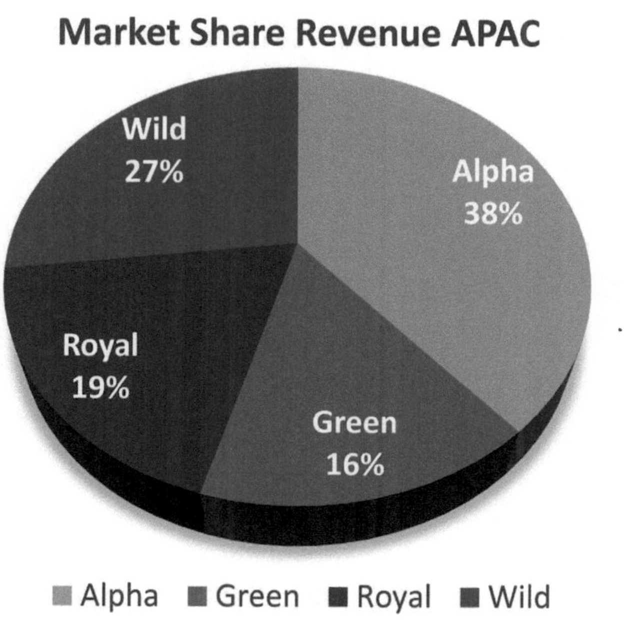

Fig. 9.6 Revenue market share APAC

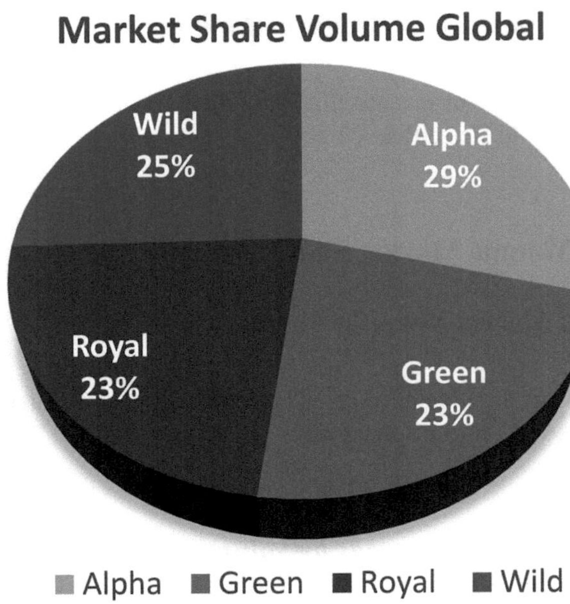

Fig. 9.7 Global volume market share

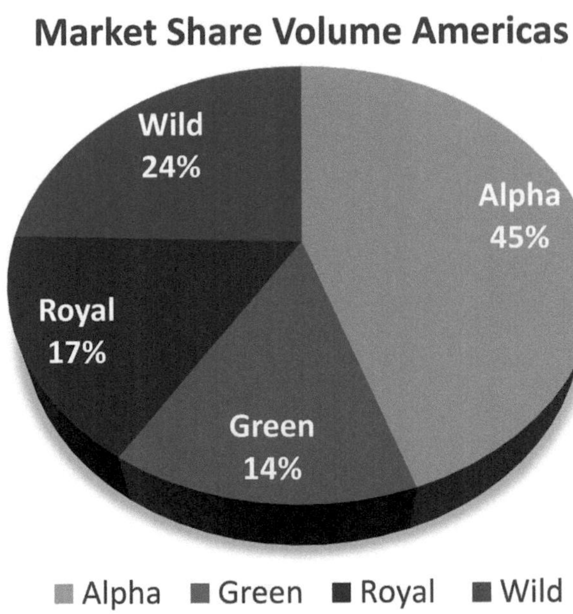

Fig. 9.8 Volume market share Americas

9.3.3 *Market Share Europe by Volume*

Market share Europe by volume (Fig. 9.9): Alpha Beer 14 %, Green Beer 33 %, Royal Beer 38 %, Wild Horse Beer 15 %.

9.3.4 *Market Share Africa by Volume*

Market share Africa by volume (Fig. 9.10): Alpha Beer 0 %, Green Beer 29 %, Royal Beer 26 %, Wild horse Beer 45 %.

9.3.5 *Market Share Asia Pacific by Volume*

Market share Asia Pacific by volume (Fig. 9.11): Alpha Beer 40 %, Green Beer 19 %, Royal Beer 9 %, Wild horse Beer 32 %.

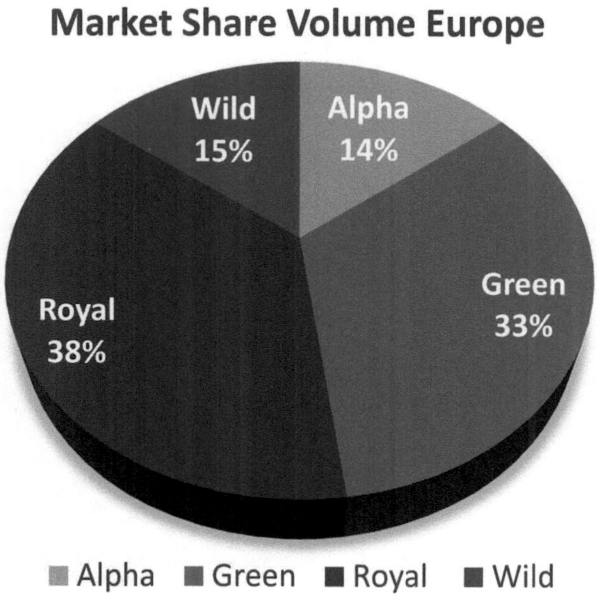

Fig. 9.9 Volume market share Europe

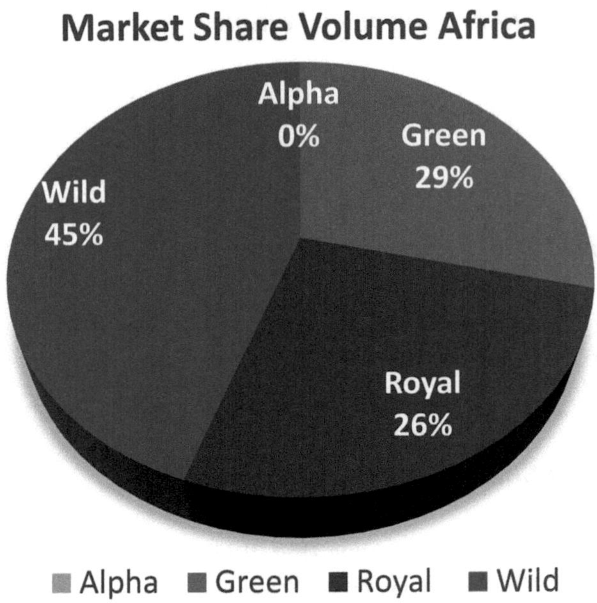

Fig. 9.10 Volume market share Africa

Fig. 9.11 Volume market share APAC

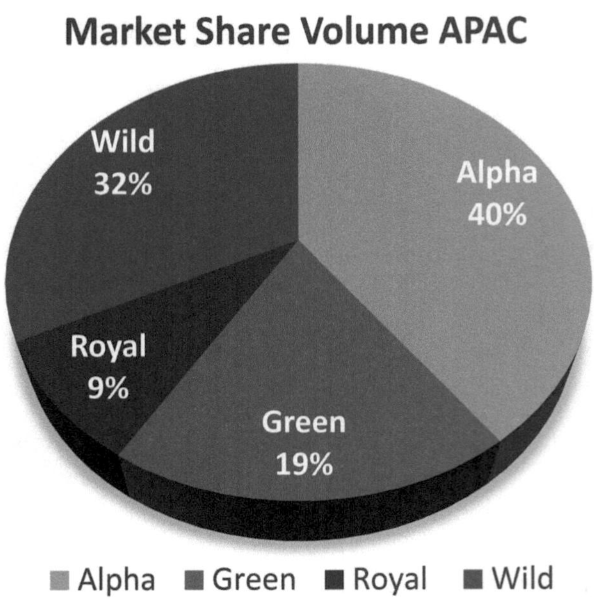

9.4 Global EBITDA Market Share

9.4.1 Global Market Share by EBITDA

Global market share by EBITDA (Fig. 9.12): Alpha Beer 30 %, Green Beer 29 %, Royal Beer 19 %, Wild Horse Beer 22 %.

9.4.2 Market Share Americas by EBITDA

Market share Americas by EBITDA (Fig. 9.13): Alpha Beer 27 %, Green Beer 26 %, Royal Beer 26 %, Wild Horse Beer 21 %.

9.4.3 Market Share Europe by EBITDA

Market share Europe by EBITDA (Fig. 9.14): Alpha Beer 26 %, Green Beer 32 %, Royal Beer 18 %, Wild Horse Beer 24 %.

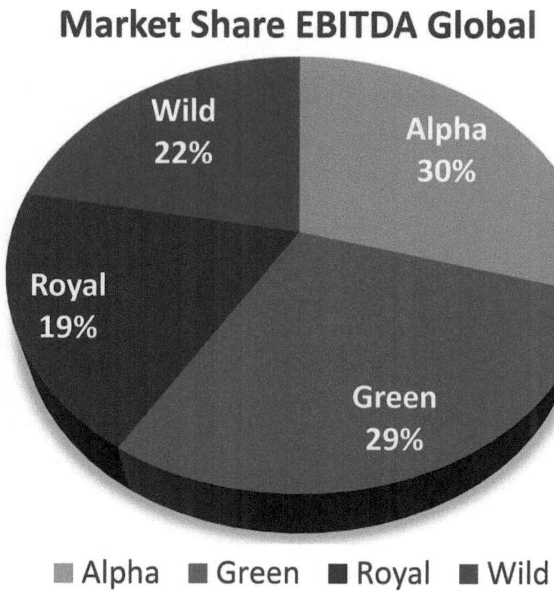

Fig. 9.12 Global EBITDA market share

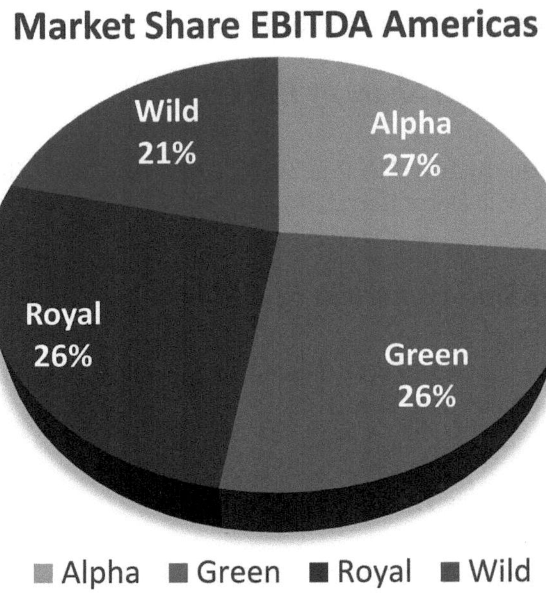

Fig. 9.13 EBITDA market share Americas

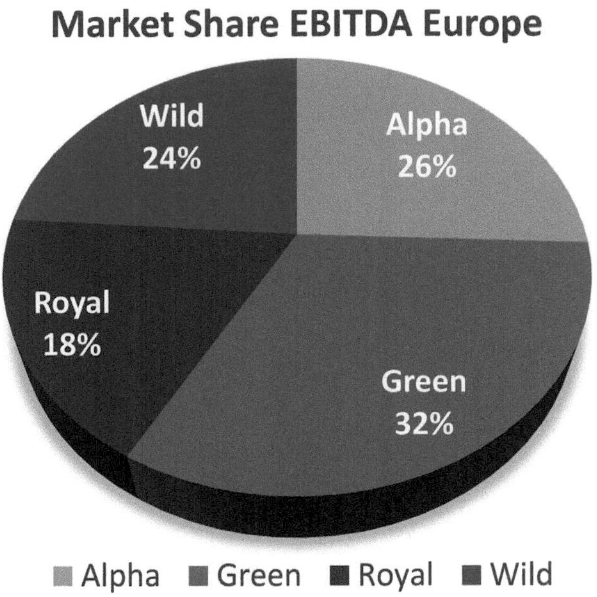

Fig. 9.14 EBITDA market share Europe

9.4.4 Market Share Africa by EBITDA

Market share Africa by EBITDA (Fig. 9.15): Alpha Beer 0 %, Green Beer 56 %, Royal Beer 27 %, Wild Horse Beer 17 %.

9.4.5 Market Share Asia Pacific by EBITDA

Market share Asia Pacific by EBITDA (Fig. 9.16): Alpha Beer 27 %, Green Beer 30 %, Royal Beer 12 %, Wild Horse Beer 31 %.

9.5 Alpha Beer

At Alpha Beer, our ambition is to build a great, enduring company. In the last year, we delivered a year of solid growth and progress against our commercial priorities. Together with our colleagues, customers and commercial partners, and thanks to our consumers' passion for our great portfolio of brands, we delivered strong organic growth in both top-line and EBITDA.

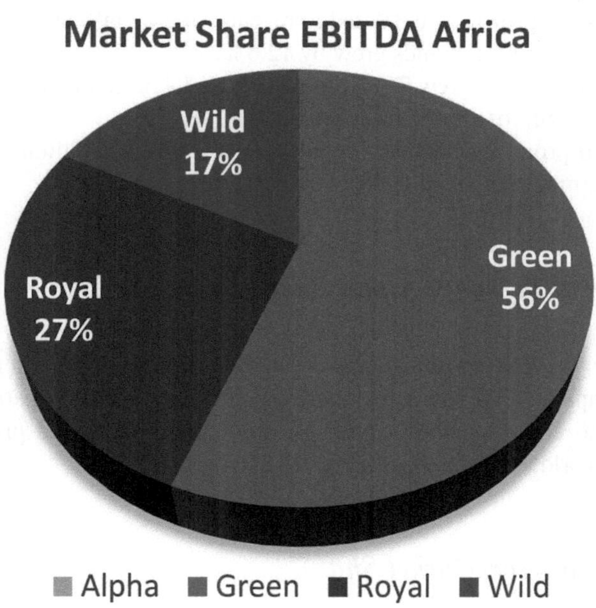

Fig. 9.15

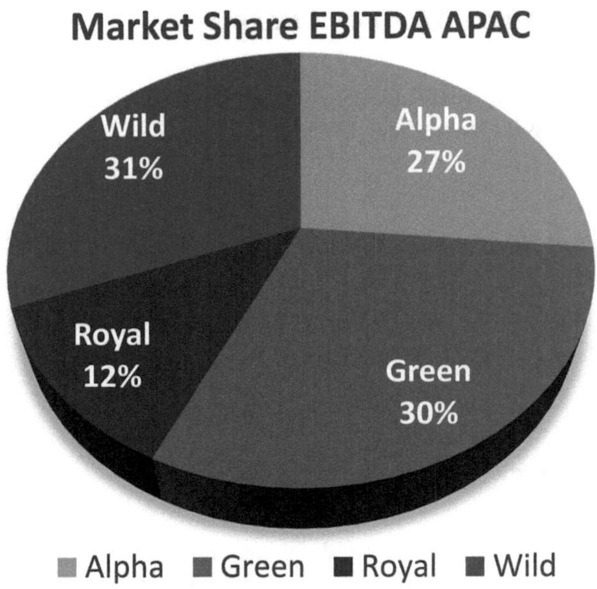

Fig. 9.16 EBITDA market share APAC

9.5.1 Alpha Beer Results

Alpha Beer results (Fig. 9.17):

- Strong top-line growth of 6.3 % led to revenue of 24.7 billion USD.
- Revenues of our 3 top brands grew by 12.6 %.
- Normalized EBITDA grew 7.8 % organically to 7.4 billion USD, and normalized EBITDA margin rose by 55 basis points to 30 %.
- Normalized profit attributable to equity holders was 4.2 billion USD, and normalized earnings per share (EPS) was 5.20 USD.

9.5.2 Global Presence Alpha Beer

Alpha Beer is the leading global brewer and one of the world's top five consumer products companies. We are a company of more than 150,000 people across 26 countries, who come together – with passion, commitment and pride – to brew many of the world's favorite beers (Fig. 9.18).

9.5.3 Alpha Beer Market Share

Market share by revenue: Americas 61 %, Asia Pacific 23 %, Europe 16 % (Fig. 9.19).

Region	Alpha Beer		
	Volume 1000hl	Revenue Million$	EBITDA %
Americas	151125	15200	40%
Europe	42900	4012	27%
Africa	0	0	0%
Asia Pacific	88218	5555	24%
Total	282243	24767	30%

Fig. 9.17 Alpha Beer results

Fig. 9.18 Alpha Beer Global presence

Market share by volume: Americas 54 %, Asia Pacific 31 %, Europe 15 % (Fig. 9.20).

Market share by EBITDA: Americas 44 %, Asia Pacific 26 %, Europe 30 % (Fig. 9.21).

9.5.4 Alpha Beer Portfolio

Portfolio Alpha Beer (Fig. 9.22):

- Premium bottle
- Premium flip-top bottle
- Non-alcoholic bottle
- Premium can

Fig. 9.19 Revenue market share Alpha Beer

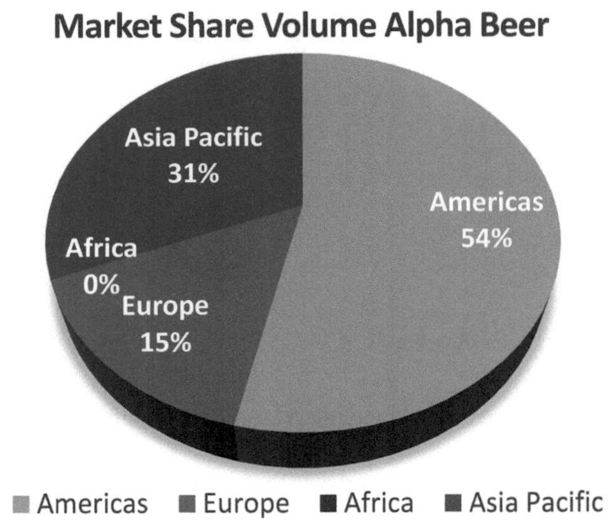

Fig. 9.20 Volume market share Alpha Beer

- Premium 6 pack
- Premium 12 pack
- Premium party
- Premium case
- Flip-top case
- Non-alcoholic case
- Keg

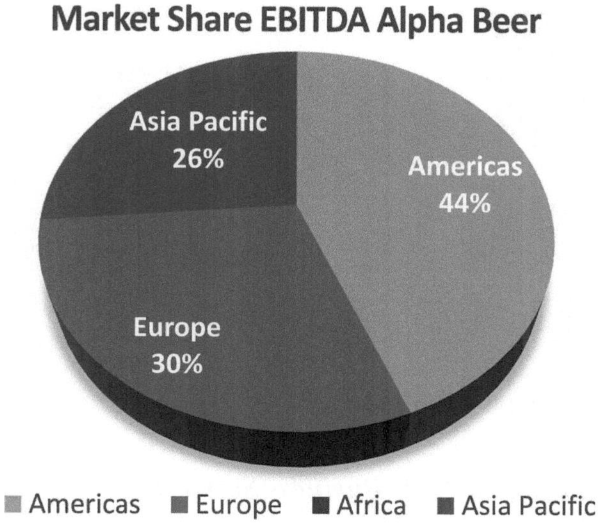

Fig. 9.21 EBITDA market share Alpha Beer

Fig. 9.22 Portfolio Alpha Beer

9.5.5 Alpha Group Organization Chart

Alpha Group Holding has two independent group companies, Alpha Beer with four divisions and Alpha Global Business and IT Services (Fig. 9.23) with two divisions.

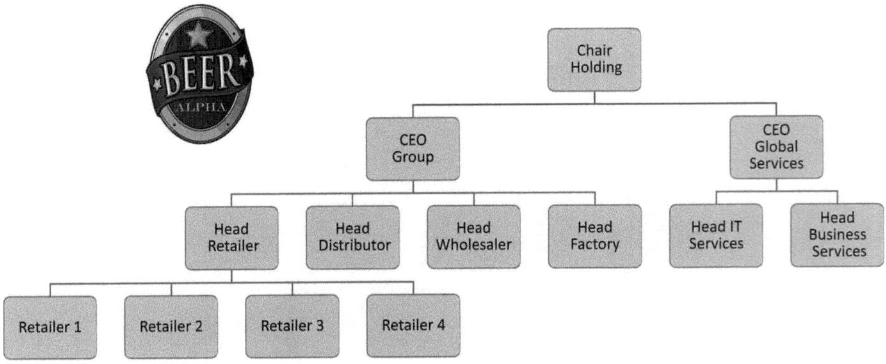

Fig. 9.23 Group organization chart Alpha Beer

9.5.6 Alpha Global IT & Business Servicers

Alpha Global Business & IT Services is located in Prague and was established in 2006 to ensure that the company provides the best possible transactional and support services to its sales activities and breweries across Europe (Fig. 9.24). The center performs selected activities within its IT, Logistics, Finance, Planning and Performance Management, Procurement and Sales Support functions globally in a multinational, multicultural environment with about 1,200 people from 32 different countries which include:

- Standardization of systems and processes
- Business services and good practice sharing
- Consistent policies, processes and rules among different countries
- Facilitating the integration of different processes per region
- More focus on products and customers

9.6 Green Beer

The Green Beer Group is committed to making decisions that have a positive impact on our business and the communities in which we operate. We want to grow our business responsibly while enhancing the quality of life for our consumers, employees and other stakeholders. The strength of the Green Beer Group is our full-range portfolio of international premium and strong local beer brands.

9.6.1 Green Beer Results

Green Beer results (Fig. 9.25):

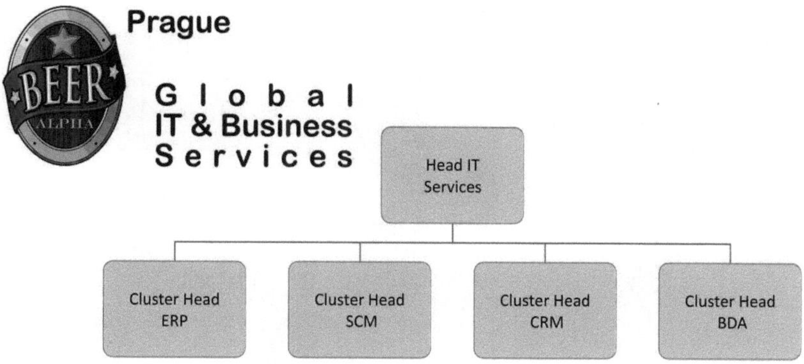

Fig. 9.24 Global IT services organization chart Alpha Beer

Region	Green Beer		
	Volume 1000hl	Revenue Million$	EBITDA %
Americas	47615	4850	39%
Europe	100400	7420	34%
Africa	31250	1500	20%
Asia Pacific	41400	2270	28%
Total	220665	16040	30%

Fig. 9.25 Green Beer results

- Net revenue grew by 2 % organically to $16.0 billion as a result of strong Asian performance and price/mix in Eastern Europe.
- Operating profit was down 7 % organically. Strong Asian growth was offset by results in Eastern and Western Europe.
- Adjusted net profit was impacted by lower operating profit and higher other financial items.

9.6.2 Global Presence Green Beer

We hold strong number one or two positions in 80 % of our markets in more than 45 countries (Fig. 9.26).

Fig. 9.26 Global presence Green Beer

9.6.3 Green Beer Market Share

Market share by revenue (Fig. 9.27): Americas 30 %, Asia Pacific 14 %, Africa 10 %, Europe 46 %.

Market share by volume (Fig. 9.28): Americas 22 %, Asia Pacific 19 %, Africa 14 %, Europe 45 %.

Market share by EBITDA (Fig. 9.29): Americas 33 %, Asia Pacific 23 %, Africa 16 %, Europe 28 %.

9.6.4 Green Beer Portfolio

Portfolio Green Beer (Fig. 9.30):

- Premium bottle
- Premium flip-top bottle
- Non-alcoholic bottle
- Premium can
- Premium 6 pack
- Premium 12 pack
- Premium party
- Premium case
- Flip-top case
- Non-alcoholic case
- Keg

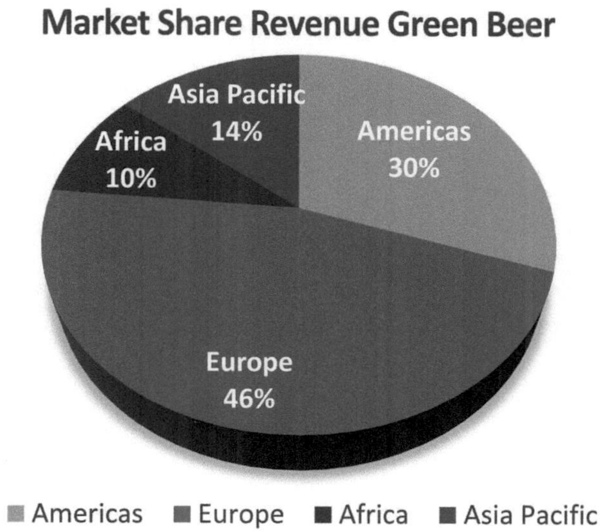

Fig. 9.27 Revenue market share Green Beer

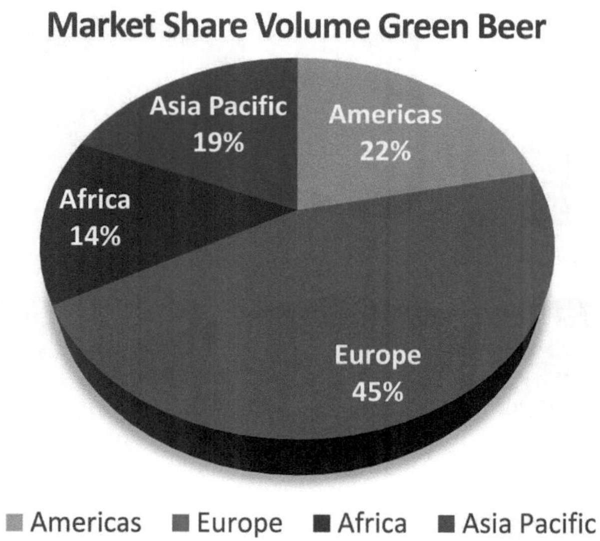

Fig. 9.28 Volume market share Green Beer

9.6.5 Green Group Organization Chart

Green Group Holding has two independent group companies, Green Beer with four divisions and Green Global Business and IT Services (Fig. 9.31) with two divisions.

Fig. 9.29 EBITDA market share Green Beer

Fig. 9.30 Portfolio Green Beer

9.6.6 Green Global IT Organization Chart

Green Global Business & IT Services is located in Copenhagen and was established in 2003 and is structured to support business outcomes, partnering deeply with Green Beer leadership and functions to shape demand for business and information services and improvements (Fig. 9.32). Improving the speed and quality of executive decisions is the main objective. We are developing business intelligence and analytics solutions that will provide our executives with the accurate and timely

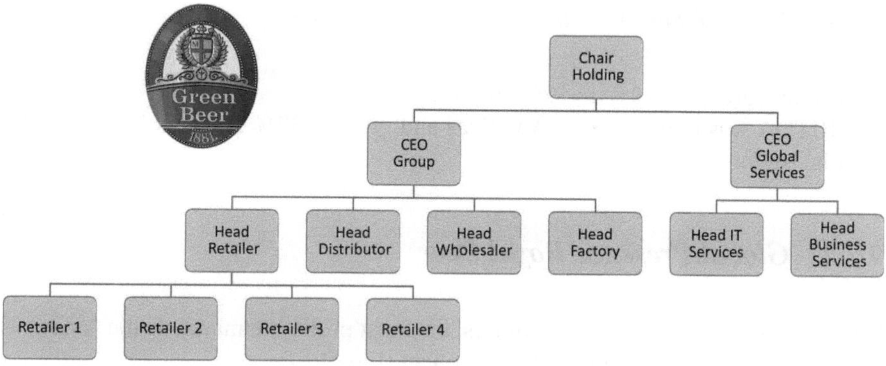

Fig. 9.31 Group organization chart Green Beer

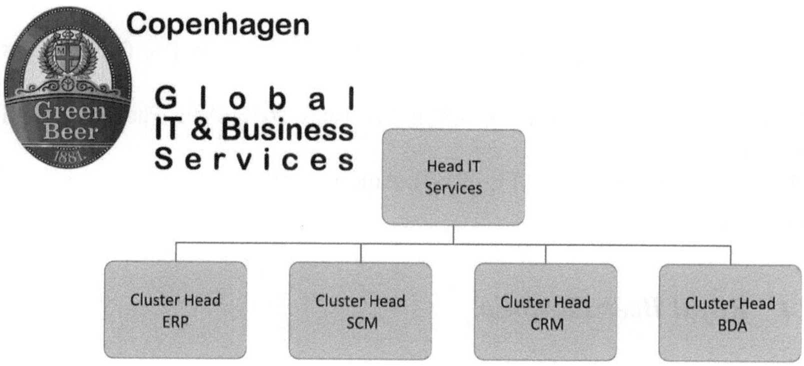

Fig. 9.32 Global IT services organization chart Green Beer

information they need to make better decisions with about 1,500 people from 42 different countries which include:

- Standardization of systems and processes
- Business services and good practice sharing
- Consistent policies, processes and rules among different countries
- Facilitating the integration of different processes per region
- More focus on products and customers

9.7 Royal Beer

Royal Beer is the world's most international brewer with brands available in 179 countries around the world. We are a proud independent global brewer committed to bringing enjoyment to consumers around the world. We value a passion for quality, brands that people love, enjoyment of life, respect for people and for our planet.

9.7.1 Royal Beer Results

- Revenue grew by 9.2 % to $26.2 billion.
- EBITDA was highest in the Americas and grew to 39 % and was 20 % globally (Fig. 9.33).

9.7.2 Global Presence Royal Beer

With a global presence in 150 countries, the most profitable market is the Americas with a focus on southern half of the continent (Fig. 9.34).

9.7.3 Royal Beer Market Share

Market share by revenue (Fig. 9.35): Americas 22 %, Asia Pacific 10 %, Africa 11 %, Europe 57 %.

Market share by volume (Fig. 9.36): Americas 26 %, Asia Pacific 9 %, Africa 13 %, Europe 52 %.

Market share by EBITDA (Fig. 9.37): Americas 50 %, Asia Pacific 14 %, Africa 12 %, Europe 24 %.

9.7.4 Royal Beer Portfolio

Portfolio Royal Beer (Fig. 9.38):

- Premium bottle
- Premium flip-top bottle
- Non-alcoholic bottle

Region	Royal Beer		
	Volume 1000hl	Revenue Million$	EBITDA %
Americas	56000	5704	39%
Europe	112500	14915	19%
Africa	28863	2900	10%
Asia Pacific	19800	2695	11%
Total	217163	26214	20%

Fig. 9.33 Royal Beer results

Fig. 9.34 Global presence Royal Beer

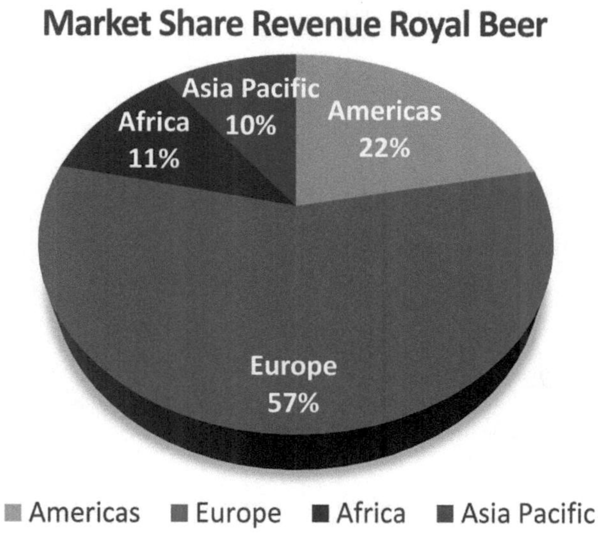

Fig. 9.35 Revenue market share Royal Beer

- Premium can
- Premium 6 pack
- Premium 12 pack
- Premium party
- Premium case
- Flip-top case
- Non-alcoholic case
- Keg

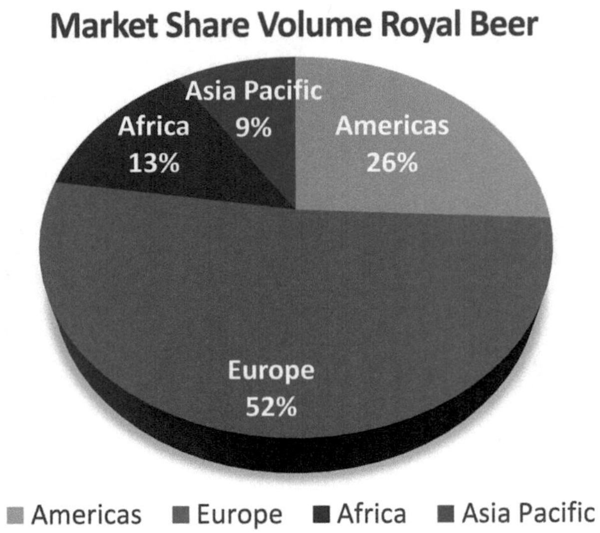

Fig. 9.36 Volume market share Royal Beer

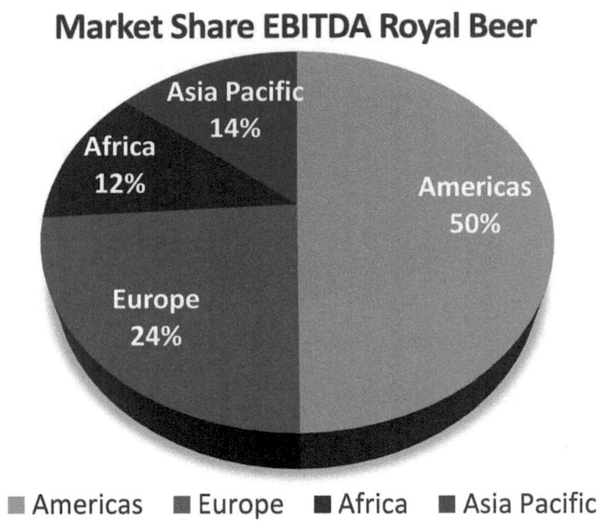

Fig. 9.37 EBITDA market share Royal Beer

Fig. 9.38 Portfolio Royal Beer

9.7.5 Royal Group Organization Chart

Royal Group Holding has two independent group companies, Royal Beer with four divisions and Royal Global Business and IT Services (Fig. 9.39) with two divisions.

9.7.6 Royal Global IT Organization Chart

Royal Global Business & IT Services is located in Budapest and was established in 2005. Our goal is to be the Global Centre of Excellence within Royal Group, that attracts and develops great people. We will deliver this through world class results with our business partners as one team (Fig. 9.40) 1300 people from 45 countries which include:

- Standardization of systems and processes
- Business services and good practice sharing
- Consistent policies, processes and rules among different countries
- Facilitating the integration of different processes per region
- More focus on products and customers

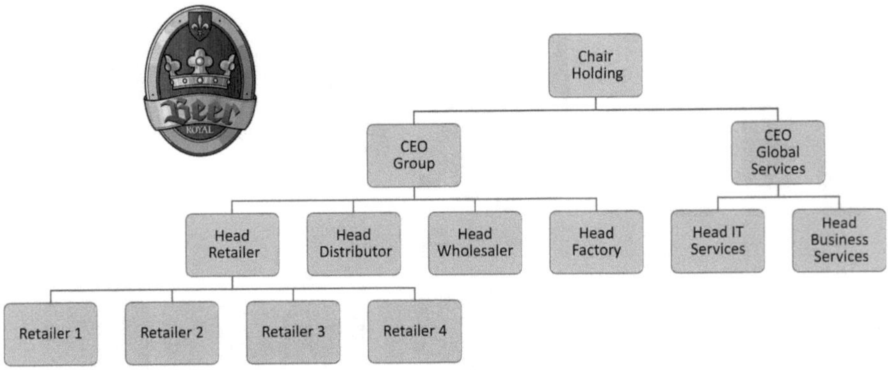

Fig. 9.39 Group organization chart Royal Beer

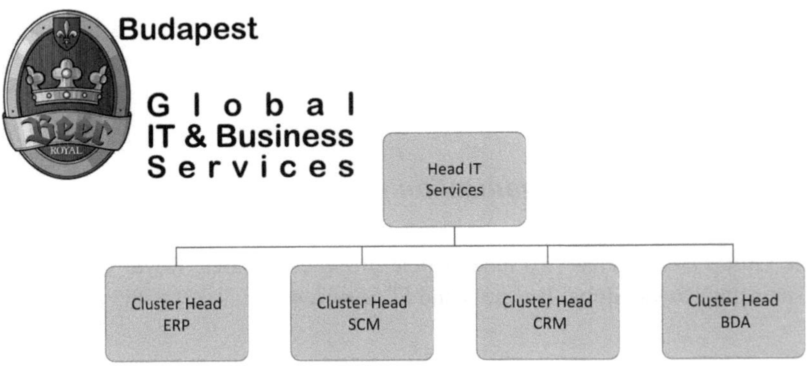

Fig. 9.40 Global IT services organization chart Royal Beer

9.8 Wild Horse Beer

We are in the beer and soft drinks business. We bring refreshment and sociability to millions of people all over the world who enjoy our drinks. We do business in a way that improves livelihoods and helps build communities. We are passionate about brewing and have a long tradition of craftsmanship, making superb beer from high quality natural ingredients. We are local beer experts from which we have carefully selected and nurtured a range of special regional and global brands.

9.8.1 Wild Horse Beer Results

Wild Horse Beer results (Fig. 9.41):

- Revenue grew by 6 % to $26.2 billion.
- EBITDA grew by 6 % to globally 23 % and the Americas leading with 32 %.

Region	Wild Horse Beer		
	Volume 1000hl	Revenue Million$	EBITDA %
Americas	82700	10450	32%
Europe	43600	4398	25%
Africa	48400	7462	6%
Asia Pacific	71200	3867	28%
Total	245900	26177	23%

Fig. 9.41 Wild Horse Beer results

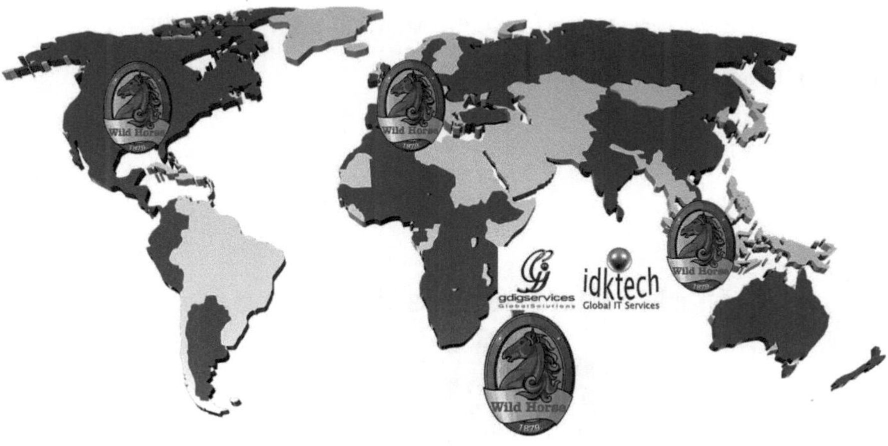

Fig. 9.42 Global presence Wild Horse Beer

9.8.2 Global Presence Wild Horse Beer

Wild Horse Beer has 69,000 employees in more than 80 countries (Fig. 9.42).

9.8.3 Wild Horse Beer Market Share

Market share by revenue (Fig. 9.43): Americas 40 %, Asia Pacific 15 %, Africa 28 %, Europe 17 %.

Market share by volume (Fig. 9.44): Americas 33 %, Asia Pacific 29 %, Africa 20 %, Europe 18 %.

Market share by EBITDA (Fig. 9.45): Americas 35 %, Asia Pacific 31 %, Africa 7 %, Europe 27 %.

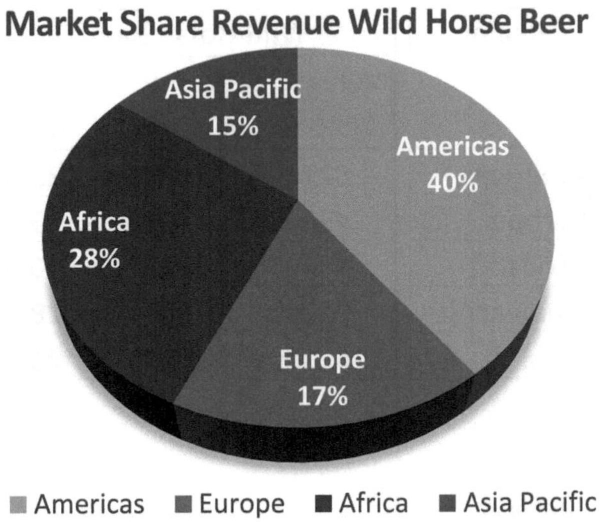

Fig. 9.43 Revenue market share Wild Horse Beer

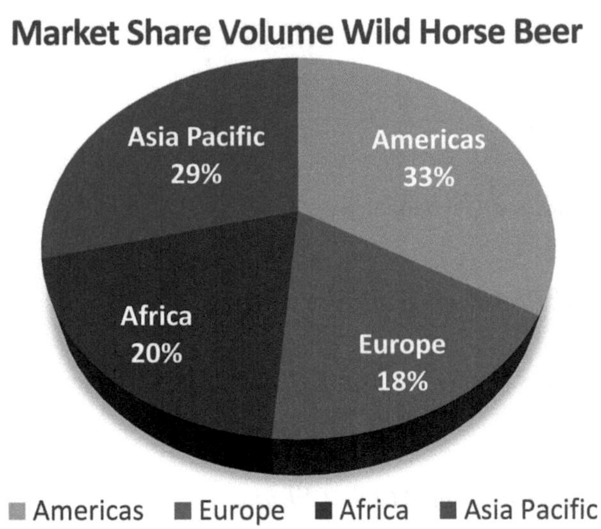

Fig. 9.44 Volume market share Wild Horse Beer

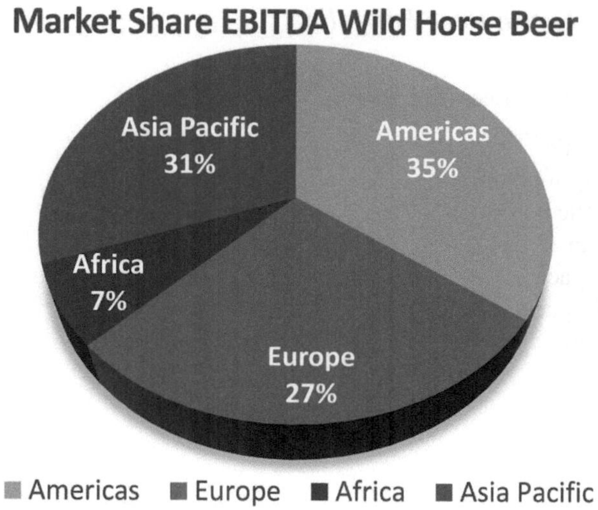

Fig. 9.45 EBITDA market share Wild Horse Beer

Fig. 9.46 Portfolio Wild Horse Beer

9.8.4 Wild Horse Beer Portfolio

Portfolio Wild Horse Beer (Fig. 9.46):

- Premium bottle
- Premium flip-top bottle
- Non-alcoholic bottle
- Premium can
- Premium 6 pack
- Premium 12 pack
- Premium party
- Premium case
- Flip-top case
- Non-alcoholic case
- Keg

9.8.5 Wild Horse Group Organization Chart

Wild Horse Group Holding has two independent group companies, Wild Horse Beer with four divisions and Wild Horse Global Business and IT Services (Fig. 9.47) with two divisions.

9.8.6 Wild Horse Global IT Organization Chart

Wild Horse Global Business & IT Services is located in Brussels and was established in 2004. Global IT Services is also transforming its own underlying capabilities. By driving improvements in its internal technical skills, vendor performance,

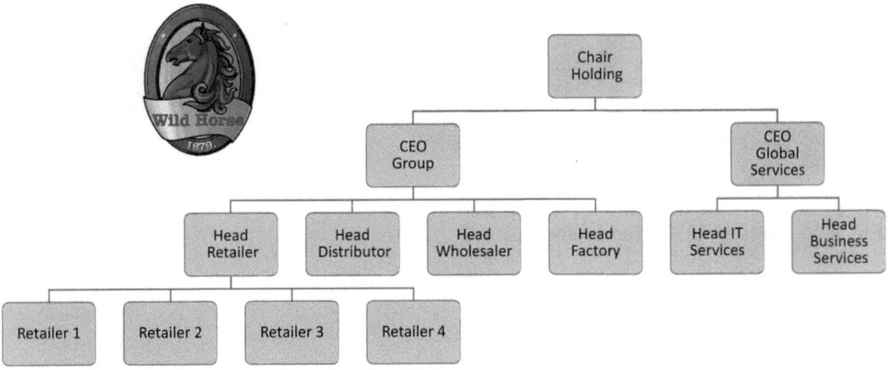

Fig. 9.47 Group organization chart Wild Horse Beer

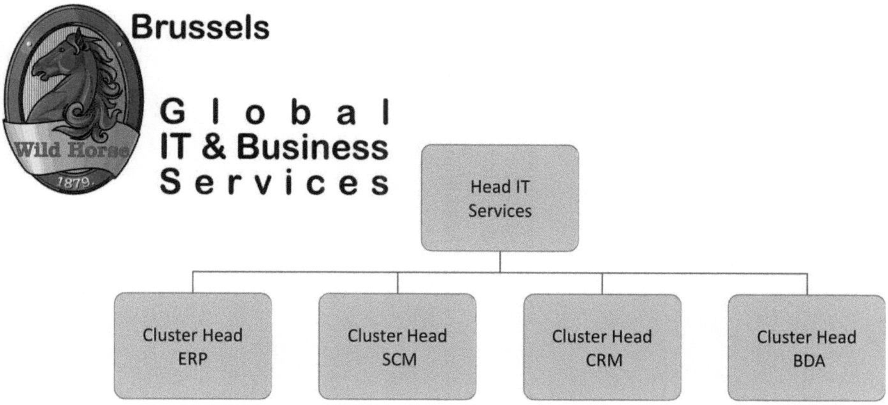

Fig. 9.48 Global IT services organization chart Wild Horse Beer

systems controls and people abilities, Global IT Services is striving to be best in class against a number of measures, including cost, efficiency and quality (Fig. 9.48). Our Global IT Services operation offers careers in these areas: Service Delivery, Solution Delivery, Strategy and Architecture, Vendor Management, and Business Partnering in a multicultural team of 1,000 people from 34 countries.

Chapter 10
Global Service Provider Profiles

Abstract Chapter 10 includes the company profiles of two India-based global service providers: Gdigservices and Idktech.

10.1 Gdigservices: Profile and Delivery Model

Gdigservices (Fig. 10.1) is a global leader in consulting, technology, and outsourcing and next-generation services. We enable clients in more than 54 countries to outperform the competition and stay ahead of the innovation curve. 197,000 experts are helping enterprises renew themselves while also creating new avenues to generate value. We provide enterprises with strategic insights on what lies ahead. We help enterprises transform and thrive in a changing world through strategic consulting, operational leadership, and the co-creation of breakthrough solutions, including those in mobility, sustainability, big data, and cloud computing.

10.1.1 History

In 1981, eight engineers started gdigservices. From the beginning, the company was founded on the principle of building and implementing great ideas that drive progress for clients and enhance lives through enterprise solutions. For over three decades, we have been a company focused on bringing to life great ideas and enterprise solutions that drive progress for our clients.

10.1.2 Global Footprint

Delivery centers in 54 countries with 50 global delivery centers and 25 near-shore centers (Fig. 10.2).

K. Gronwald, *Global Communication and Collaboration*,
DOI 10.1007/978-3-662-53150-1_10

Fig. 10.1 Gdigservices logo

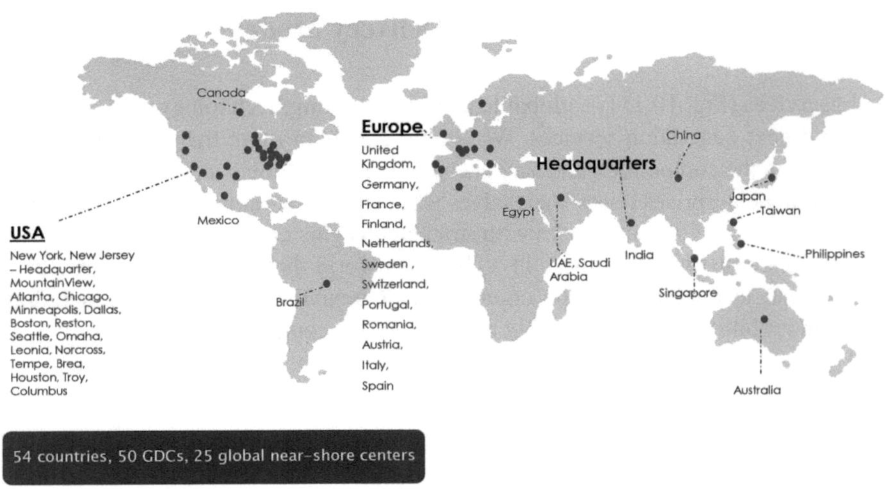

Fig. 10.2 Gdigservices global footprint

10.1.3 Building Right Capability and Leadership

More than 90,000 associates in 54 countries (Fig. 10.3).

10.1.4 Globally diversified service portfolio

The service portfolio includes application development, business process outsourcing, testing services, package implementation, consulting, and technology infrastructure services (Fig. 10.4).

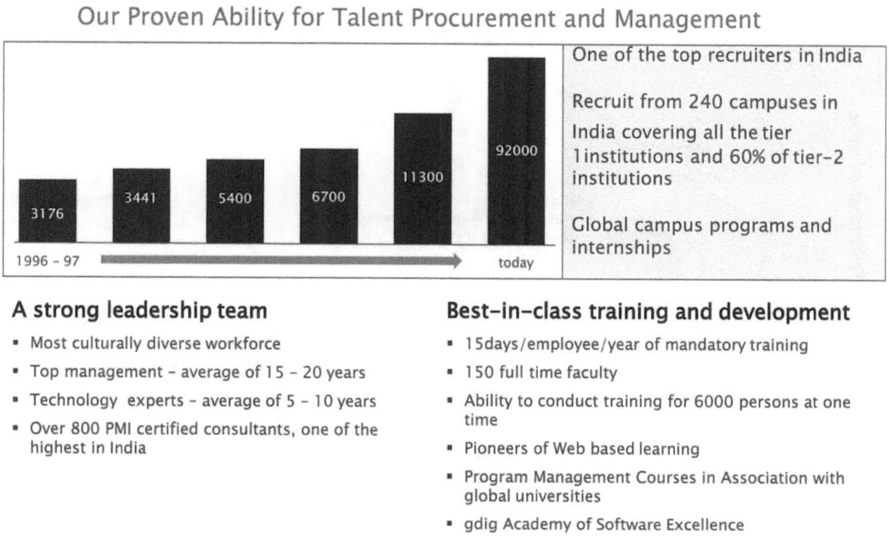

Fig. 10.3 Gdigservices building right capability and leadership

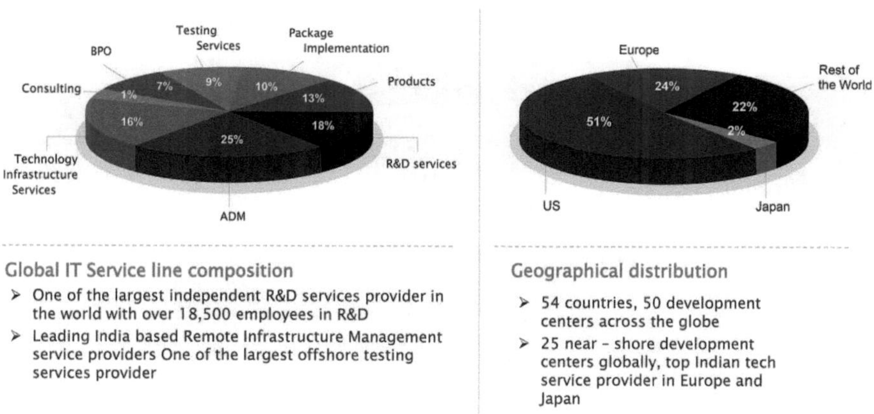

Fig. 10.4 Gdigservices globally diversified service portfolio

10.1.5 Engagement Roadmap

The engagement roadmap is an evolutionary process, starting with a simple staff augmentation and evolving into a risk share partnership (Fig. 10.5).

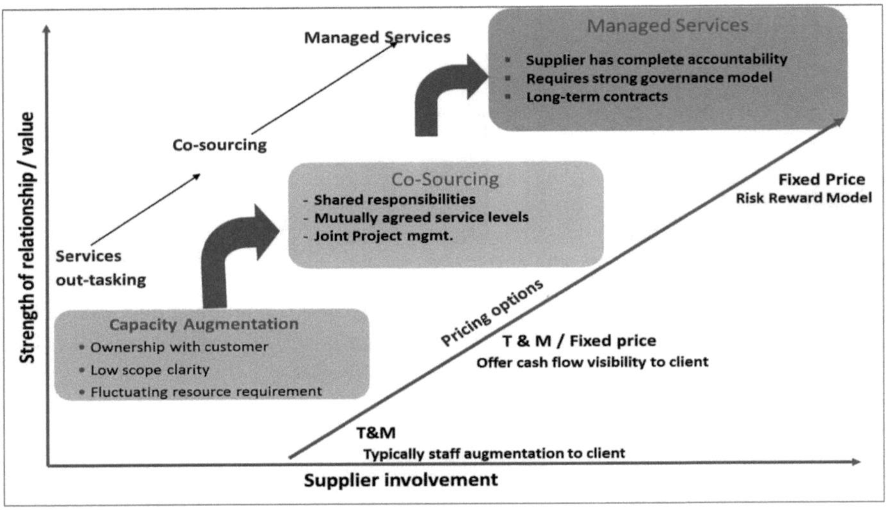

Fig. 10.5 Gdigservices engagement roadmap

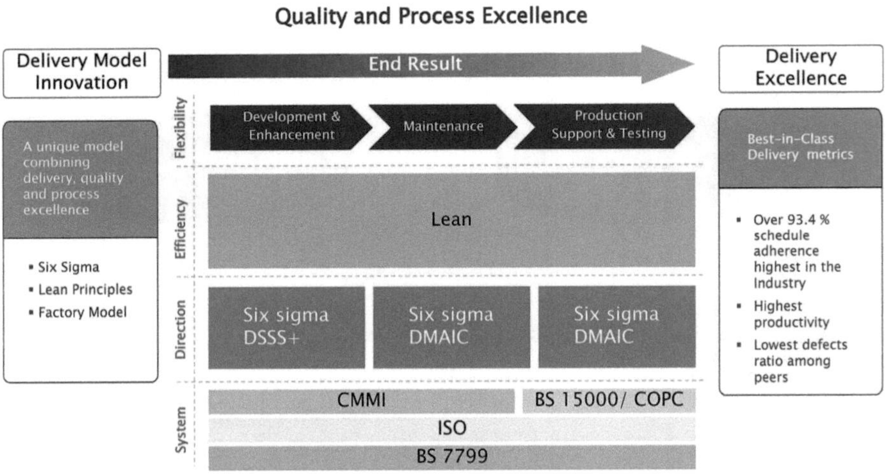

Fig. 10.6 Gdigservices investing in optimized global delivery model

10.1.6 Investing in Optimized Global Delivery Model

Best practices process models matching the organizational maturity of the customer (Fig. 10.6).

10.1.7 Gdigdelivery: Applied Innovation to Application Support

- An innovative delivery model to maintain and support enterprise applications.
- Designed to handle variability in work volume typical to application support.
- Virtualized delivery across 4 delivery centers around the globe.
- Standardized gdigDelivery platform of tools and processes.
- Leverage industry best practices.
- Improve productivity.
- Support SAP, Oracle Applications, PeopleSoft and JD Edwards.

10.1.8 Outsourcing Challenges and Traditional Delivery Models

Comparing outsourcing models (Fig. 10.7).

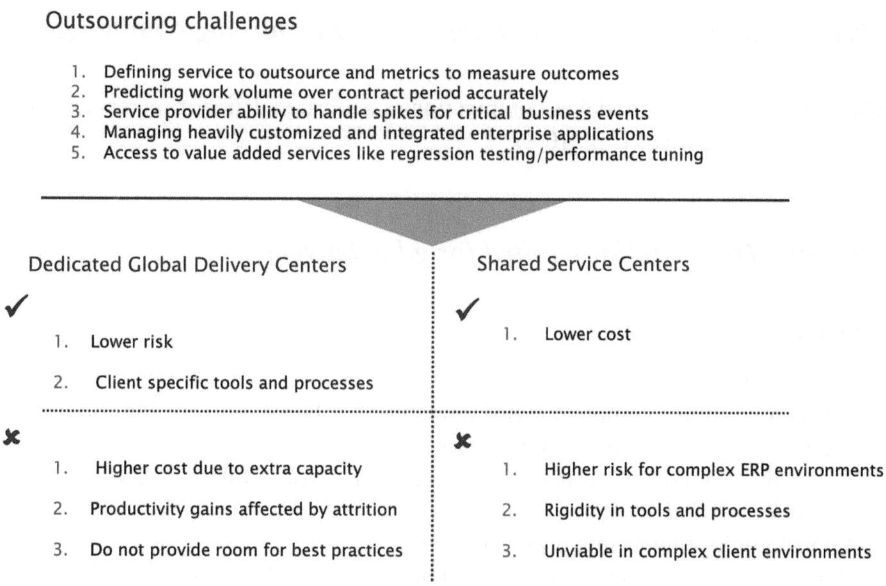

Fig. 10.7 Gdigservices outsourcing challenges

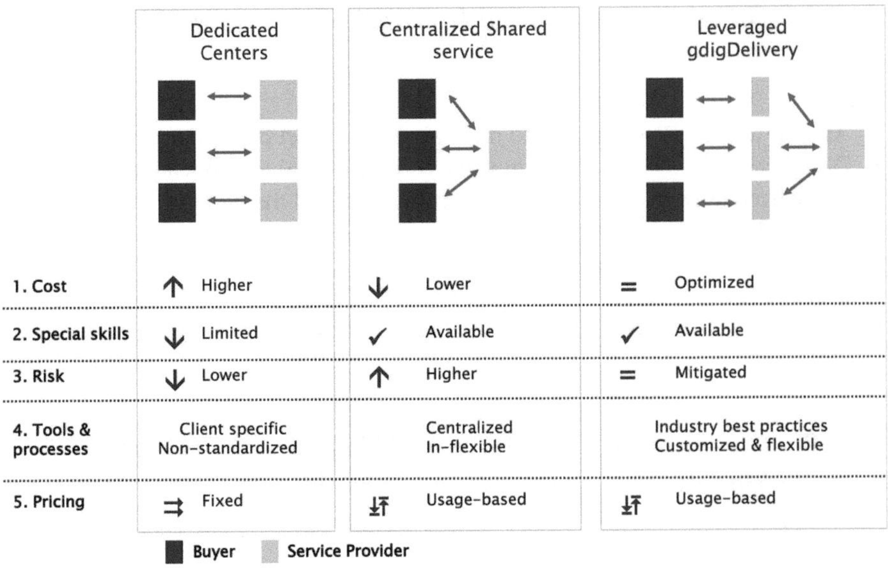

Fig. 10.8 gdigDelivery versus traditional outsourcing challenges

10.1.9 gdigDelivery Versus Traditional Outsourcing Challenges

Gdigservices delivery model as combination of dedicated delivery centers and centralized shared services (Fig. 10.8).

10.1.10 Organizations suited for gdigDelivery

Organizations Best Suited

- Non-regulated industries
- Firms looking for complete ownership and SLA based delivery for application management and infrastructure hosting
- Firms that would like to take advantage of increasing their variable costs via transaction-based pricing
- Global, multi-lingual support is required
- Application administration is included in scope (SAP Basis or Oracle DBA)
- 24/7 physical support requirement

Organization Not Suited

- Regulated business environment
- Firms that are not clear on the service being outsourced and benchmark costs for the service
- Firms that typically only want staff augmentation or co-sourcing type engagement models

10.1.11 gdigDelivery Service Offerings

Service Desk

- Providing first line of support for end users of ERP applications
  - 24/7 multilingual support
  - ERP specific help desk to improve user experience
  - Standard service management process and tool to improve productivity by 5 % to 10 %

Business Support

- Working on more specific business issues related to application configuration, data and other complex issues
  - Enhanced support for specific business windows like period close, peak sales periods
  - Proactive end user training and self-service enablement
  - Business process specific SLAs

Application Corrective Support

- Correcting any bugs that might have been introduced while customizing the ERP application
  - Universal known error database to reduce *mean time to resolve*
  - Dedicated problem management team to reduce incidents

Preventive Maintenance

- Focused on proactive monitoring of the application, batch and interface jobs, improving system performance and uptime
  - Proactive benchmarking and monitoring of system performance and uptime
  - Best practices to simplify architecture and stabilize systems
  - Specialist teams for performance tuning and niche products

Application Enhancements

- Providing minor enhancements to ERP application based on priority set by business
  - *On time* delivery of enhancements in spite of spikes in ticket volumes
  - Variable *per enhancement* pricing

Regression Testing

- Automation and testing of new releases prior to deployment in production
  - Flexible ramp up and ramp downs to support major releases
  - Independent validation and verification for all new releases
  - Automated test script library

Application Administration

- Monitoring application landscape and system performance and availability. This service includes application patch management, database administration, instance management, user and security management
  - Proactive performance monitoring and tuning to improve the overall health of the application
  - Web based integration single view dashboard for tracking application health

Infrastructure Services

- Providing integrated hosting of the ERP applications and the related network and operating system related services
  - Optimizing TCO by providing support of infrastructure, database and applications
  - Integrated SLAs to the business

10.1.12 Gdigservices Execution model

Execution model as combined dedicated and shared team supported by tools and processes (Fig. 10.9).

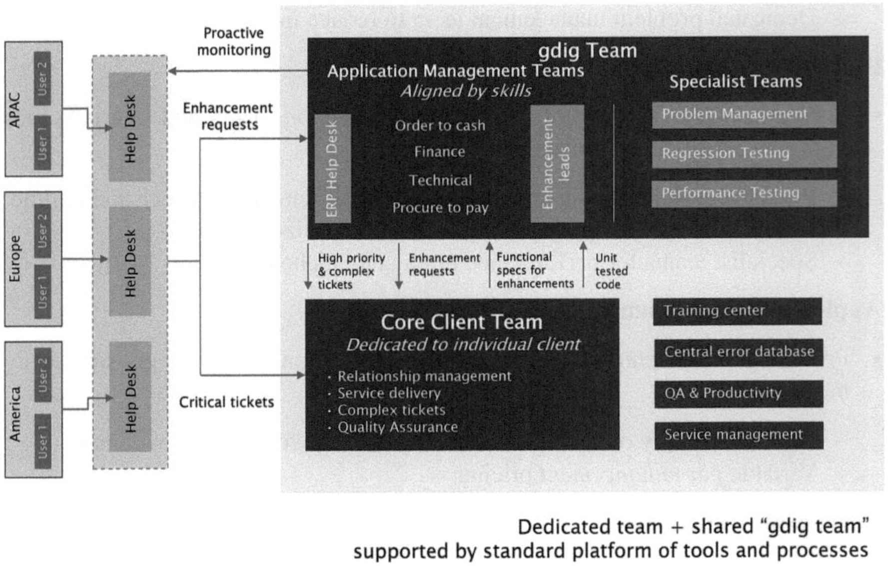

Fig. 10.9 Gdigservices execution model

10.1.13 Gdigservices Tools

Merged processes and tools between provider and client as part of a shared reward partnership (Fig. 10.10).

10.1.14 Pricing Models

Variable pricing models linked to the maturity of the engagement (Fig. 10.11)

10.1.15 Operational Model: Security and Ticket Allocation

Security

- All shared resources to be on named basis and accounts created for client application access
- gdigDelivery centers in the process of being BS7799 certified
- Can provide SAS 70 audit as per customer requirements

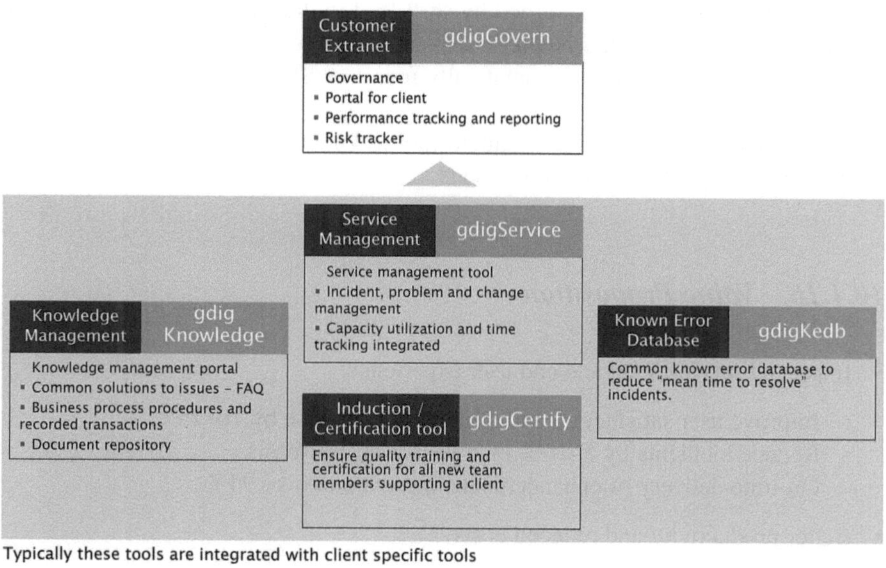

Fig. 10.10 Gdigservices tools

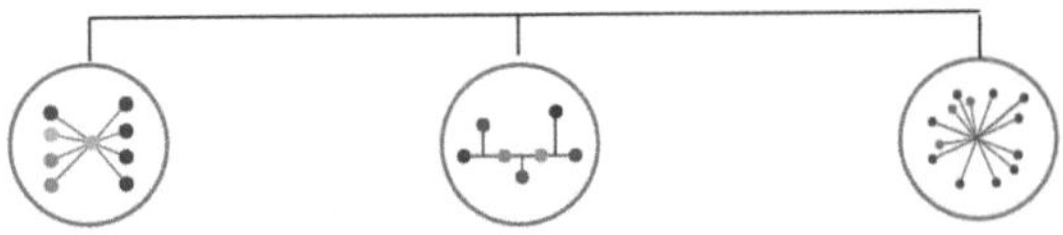

	User-based pricing	Transaction-based pricing	Application instance based pricing
Suitability	Usage and support volume not easily predictable	Mature systems & ticket volumes predictable	Typically for application administration and infrastructure services
Advantages	▪ Predictable budget outlay ▪ Vendor owns support and takes on risk of varying work volume ▪ Reduced management overhead	▪ Can leverage savings related to ticket reductions ▪ Transparent pricing – clear visibility to vendor productivity	▪ Predictable costs for managing an application landscape ▪ Transparent pricing and productivity ▪ Easy charge back to business units
Disadvantages	▪ Could pay premium for vendor taking on variability risk	▪ No incentive to vendor to reduce tickets ▪ Higher management overhead for client	▪ Certain constraints in terms of variable services

All pricing models can be offered as fixed monthly price with an assumed baseline scope for variable parameters (user, transaction, etc.)

Fig. 10.11 Gdigservices pricing models

Ticket Allocation & Prioritization Process

- Severity 1 issues assigned/paged to identified core team members/leads
- All other severity issues assigned by shift lead to the team members directly in the service management system
- Service management tool automatically monitors SLA slippage and alerts shift leads
- Direct link from service management tool to knowledge base and known error database for quick resolution of tickets

10.1.16 Value Proposition

- Improved service level and end user experience:
  - Improve user satisfaction and system performance by 10–15 %.
  - Reduce incidents by 5–10 % on a year over year basis.
  - On-time delivery of enhancements improved to over 95 %.
- Better productivity and reduced costs:
  - Standardized service management tools and processes increase productivity by 5–10 %.

  - Common known error database helps reduce *mean time to resolve* increasing productivity and reducing incident occurrence by 5–10 %.
  - Using flexible teams helps addressing spikes instead of maintaining additional fixed capacity.

- Flexible pricing options:

  - Fixed price based on a fixed scope of services.
  - Flexible pricing based on users, tickets or application instances. Addresses situations where volume of work across services cannot be predicted.

10.1.17 Governance Structure

Three tier governance structure (Fig. 10.12).

10.1.18 Governance Organization

Governance organization reflecting the tree tier governance structure (Fig. 10.13).

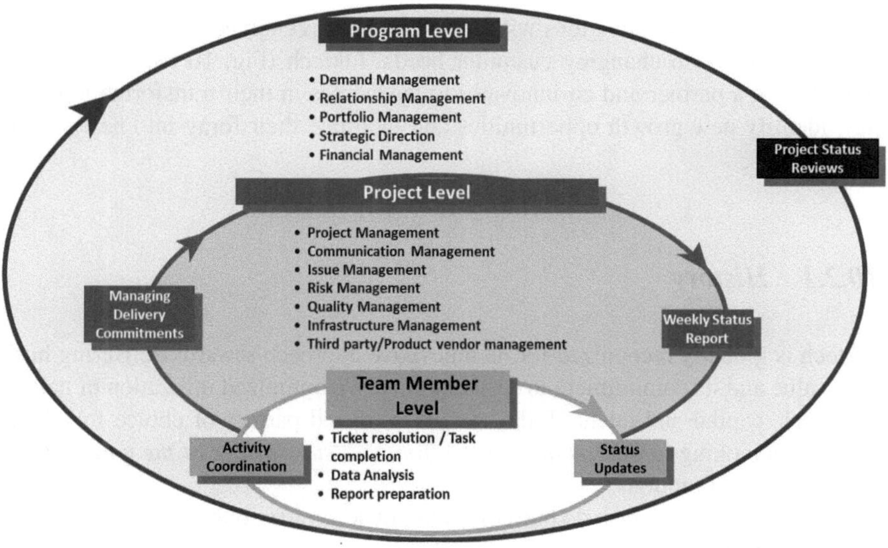

Fig. 10.12 Gdigservices governance structure

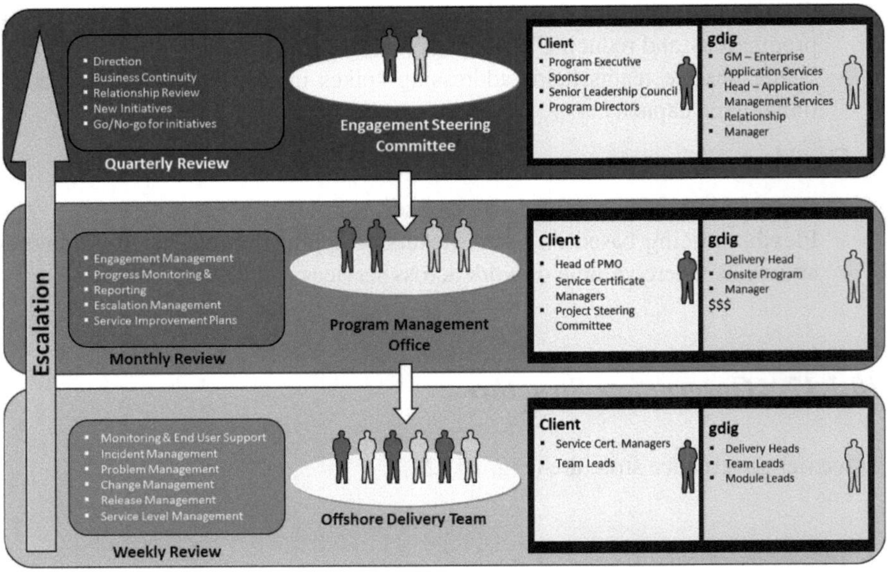

Fig. 10.13 Gdigservice governance organization

10.2 Idktech: Profile and Delivery Model

In today's world, organizations will have to rapidly reengineer themselves and be more responsive to changing customer needs. Idktech (Fig. 10.14) is well positioned to be a partner and co-innovator to businesses in their transformation journey, identify new growth opportunities and facilitate their foray into new sectors and markets.

10.2.1 History

Idktech is globally recognized for its innovative approach towards delivering business value and its commitment to sustainability. We optimized utilization of natural resources, capital and talent. Today we are a trusted partner of choice for global businesses looking to *differentiate at the front* and *standardize at the core* through technology interventions.

Idktech helps customers do business better by leveraging our industry-wide experience, deep technology expertise, comprehensive portfolio of services and vertically aligned business model. Our 170,000 workforce in 75+ dedicated technologies *Centers of Excellence* in 175+ cities across 6 continents enable us to harness the latest technology for delivering business capability to our clients.

Fig. 10.14 Idktech logo

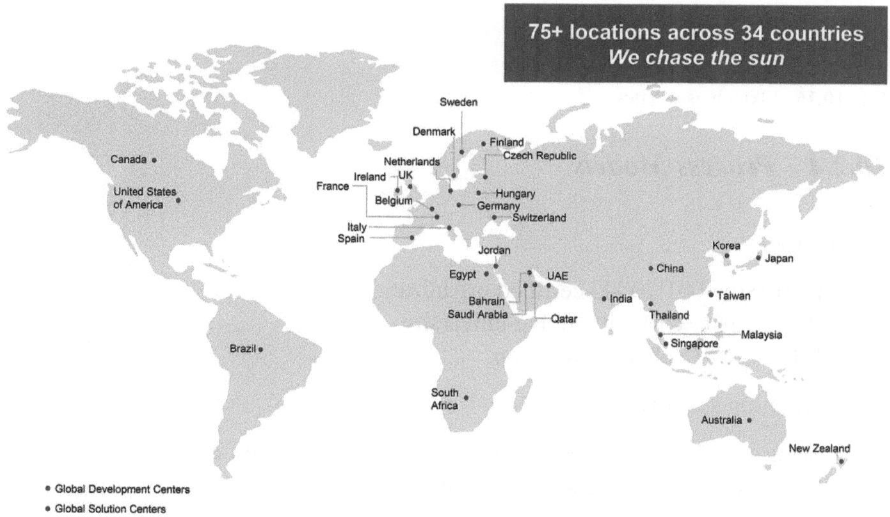

Fig. 10.15 Idktech global presence

10.2.2 Global Presence

Idktech presence in 34 countries with global development and solution centers in 75 locations (Fig. 10.15).

10.2.3 Associates

Globally 29,000 employees, more than 60 nationalities, 80 % with more than three years experience (Fig. 10.16).

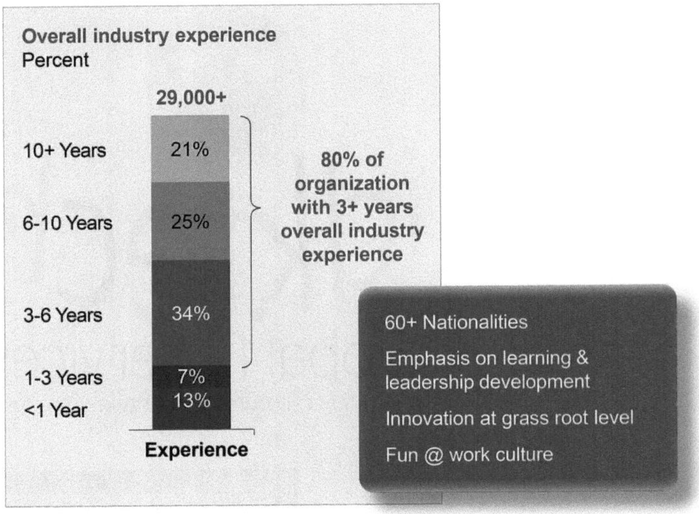

Fig. 10.16 Idktech associates

10.2.4 Process Models

- Quality:
  - First ISO 9001:20000 certified organization.
  - Pioneered eSCM with global university.
  - ISO 27001 Global certification.
- Information security:
  - Security discipline embedded in the organizations culture.
  - Security process integrated into quality management system.
  - Compliance verified periodically through external and internal audits.
- Business continuity:
  - BS 25999 certification on business continuity.
  - BCM processes integrated into the quality management system.
  - Multi-layered crisis management teams.
  - Integration of customer and location business continuity plans.

10.2.5 Full Life Cycle Offering

Full life cycle offerings: Enterprise business solutions, application development and management services, infrastructure management services, integrated engineering solutions, business process outsourcing (Fig. 10.17).

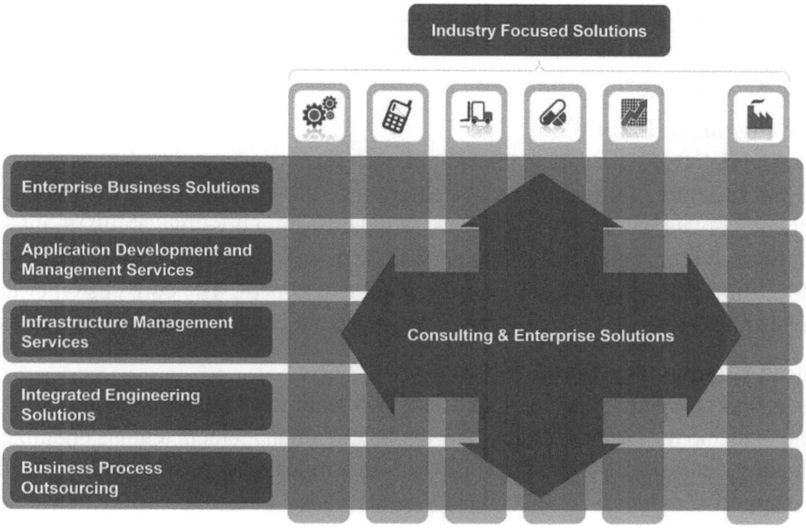

Fig. 10.17 Idktech full life cycle offering

10.2.6 Lines of Business

Consulting
Idktech turns vision into action, creating and sustaining stakeholder value. We deliver insights and help our customers achieve strategic and operational excellence, using our in-depth industry knowledge and expertise.

IT Services
Idktech helps companies leverage IT to realize their business strategies, explore new opportunities, create virtual enterprises, grow competencies, and forge closer ties with their customers. We help clients architect change and implement solutions across multiple platforms.

Outsourcing
Idktech offers a wide range of outsourcing services that enable companies to focus on core competencies, free up resources, enhance productivity, and improve profitability. The Idktech BPO provides access to unmatched infrastructure, world-class resource, and highly talented, committed professionals.

10.2.7 Advanced Shared Competency Delivery Model: ASCDM

Advanced Shared Competency Delivery
is a competency based delivery model with focus on support and maintenance extended to project execution. The fundamental concept is to provide application management services and projects using virtualized delivery centers across the globe

with a standard platform of tools and processes leveraging industry best practices. The model is capable of handling variability in work volume; and provides committed year on year productivity gains.

Core Customer Team
In this model, there is a core team from Idktech that is dedicated to the customer. The size and structure of this team will be determined based on the maturity and stability of client's organization, level of process standardization possible, ability to integrate with Idktech tools and other parameters. Idktech will recommend the size, structure and location for the core team after an initial assessment. The core customer teams can be either located at the customer sites or at Idktech global delivery locations.

Shared Competency Team
The shared competency team is split into two main teams, the application management team and the specialist team. The application management team is organized by technology and skills. There are shift leads that manage teams that address application support activities while the enhancements leads address enhancement and development work. The specialist teas are very critical to the value proposition of the shared competency center. These teams can provide high-end value added services on an on-demand model. So access to these specialists is available at short notice and at lower cost.

10.2.8 ASCDM: Utilization with Maximized Profitability and Zero Bench

All billable resources are part of a shared competency pool and can be utilized in projects as needed. Once their project assignment has finished, they return to the pool and will be utilized virtually for various customers (Fig. 10.18).

10.2.9 Advanced Shared Competency Delivery Versus Dedicated Support

Idktech delivery model as combination of dedicated delivery centers and centralized shared services (Fig. 10.19).

10.2.10 Advanced Shared Competency Delivery Model Comparison

Comparing delivery models (Fig. 10.20)

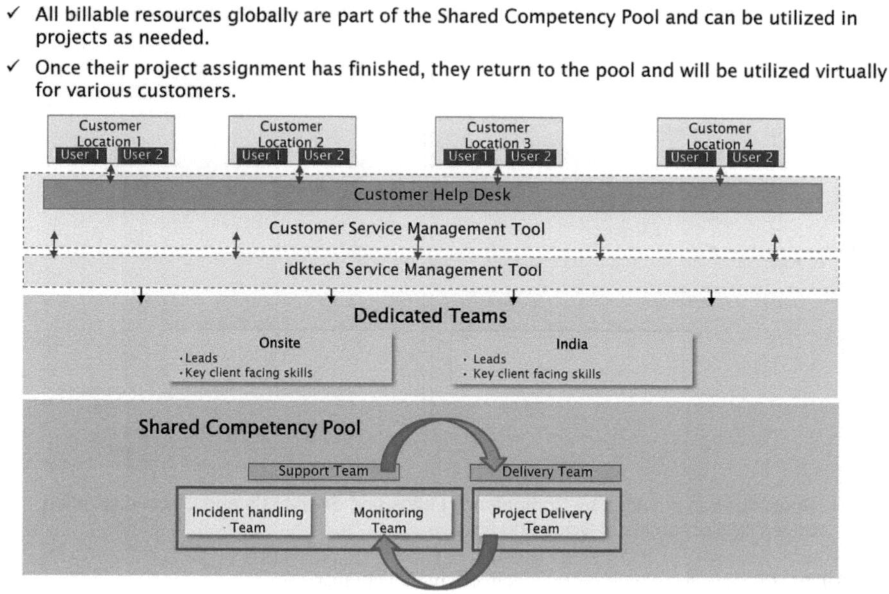

Fig. 10.18 Idktech utilization

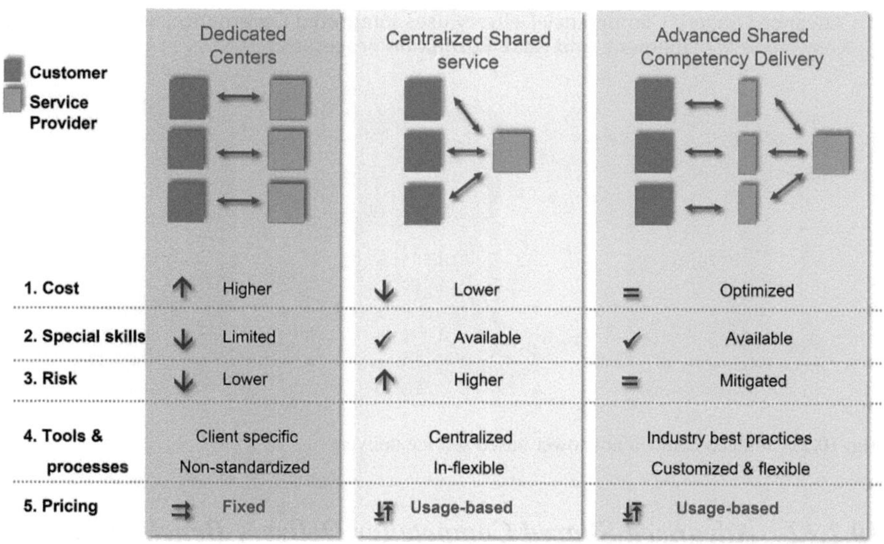

Fig. 10.19 Idktech ASCDM versus dedicated support

10.2.11 Competency Tower based Service Delivery

Global competency tower based service delivery uses shared integrated processes (Fig. 10.21)

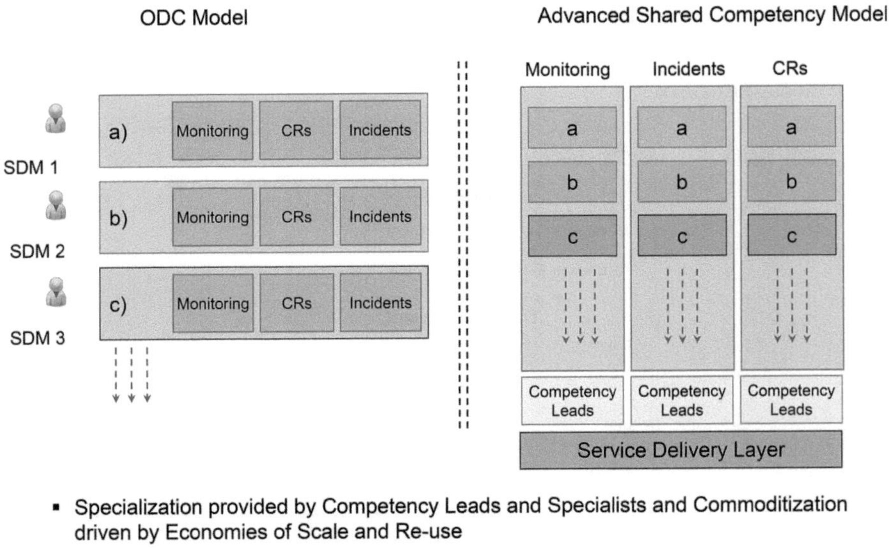

Fig. 10.20 Idktech shared competency delivery model comparison

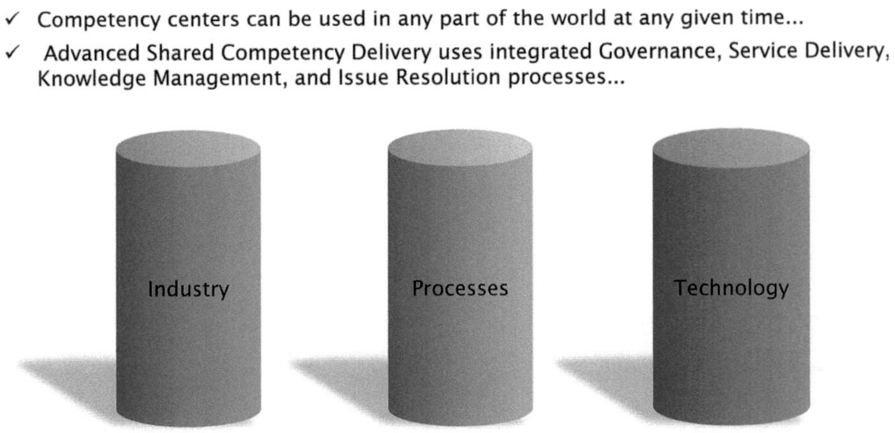

Fig. 10.21 Idktech competency tower based service delivery

10.2.12 Advanced Shared Competency Delivery Benchmark

Compares a typical Offshore Development Centre (ODC) model with the idkTech Advanced Shared Competency Delivery (ASCD) model (Table 10.1).

Table 10.1 Idktech ASCDM benchmark

Parameters	Typical ODC Model	Typical ASCD Model	% ASCD Gain
Productivity Parameters			
Enhancements/FTE per month	4	4.2	5.0 %
Tickets/FTE per month	24.0	30.5	27.3 %
Active Users Supported/FTE Year 1	60	70	16.7 %
Operational Parameters			
Onsite Percentage Year 1	30–35 %	20–25 %	8 %
Bulge Avg. Exp. in years	5.5	4.5	18.2 %
Dollar Metrics			
Price/Ticket	350	270	22.9 %

10.2.13 ASCDM Tool Support

Service Level Management

- Service level management is the primary management of IT services, ensuring that agreed services are delivered when and where they are supposed to be delivered.
- The service level manager is dependent upon all the other areas of service delivery providing the necessary support that ensures the agreed services are provided in a secure, efficient and cost effective manner.
- The following activities can be performed using tool support to ensure service level management:
  - Transparent automated process to track service delivery at each incident level
  - Auto escalations at potential failure points driven by a workflow and threshold levels
  - Alerts to the consultant for follow-up and closure of open tickets
  - Inbuilt capacity planning features for effective shift/day/week planning
  - Reduction in mean time to resolve
  - Features to track & eliminate respective tickets
  - Integration with communication devices for notifications & escalations

Productivity Management

- Productivity management systematically explores complex service issues and suggests the most appropriate methods to improve service productivity, quality, and customer satisfaction. Tool support can be used to improve productivity of the engagement.
- The activities are as follows:
  - Defining productivity benchmarks based on incident category
  - Weekly performance (team & individuals) reporting against set benchmarks

- Frequent updating to benchmarks to raise the bar on performance
- Granular level details to support new estimations for new projects
- Automated daily timesheet for each consultant on each task based on inbuilt automated time tracking

Demand Management

- The demand management framework will be used to manage the demand and the customer's incident/development/project pipeline.
- This framework is capable to address sudden change/requirements of demand at the customer's environment.
- The demand management framework consists of two major areas: demand planning, demand execution
- Demand planning consists of demand prioritization and demand aggregation.
- The demand planning will be driven by the business process managers, customer's IT managers, AD (application development) and AM (application management) teams
- The demand forecast along with the prioritization will be used for planning.
- Demand planning will cover both long range planning for a time horizon of 3-6 months ahead and short range plans for next 4-12 weeks time.
- Demand planning includes the following activities:
  - Capture, catalogue, evaluate, and approve product or technology ideas, project requests, and early-stage initiatives.
  - Manage unplanned work by capturing incidents and service requests from the help desk and qualify them for impact, urgency, and priority.
  - Output from the demand planning process will work as the input for demand execution and capacity management.
  - The planning process will also generate a demand dashboard providing the status of demand generated from each source.
- Demand execution consists of actual staffing of the project, possibly in different offshore/low cost/near shore locations.
- This is managed by the respective project delivery team working closely with the customer and the customer's other suppliers.

Capacity Management

- The objective of capacity management is to ensure that the organization has, at all times, sufficient capacity to meet the current and future agreed demands of the customer at agreed performance level.
- The tool support helps in capacity planning in the following ways:
  - Resource management – match people to AD/AM work requirements based on role, availability, and skill.

- Assess employees' alignment with customer initiatives by reviewing and tracking the resources' skills, experience, and certifications.
- Communicate resource requirements efficiently to internal resource managers.
- Focus on critical areas by highlighting capacity and demand overloads by organization units, project, or roles.
- Gain insight into customer portfolio by showing how work (demand) compares with resources available (capacity).
- Perform what-if analyses on projects to simulate different scenarios, such as when demand is shifted, to prevent overcapacity.
- Demand dashboard – Connect service and project functions from a single view through which all demand is evaluated and managed, while offering total visibility to resource utilization.
- Prioritize work and allocate resources to the highest value opportunities.
- Conduct periodic reviews with the customer and planning teams to arrive at an updated capacity management plan.

10.2.14 Sourcing Model

Pioneers in remote offshore development and global delivery model. Strengthening idkSourcing model and delivering services from our offshore delivery campuses (Fig. 10.22).

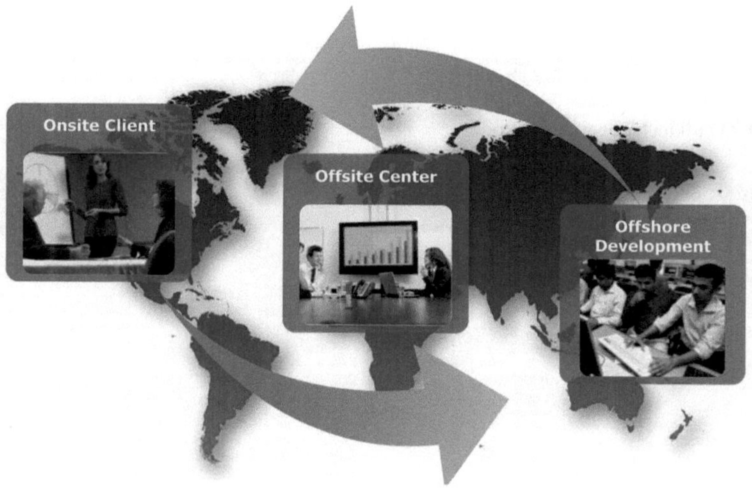

Fig. 10.22 Idktech sourcing model

10.2.15 Governance Model

Three tier governance structure (Fig. 10.23).

10.2.16 Governance Participants

Governance organization reflecting the tree tier governance structure (Fig. 10.24).

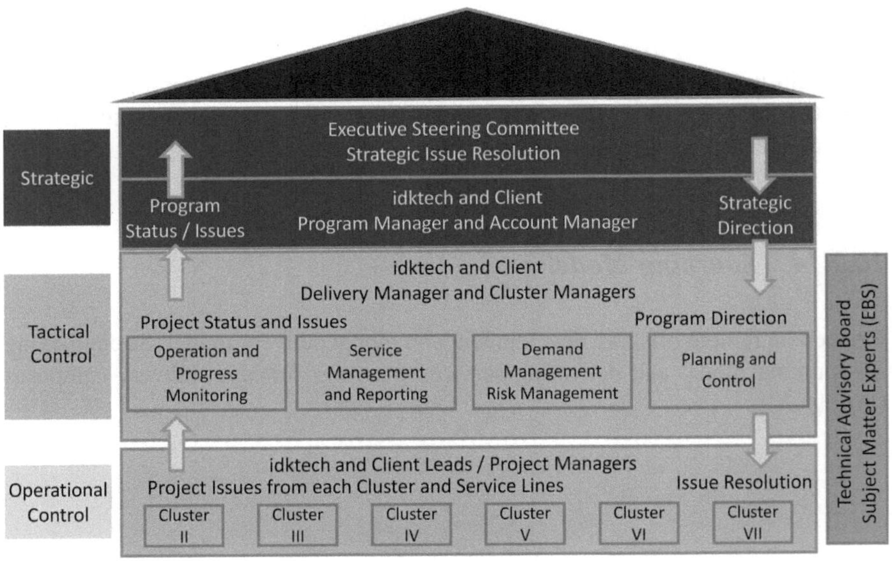

Fig. 10.23 Idktech governance model

Level / Objectives	Frequency of Meetings	Client IT Services	idktech
Executive Steering Committee • Decision-making body for all strategic and fundamental operative topics • Preparation of information for the Managing Board • Highest escalation level in collaboration with the Managing Board	Quarterly	Chair: • Supplier Manager GSP Participants: • Directors of the service clusters	Participants: • Executive Sponsors • Principal Relationship Manager • Program Manager
Management Committee • Global monitoring for provision of services, quality assurance • Continuous service improvements (Best Practice) • Contract controlling and management • Approval of change requests • Second escalation level	Monthly	Chair: • Supplier Manager GSP Participants: • Supplier Contract Manager • Supplier Demand Manager • Supplier Cluster Owner	Participants: • Program Manager • Principal Relationship Manager • Onsite Delivery Manager • Offshore Delivery Managers
Service Delivery Committee • Ensuring realization of daily operations • Service level review/monitoring • First escalation level	Monthly	Chair: • Service Cluster Owner Participants: • Service Owner	Participants: • Delivery Managers • Cluster Managers

Fig. 10.24 idktech governance participants

Index

Symbols
(M-time), viii

A
Administrative and Political Distance, 56
Alpha Beer, x
Assigned Reading, 78

C
Cage Distance Framework, 56–57
Capability Maturity Model Integration, 34–37
Chaos Reports, 67
CMMI, 34–37
Continual Service Improvement, 31, 33
cross-cultural, vii
cultural differences, 1
cultural distances, 44, 56

E
Economic Distance, 56
emerging economies, vii, ix, 2, 43–49
engagement roadmap, 159, 160

F
Firm Internationalization, 51

G
Gdigservices, 20, 22, 157–167
Geographic Distance, 56
Gini Index, 44–45
globalization, 51
Global sourcing, ix, 1, 7, 13, 17–19, 39
Governance, 167
Green Beer, x

H
High and low context culture, 63
Hofstede, 79–81

I
Idktech, 25, 168–178
Indulgence versus restraint, 79
intercultural competencies, ix, 48
international business, 51, 54–55
International Trade, 51–53
ITIL, 31–34

L
Lean IT, 38–39
Long-Term Orientation, 79

M
Masculinity versus Femininity, 79
monochronic time, 117
Multinational Companies, 54

N
nearshore centers, 20

O
Organizational change management, 29

K. Gronwald, *Global Communication and Collaboration*,
DOI 10.1007/978-3-662-53150-1

organizational readiness, 1, 27–30
outsourcing, x, 1–2, 11, 17–19, 25, 43, 157, 161–162

P
Power Distance, 79

R
Royal Beer, x

S
Service Design, 32
Service Operation, 33
service portfolio, 20
Service Strategy, 32
Service Transition, 33
Six Sigma, 37–38
stakeholder, 67–68
Standish Group, 67

T
Time Orientation, 62

U
Uncertainty Avoidance, 79

V
virtual teams, ix, 1–2, 56, 69–77, 74, 102–110

W
Wild Horse Beer, x, 2

MIX
Papier aus verantwortungsvollen Quellen
Paper from responsible sources
FSC® C105338

If you have any concerns about our products,
you can contact us on
ProductSafety@springernature.com

In case Publisher is established outside the EU,
the EU authorized representative is:
Springer Nature Customer Service Center GmbH
Europaplatz 3, 69115 Heidelberg, Germany

Printed by Libri Plureos GmbH
in Hamburg, Germany